HANDBOOK ON
EMERGING ISSUES IN
CORPORATE GOVERNANCE

T0358651

HANDBOOK ON
EMERGING ISSUES IN
CORPORATE GOVERNANCE

edited by

Alireza Tourani-Rad • Coral Ingley
Auckland University of Technology, New Zealand

 **World Scientific**

NEW JERSEY · LONDON · SINGAPORE · BEIJING · SHANGHAI · HONG KONG · TAIPEI · CHENNAI

Published by

World Scientific Publishing Co. Pte. Ltd.

5 Toh Tuck Link, Singapore 596224

USA office: 27 Warren Street, Suite 401-402, Hackensack, NJ 07601

UK office: 57 Shelton Street, Covent Garden, London WC2H 9HE

British Library Cataloguing-in-Publication Data
A catalogue record for this book is available from the British Library.

HANDBOOK ON EMERGING ISSUES IN CORPORATE GOVERNANCE

ISBN-13 978-981-4289-34-4
ISBN-10 981-4289-34-5

Typeset by Stallion Press
Email: enquiries@stallionpress.com

Printed in Singapore by World Scientific Printers.

CONTENTS

Chapter 1

EMERGING TOPICS IN CORPORATE GOVERNANCE

ALIREZA TOURANI-RAD AND CORAL INGLEY

Auckland University of Technology

Corporate Governance has been commonly defined as the rules and procedures in place for governing an organisation. However, given the rapid developments within the field and the increasing prominence of corporate governance in the modern world, this definition may be considered too narrow. Corporate governance, while a topic that has been examined in considerable depth in many areas, is widely applicable to a vast array of topics and issues, some of which are the focus of this handbook. We seek to address new and emerging topics which have yet to be closely examined and have, to a degree, been overlooked. The purpose of the handbook is to raise awareness of these issues, drive new research and potentially spark debate regarding the shape of corporate governance in the future. For instance, how should the governance structures of closely held entities and public-private partnerships differ from the dominant views regarding governance architectures? What is the link between the democratisation of countries and higher standards of corporate governance? How important are geographic proximity and other factors, such as soft information and personal relationships, for access to financial markets, and what are the implications for economic development both domestically and internationally? How should governments and regulators address such issues?

The handbook highlights four key themes as the basis around which we have organised the chapters. The first part examines the relationship between corporate governance and the capital markets, presenting the existing literature on areas, such as the role of debt and equity financing, geographic proximity and fraud against minority shareholders, and raising key areas for future research. The second part explores the role of regulators in establishing, reforming and enforcing corporate governance standards. Areas covered include the implications of proposed regulations for the financial sector, the definition and role of independent directors and audit committees, insider trading and dealing laws, and the relevance of existing corporate governance structures for other types of entities- such as small, and medium-sized firms. Part three discusses the costs and benefits of stakeholder engagement and socially responsible investing. Chapters in this part explore the role of institutional investors, one within the setting of shareholders resolutions and their impact on firm policy, and another by examining the importance of environmental, social and governance factors in investment decision making by pension funds. This part also explores the importance of governance in Public-Private Partnerships where other objectives in addition to financial goals are involved. Part four contains a selection of topics exploring how corporate governance systems and structures can be applied for better performance of both firms and countries.

The chapters in each part are summarised below.

Part 1 Corporate Governance and the Financial Markets

Chapter Two examines the interaction of law and finance, and provides an extensive overview of the latest literature on how legislation impacts investor protection, as well as the development of capital markets and individual firms. The authors highlight the rights and remedies conferred in private contracts which provide protection to investors. However, the value of these rights and remedies depend on the extent to which they are enforceable within the public domain. The authors report strong evidence showing that the legal protections given to outside shareholders affect the availability and cost of equity financing, as well as the size and efficiency of stock markets around the world. Both preemptive and remedial rights conferred on outside shareholders are shown to be significantly associated with the size of stock markets and control premiums. In so far as it relates to debt markets, the relative importance of preemptive and remedial rights remains unclear.

The third chapter deals with the novel idea concerning the link between location and finance, where 'near' is better than 'far'. The authors review the scant literature on this topic showing that the geographic location of firms and financiers plays an important role in financial decision making. They demonstrate a strong link between geographical proximity of firms and financiers, the degree of asymmetric information and the agency costs of the firms. Both information asymmetries and agency costs appear to decrease when capital providers reside closer to the firm. The authors highlight from the results of their study a potential geographic segmentation of capital markets based on the location of financiers which, in turn, could impact the firm in a variety of ways.

The final chapter in this section presents a classification of tunneling (shareholder expropriation) techniques used in both emerging and developed markets around the world. Adopting the model developed by the author in a previous study, the techniques are grouped under three categories: equity, asset, and cash flow tunneling. The impact of tunneling on firm valuation and capital market development is discussed. The analysis of existing tunneling studies is followed by a set of policy implications with a focus on the design of anti-tunneling protections. The chapter concludes with an agenda for future research in this area.

Part 2 Corporate Governance and the Regulatory Environment

Chapter Five presents an overview of the debate on the positive and negative aspects of insider trading in general. It then investigates practical aspects of the regulation of insider trading. The main aim is to provide evidence regarding the elements of insider trading laws that are most effective in limiting harm from insiders. Existing laws have been developed on a relatively ad-hoc basis without specific thought or understanding of the potential impacts on financial markets and with little guidance from the literature on how to minimise harmful insider trading. It also appears that much of the evidence cited when regulatory changes are made relates to anecdotal examination of the performance of specific definitions, rules and punishments in other markets. As such, there has been a lack of detailed evidence used in the construction of these regulations despite the potential for significant harm where poorly designed regulations are implemented. Using their own multi-country analysis, the authors provide evidence for the legal elements that constitute good insider trading rules.

Chapter Six examines regulatory responses to the global financial crisis and proposed corporate reforms. The chapter offers an overview of some of the causes of the crisis and perceived failures in corporate governance in a context of inadequate risk management and weak regulation. The authors then survey the reforms proposed in the wake of the financial crisis, suggesting that these will become corporate best practice. Such reforms are likely to include improvements in risk management and disclosure, supervision of executive remuneration and its alignment with corporate risk, prudential regulation and accounting standards specific to complex financial products, extended scope in regulatory oversight to include credit rating agencies and hedge funds, as well as a new emphasis on systemic risk and cooperation between supervisory bodies. However, regulators and policy makers face a challenge in finding the right balance between stability and growth.

Chapter seven reviews the literature on the association between independent directors on the audit committee and financial reporting quality in an international context. The authors find that given each country has its own set of regulations, laws and corporate culture, there is no consensus on the definition of an independent director. They argue that there will not be global convergence on the specification of director independence nor do they expect to see the establishment of a global corporate governance standard. For this reason, the authors encourage further cross-country studies on director independence. They contend that further research is important because regulations governing director independence have been introduced hastily based on anecdote rather than systematic scientific evidence. Future research could provide feedback on past policies and regulations and also help shape new legislation.

Small and medium enterprises (SMEs) are the focus of corporate governance in Chapter Eight. This chapter questions the relevance of the dominant framework for SMEs, and argues that the purpose and function of a board in the context of the smaller firm may differ significantly from the board's role in large companies. The debate over issues, such as board composition and independence as well as different board role perspectives, is analysed along with the theoretical underpinnings, against a backdrop of growing corporate complexity and emerging new forms of business. A resource-based view appears to provide a more relevant theoretical framework for boards in smaller firms, which although not essential, can provide valuable strategic leadership and strengthen such firms. The authors propose a staged legal governance framework that could address some of the major issues associated with a one-size-fits-all approach to corporate governance and value creation.

Part 3 Corporate Governance and Stakeholder Engagement

The first chapter in this section provides an overview of the development of corporate governance in the UK and highlights recent changes with their accompanying consequences. The chapter also looks at developments that impact institutional shareholders and how the role of the institutional investor is evolving. The author highlights a variety of issues relating to corporate governance that are important to institutional investors who are increasingly aware of social, environmental and ethical issues that have an impact on the long-term sustainability of the business. Many funds now screen companies for good corporate social responsibility practices and the potential risks they may be exposed to either through the nature of the business or the geographical locations in which the companies operate. The chapter further discusses recent examples of investor activism, including efforts to limit excesses in executive directors' remuneration.

The impact of sustainable investment on the risk and return in pension funds is the focus in Chapter Ten. The authors examine different forms of sustainable investment based on environmental, social and governance (ESG) considerations. It is argued that this information should be a component of the information set used by fund managers in making investment decisions. However, this can be a complicated process with a need to consider the impact on portfolio diversification and a potential loss of focus in companies pursuing corporate social responsibility practices. After reviewing the costs and benefits of including non-financial information in the investment decision making process, the authors argue that implementing a sustainable investment policy does not necessarily conflict with the fiduciary duty of a pension fund board and should not impact negatively on the portfolio risk and return profiles.

Chapter Eleven links the idea of corporate engagement with sustainability — a concept that has passed into mainstream thinking in recent years. The idea that primary stakeholders need to be taken into account by companies and that companies can make a valuable contribution to their communities' economic health and well-being is central to the concept of sustainable governance, seen as part of civil society and linked with concepts of corporate social responsibility (CSR), socially responsible investment (SRI) and triple bottom line reporting (TBL). Yet surveys indicate a public perception that industry and commerce do not pay sufficient attention to their social responsibilities. The author argues that in an interconnected, globalised world, a company that integrates sustainability into its strategy will be perceived as less risky and a better investment option. One concern about sustainability reporting at present is the relative lack of sophistication in reporting methods and the potential for companies to project a misleading image of being socially responsible. True sustainable reporting, however, will offer companies the ability to engage meaningfully with stakeholders to their mutual benefit. The author concludes that boards in companies that have a deep understanding of environmental, social and governance issues have a powerful role to play in shaping and overseeing strategies for value creation.

Chapter Twelve reviews the prospects and problems facing public-private partnership (PPP) organisations. In order to reduce the gap between the huge costs involved in public infrastructure projects and the available financial resources, PPP arrangements have been increasingly employed to deliver new infrastructure projects. The expectation is that PPPs deliver better value for money than alternative arrangements. The Chapter provides an overview of PPPs in various countries and sectors and its determinants. It further discusses the risk, financing and governance issues in PPP and provides solutions to enhance the feasibility of these public/private arrangements.

Part 4 Corporate Governance in Different Contexts

Extending the theme of corporate social responsibility and corporate citizenship from the previous section, Chapter Thirteen examines the link between democratisation of countries and higher standards of corporate governance, using Africa and the UN Global Compact as a basis for the discussion. Taking the desirability of a democratic political system as a given for better private sector governance, the chapter highlights ways in which private corporations can contribute to strengthening democracy using the Global Compact as a framework for improving their standards of corporate social responsibility. Drawing also on the Ibrahim Index, the King Reports on Corporate Governance (South Africa) and the Global Reporting Index (GRI), a basic model is developed which could assist corporations in their strategic thinking about the value of CSR and the link between good corporate citizenship and improved corporate governance. By acting as positive role models for good governance, corporations can make both direct and indirect contributions to democracy and, in turn, benefit from a virtuous cycle that they co-create with governments and other stakeholders.

Chapter Fourteen adopts a practitioner perspective, highlighting an integrated process for enhanced governance performance with a particular focus on the interplay between strategy, structure and corporate systems. A central element in this chapter is the notion that corporate performance is driven by stakeholder expectations and competitiveness based on the productive use of resources. According to this perspective, high performing boards are those which understand that stakeholders expect more than mere oversight for compliance. They are boards which are actively involved in delivering sustained returns, at least in line with, or higher than, expectations. Taking a structured approach to value creation, effective governance is encapsulated within three interconnected sets of dimensions that balance the compliance-performance nexus. These board processes are best developed within an organisational learning context where learning to renew competitiveness (the essence of achieving sustainable returns) is embedded within designing and implementing plans that embody management excellence and people development. The author argues that the model and methodology is well-aligned with existing systems and indices such as Six Sigma, Balanced Scorecard and Economic Value Added (EVA). For practitioners, a key benefit in using the methodology is its ability to apply effectively a systematic process to a complex activity, while helping the board avoid interfering with management.

The final chapter, Chapter Fifteen, debates issues in corporate governance reform, which, it argues, is an unfinished and ongoing process. The author is critical of many of the reforms to date, suggesting them to be "ill-considered demands for instantaneous solutions" to somewhat intransigent problems relating to current socio-economic systems by which wealth is created and distributed. This chapter highlights risk and sustainability as two central themes in the direction of corporate governance reform. The chapter presents a theoretical basis for reconciling the two seemingly disparate concepts within a refined version of the existing business model, in conjunction with the notion of a "risk tax" which seeks to moderate ill-considered or excessive risk by setting a limit for systemic risk through the market price mechanism. Practical recommendations are also presented that emphasise the duties of a statutory director and the benefits of a contract for services specifying roles, time commitments and primary loyalty based on higher levels of strategic thinking, environmental sense-making and judgment under conditions of uncertainty. The duties and liabilities of owners combined with skilled directors and a strong regulatory system are necessary components of a new agenda for better corporate governance.

The four parts of this volume combine a range of topics, conceptual perspectives and practical frameworks from different disciplines that highlight current and emerging issues in corporate governance. While diverse in their coverage, there is, at the same time, a consistency across the topics regarding the challenges facing corporations and their boards of directors, shareholders, investors and other stakeholders, as well as regulators and policy makers around the world. The global financial crisis has accentuated both this interrelatedness and drawn attention to the risks inherent in economic growth and capital market development on a scale that has not previously been encountered. With heightened complexity in financial markets and the requirement for constant innovation in products to build competitive advantage, the need for wise, competent and ethical governance of corporations and other organisations is imperative. In highlighting these issues, this volume aims to inform and stimulate thinking on how such emerging challenges may best be met.*

*The editors wish to acknowledge the special assistance of Dr Aaron Gilbert, Auckland University of Technology, for his expert contribution of editorial support to this book.

Chapter 2

INVESTOR PROTECTIONS AND THEIR IMPACT ON CAPITAL MARKETS

MANU GUPTA, OGHENOVO OBRIMAH,
PUNEET PRAKASH AND NANDA K. RANGAN

Virginia Commonwealth University

2.1 Introduction

By design, debt contracts confer superior claims on debt holders regarding a firm's assets, in comparison to the firms' shareholders. Whenever a firm defaults on its debt obligations, debt holders, in order of priority (secured creditors hold superior claims to unsecured creditors) have the right to seize the firm's assets in an attempt to recoup their investment, with shareholders holding residual claims to the firm's assets. Hence, the rights conferred on debt holders are remedial rights. That is, debt holders cannot seize a firm's assets until the firm actually defaults on its debt covenants or obligations.

In countries where ownership of publicly traded companies is highly diffused, the day-to-day management of firms is delegated to the board of directors and professional managers. Given that shareholders delegate the management of the firm to the board of directors and other senior management, but bear the risk of firm failure, certain rights are conferred on shareholders to enable them to manage their risk. Hence, by design, these rights conferred on shareholders, which either afford the right to vote or the right to legal recourse are, respectively, preemptive and remedial. The rights conferred on shareholders thus differ from the rights conferred on creditors in that shareholders' rights are both preemptive and remedial.

In contrast to mature economies such as the United States and the United Kingdom, in many less developed and emerging countries, ownership of publicly traded firms is highly concentrated, with large shareholders (inside shareholders or insiders) having a significant role in the firm's senior management. Insiders' role in the firm's senior management thus creates conflicts of interest and has the potential for insiders to focus on their returns at the expense of maximizing overall firm value, for instance, by increasing managerial perks at the expense of firm performance, or by tunneling firm resources to affiliate firms that are wholly owned by them. Given that they hold majority stakes in the firm, the potential for inside shareholders to act in their own interests, and to the detriment of outside shareholders (minority shareholders not involved with firm management) is high. As a consequence this may result in the expropriation of wealth from outside shareholders. Outside shareholders, given their minority stakes, have little power to preempt expropriation by inside shareholders and, hence, are no different from debt holders. The rights that are effective in deterring expropriation are thus more likely to be remedial, rather than preemptive.

Rights and remedies conferred in private contracts have value in that they provide protection to the contracting parties. However, the financial economics literature has demonstrated that the values of these rights and remedies depend on the extent to which they are enforceable within the public domain. The extent to which legal protections conferred in private contracts are enforceable is thus expected to affect the intrinsic value of these contracts, with the quality of the legal environment being either advantageous or disadvantageous for equity and/or debt financing.

In a survey of corporate governance practices, Shleifer and Vishny (1997) document that richer and mature economies like the United States, United Kingdom, Germany and Japan have some of the best corporate governance practices, in comparison with less developed, emerging, and transition economies. They attribute the observed differences in corporate governance practices to strong legal protection in developed countries that protect outside shareholders from expropriation by corporate insiders.

In this survey chapter, we summarize the evidence on how sovereign laws and their enforcement affect the development and structure of capital markets around the world. Specifically, we focus on the following three questions: First, what legal protections are afforded to outside investors across mature and developing economies? Second, how do differences in the legal protections afforded to outside investors and creditors affect the size and structure of capital markets, particularly in emerging and transition economies? Third, are preemptive and remedial rights equally important in terms of their effect on the size and structure of capital markets around the world? While we recognize that the size and structure of capital markets have been associated with differences in economic growth across countries, the vastness of the literature and the scope of this survey limit our focus in this chapter to these three questions. In terms of its scope, our study focuses on the evidence in the extant literature on the impact of investor protection laws and their enforcement on the development of capital markets and individual firms.

Our chapter is organized as follows. Section 2.2 describes different metrics developed in the extant literature to measure the strength of legal protection available to outside shareholders and creditors. Section 2.3 discusses how the legal protection available to outside shareholders affects the cost of equity, the size and structure of stocks markets, with particular emphasis on the effects of tunneling (expropriation of wealth by controlling shareholders at the cost of minority shareholders and creditors using related party transactions) and cross-border listings. Section 2.4 discusses how the legal protection afforded to creditors affects the flow of capital to firms and the structure of capital markets. Section 2.5 concludes the discussion.

2.2 Measures of Outside Shareholder Protection

2.2.1 *The Anti-director Rights Index*

La Porta *et al.* (1998) examine differences in investor protection laws and their enforcement across 49 nations. They classify the origins of investor protection laws according to two broad categories: common (English origin) and civil (Roman origin). Civil law countries are further classified by those with French, German and Scandinavian origins. They construct an index of shareholders' voting (preemptive)[1] and remedial rights against entrenched directors of a firm, which they term, the Anti-director rights index. The Anti-director rights index adds one for each of the following provisions in a country's corporate law: existing shareholders have first right of refusal in the event that the firm decides to issue new equity; shareholders are allowed to mail their proxy vote to the firm; shareholders are allowed cumulative voting; the minimum percentage shares that a shareholder can own in order to call for an extraordinary meeting of shareholders is less than or equal to 10 percent; shareholders are not blocked from trading their shares before the general meeting of the company; and minority shareholders (those with less than 10 percent ownership)

---

[1] In legal parlance, preemptive rights refer to anti-dilution rights. Within our context, however, preemptive rights relate to rights that enable outside shareholders to preempt expropriation by large shareholders. These preemptive rights are all associated with shareholders' voting rights and, to that extent, our usage of the term "preemptive rights" is not completely devoid of its usage within the context of legal parlance.

can seek judicial intervention, or force the firm to purchase their shares in the event of certain major changes in the firm. While the first five provisions considered in constructing the Anti-director rights index are primarily preemptive rights, the last provision is primarily a remedial right.

2.2.2 *The Anti-self-dealing Index*

Djankov *et al.* (2008) develop an alternative measure of the legal protection of minority shareholders, which they term the anti-self-dealing index. This index has the advantage of explicitly separating shareholders' rights into preemptive rights (rights that relate to the ability to vote) and remedial rights (rights that enable shareholders to recoup losses incurred consequent to self-dealing by controlling shareholders). The anti-self-dealing index is constructed from private enforcement mechanisms against self-dealing, which include disclosure practices, approval procedures for firm transactions, and the ease of litigation against suspected cases of self-dealing. The public enforcement index measures fines and prison terms for self-dealing. As is the case with the Anti-director index, common law countries have significantly higher anti-self dealing index scores than French civil law countries.

La Porta *et al.* (1998) also examine the quality of legal enforcement across sample nations. Specifically, they include in their study an assessment of the rule of law, the efficiency of the judiciary, a corruption index, an index of expropriation risk, and a measure of the risk of repudiation of contracts by country governments.

2.3 The Impact of Shareholder Protection on Equity Markets

Given that contracts cannot address every possible state of the world (see for example, Hart, 1995), they are necessarily incomplete. The value of a contract, particularly one that exchanges the rights to a firm's assets for financing, thus depends on the rights and/or remedies conferred on investors providing the financing. Because rights and/or remedies conferred in contracts have value only if they are enforceable, the theoretical framework in Hart (1995) predicts that security values will be affected by the legal protections conferred on investors within the public domain. Hart (1995), therefore, is suggesting that systematic risk will be higher in countries with poor legal protection, in comparison with countries with strong legal protection. If the risk of expropriation is sufficiently high that it engenders significantly high adverse selection problems, some investors in countries with relatively weak legal protection may shy away from capital markets altogether.

2.3.1 *Shareholder Protection and Ownership Concentration*

La Porta *et al.* (1998) find that common law countries, in general, provide shareholders with better legal protection than civil law countries. Consistent with the notion that the quality of legal protection affects investors' willingness to invest, they find that, relative to countries with better legal protection, small investors are less likely to participate in the capital markets of countries with weak legal protection, thus resulting in more concentrated ownership in these countries. One potential explanation of the finding that ownership is more dispersed in countries with better legal protection for minority shareholders is provided in La Porta *et al.* (2000). They find that firms in countries with better minority shareholder protection pay more dividends as a percentage of cash flows, earnings or sales than firms located in countries with relatively weak minority shareholder protection.

2.3.2 *Shareholder Protection, the Cost of Equity, and the Size of Equity Markets*

La Porta *et al.* (1997) examine the effect of investor protection laws on a firm's ability to raise capital. They find that firms in countries with strong anti-director rights have more dispersed ownership and better access to debt financing. Countries with strong anti-director rights are also associated with a larger number of domestic firms and a larger number of initial public offerings, as a percentage of country population. Smaller capital markets associated with weaker investor protection also have an impact on corporate cash holdings. Dittmar *et al.* (2003) find that corporate cash holdings are twice as large in weak investor protection nations than in strong investor protection nations.

Using a sample of firms with controlling shareholders from 27 wealthy nations, La Porta *et al.* (2002) find that firms in countries with better minority shareholder protection have higher valuations as measured by Tobin's q, and allocate capital more efficiently. They also find that firms where controlling shareholders have higher cash flow ownership, have higher valuations, indicating that higher cash flow ownership by controlling shareholders may decrease insiders' incentive to expropriate minority shareholders. Consistent with the findings in La Porta *et al.* (2002), Wurgler (2000) finds that firms in countries with better shareholder protection reallocate capital away from declining industries more efficiently than firms in countries with weak shareholder protection. In line with the expectation that systematic risk is higher in countries with relatively weak legal protection for investors, Morck *et al.* (2000) find that stock returns in countries with weak investor protection are more highly correlated than stock returns in countries with strong investor protection. The observation that systematic risk is higher in countries with weak investor protection is consistent with higher costs of capital in such countries.

Using the anti-self-dealing index, Djankov *et al.* (2008) examine the roles of private and public enforcement in addressing corporate self-dealing. By comparing ex-ante (preemptive) and ex-post (remedial) measures of anti-self-dealing, they find that both preemptive and remedial measures of anti-self-dealing are associated with higher stock market capitalization to GDP ratios and lower control premiums, indicating that legal protections conferred on minority shareholders have a positive impact on the size of capital markets and the cost of equity financing. La Porta *et al.* (2006) also find that laws governing disclosures in IPO prospectuses and remedial rights afforded to investors participating in IPOs, are associated with larger stock markets.

Differences in shareholder protections across nations also have an impact on private equity participation. Lerner and Schoar (2005) report that greater shareholder protection is associated with more private equity participation in the form of preferred stocks with covenants. In the absence of legal protection, the private equity is more likely to be in the form of common stock and debt with broader control.

Overall, the evidence in the literature is consistent with the notion that outside shareholders of firms located in countries with weaker investor protection laws are more exposed to expropriation by inside shareholders. The potential for expropriation is, however, priced, resulting in lower individual firm valuations, smaller and less efficient capital markets, higher costs of equity financing, consequent upon higher levels of systematic risk and less participation by small or individual investors. Weak legal protection for minority or outside shareholders thus has a negative effect on the availability and cost of equity financing, as well as the size and efficiency of stock markets around the world. Both preemptive and remedial rights conferred on outside shareholders are shown to be significantly associated with the size of stock markets and control premiums. As yet, however, there is little or no evidence of the relative importance of preemptive and remedial rights in deterring expropriation.

In the following two sub-sections, we discuss in some detail the empirical evidence of the relation between tunneling and investor protection. We also discuss the evidence on alternatives to investor protection, such as corporate governance, the use of debt and the decision to cross-list on more developed stock exchanges that help mitigate expropriation risk in countries with weak investor protection.

2.3.3 *Weak Investor Protection and Tunneling*

Expropriation of wealth by controlling shareholders (insiders) at the expense of minority or outside shareholders using related party transactions is referred to as Tunneling (see for example, Johnson *et al.* 2000b). Tunneling can be achieved using several different mechanisms including transfer pricing, dilution of equity via the issuance of underpriced equity to insiders, share buybacks at prices below market value, and insider trading.

Although tunneling has been observed in many different countries, it has been shown to be more prevalent in countries where investor protection laws and their enforcement are, in general, weak. For instance, Bertrand *et al.* (2002) find evidence of tunneling by controlling shareholders in India, while Black (1998) reports significant diversion of cash flows by controlling shareholders in Russia. Bertrand *et al.* (2008) report significant diversion of funds by family-controlled firms in Thailand, while Bae *et al.* (2002) report tunneling by Korean chaebols during merger and acquisition transactions.

In countries where tunneling is anticipated, empirical evidence shows that tunneling is priced. Atanasov (2005) finds that those Bulgarian firms that are more prone to tunneling, trade at a significant discount relative to other firms. Claessens *et al.* (2002) and Lins (2003) document lower firm valuations in weak minority shareholder regimes when controlling shareholders have more voting power than their cash flow rights; that is, in countries where the one-share-equals one-vote right is not in force. Johnson *et al.* (2000a) find Asian countries which restricted tunneling practices suffered less during the East Asian currency crisis. However, Cheung *et al.* (2006) find tunneling is unanticipated by investors and, therefore, not priced prior to its occurrence.

Dyck and Zingales (2004) quantify the value of expropriation for controlling shareholders by measuring the premium insider shareholders pay for controlling a firm. They report that the premiums can be as high as 65 percent, with strong anti-director rights significantly decreasing the control premium, indicating that strong anti-director rights decrease the probability of expropriation by controlling shareholders. Nenova (2003) examines a sample of firms with dual-class shares and finds that the premiums attached with the control-block votes are significantly lower in nations with strong minority shareholder protection. These findings lend support to the notion that the quality of the legal environment can mitigate the risk of expropriation by controlling shareholders. Stulz (2005) adds another dimension to the tunneling phenomena. In his model, not only do corporate insiders pursue their own interests, but also the rulers of sovereign states enact laws and regulate to enhance their own welfare by reducing the return on corporate investments.

The two problems, together, are called "twin agency problems." When these problems are significant, the author finds that diffuse ownership is actually inefficient. The resulting concentrated ownership then limits economic growth and financial development.

2.3.3.1 *Tunneling and the Quality of Financial Statements*

Given that controlling shareholders have the incentive to divert cash flows using various means, it is expected that the financial statements of firms, where controlling shareholders are also part of management, will be less transparent than those of firms with diffused ownership. If the lack of transparency in financial statements is systemic, arbitrageurs and fundamental analysts will likely not devote resources to gathering firm-specific information, resulting in less efficient prices, and higher systematic risk (market risk premiums).

Leuz *et al.* (2003) examine the reliability of financial statements across countries. They report higher earnings management, i.e. low matching of accruals and cash flows, and thus lower reliability of financial statements in countries with weak investor protection. Bhattacharya *et al.* (2003) find evidence that supports the notion that lower quality financial statements are associated with higher costs of equity and lesser trading in stock markets of that country. In addition, Bhattacharya and Daouk (2002) report a decrease in the cost of equity in countries that enforce insider trading laws.

2.3.4 *Self-Bonding Mechanisms that Signal Low Expropriation Risk*

2.3.4.1 *Corporate Governance*

Firms in weak minority shareholder regimes can, however, adopt stronger corporate governance mechanisms to assuage fears of expropriation by insider or controlling shareholders. Durnev and Kim (2005) find that firms in countries with weak minority shareholder protection improve their valuation by voluntarily improving their disclosure practices, as well as their governance and transparency rankings. In Ferreira and Matos (2008), firms with good governance practices, but which are located in countries with weak minority shareholder protection, attract more institutional ownership. Dahya *et al.* (2008) find that, among firms located in countries with weak minority shareholder protection, firm valuations increase with an increase in board independence. Similarly, Klapper and Love (2004) report higher valuations for firms with good corporate governance practices, with the valuation differential being more significant in countries with relatively weak investor protection. These findings demonstrate that good corporate governance practices help mitigate the risk of expropriation in countries where legal protection conferred on outside shareholders is weak.

2.3.4.2 *Debt*

Jensen and Meckling (1976) propose debt as a mechanism for curbing expropriation by insiders of the company. Harvey *et al.* (2003) study the effect of leverage on firm valuations in emerging markets that are characterized by poor corporate governance. They report a positive relationship between firm leverage and firm valuations in countries where minority shareholders are more prone to expropriation at the hands of insiders, with the leverage-induced increase in valuations becoming more pronounced if the debt contracts are in the form of internationally syndicated term loans. The findings in Harvey *et al.* (2003) indicate that debt can be a substitute for good corporate governance practices and, hence, can help mitigate the risk of expropriation in countries where legal protections conferred on outside shareholders are weak.

2.3.4.3 *Cross-Listing*

In the preceding sub-section, the empirical evidence from the extant literature indicated that good corporate governance practices can mitigate the negative effect of weak investor protection on firm valuations. According to Coffee (1999), and Stulz (1999), yet another way in which firms located in countries with weak investor protection laws can signal commitment to good corporate governance practices, is by cross-listing on stock exchanges of countries with strong investor protection laws. By cross-listing, these firms commit themselves to more stringent disclosure requirements, such as the Generally Accepted Accounting Principles (GAAP); more stringent corporate governance requirements (for instance, the requirement by the NYSE and the NASDAQ that independent directors constitute the majority on a firm's board of directors. See for example, Gupta and Fields (2009), and the Sarbanes Oxley Act of 2002.

Firm-specific and market-wide benefits of cross-listing. Empirical evidence of the decision to cross-list in foreign exchanges suggests that cross-listing is beneficial for the listing firms as well as the home country stock markets. Both Miller (1999) and Doidge *et al.* (2004) document positive stock price reactions in the home market for firms cross-listing on an exchange in the United States. They interpret this finding as evidence that firms which choose to cross-list implicitly commit to good corporate governance practices.

Klapper and Love (2004) also report higher valuations for firms that cross-list in the United States, particularly for firms located in countries with relatively weak legal systems. Errunza and Miller (2000) find significant reductions in the cost of capital for firms that cross-list in the United States.

The documented increase in firm valuations, consequent upon the cross-listing decision, are shown in Baker *et al.* (2002) and Lang *et al.* (2004) to be associated with increased analyst coverage and print media visibility for the cross-listing firms. Fernandes and Ferreira (2008) find, however, that the benefits of the increased analyst coverage of cross-listing firms is market-wide, rather than firm-specific, indicating that the decision to cross-list on a foreign country's exchange results in positive externalities for all firms in the home country. Bailey *et al.* (2006) report increased response to earnings announcements for firms that cross-list in the United States, indicating that the financial statements of firms that choose to cross-list are considered more reliable than those of other firms. Doidge *et al.* (2004) find lower voting premiums for firms with dual-class shares that choose to cross-list in the United States, suggesting that the decision to cross-list in the United States improves minority shareholder protection.

Commitment to better protection for minority shareholders also increases access to capital. Resse and Weisbach (2002) report larger increases in seasoned offerings for cross-listed firms from weak investor protection nations. Similar increases in access to capital for cross-listing firms are also reported in Lins *et al.* (2005).

The decision not to cross-list has been associated with expropriation risk. Doidge *et al.* (2009a) find evidence which indicates that firms that decide not to cross-list in the United States have controlling shareholders with significantly greater opportunities for the expropriation of minority shareholders. Lel and Miller (2008) report that poorly performing firms in countries with weak investor protection laws that choose to cross-list in the United States are more likely to remove the CEO from office, in comparison with poorly performing firms that do not cross-list.

There is evidence, however, that cross-listing is a 'reputational bonding' mechanism, rather than a 'legal bonding' mechanism. Using a sample of Mexican firms that are cross-listed in the United States, Siegel (2005) documents limited enforcement by the SEC, even though insiders in some of the cross-listed firms grossly exploited weak legal enforcement in Mexico. Given that some cross-listed firms did not expropriate minority shareholders, Seigel thus categorizes cross-listing as a 'reputational-bonding' mechanism.

Foucault and Gehrig (2008) posit that increases in firm valuations experienced by cross-listed firms are driven by better investment decisions. The higher valuations are facilitated by the firm's ability to obtain superior information about the value of its assets. However, Gozzi *et al.* (2008) document increases in Tobin's q for cross-listing firms both before, and at the time of, cross-listing but these increases do not persist after the cross-listing decision. They conclude that firms cross-list to circumvent capital raising constraints in their domestic markets. The evidence thus suggests that firms in countries with weak investor protection that choose to cross-list are precisely the firms that are committed to maximizing total firm value, as opposed to the maximization of insiders' returns.

The costs of cross-listing. Cross-listing in more developed capital markets like the United States may result in higher costs for the firms. The SEC requires reporting of financial statements under GAAP, which may add to the cost of reporting or disclosure if reporting standards in the cross-listing firms' home countries are not as extensive as those required under GAAP. The costs are primarily associated with changes in regulations. The implementation of the Sarbanes and Oxley Act of 2002 is one such instance where the cost of disclosure increased significantly, particularly for small firms. Zingales (2007) reports a significant drop in foreign IPOs in the United States and an increase in the number of US companies listing in London after the passage of the Sarbanes and Oxley Act in 2002. Marosi and Massoud (2008) also report an increase in the number of foreign firms that deregister from exchanges in the United States after 2002, in response to the significant increase in the cost of disclosure following the passage of the Sarbanes and Oxley Act. Doidge *et al.* (2009b) take the enquiry further, and examine the characteristics of firms cross-listing outside their home markets. They find similar decreases in cross-listings on the New York and London exchanges, but after controlling for firm characteristics, find no evidence that the decrease in the number of cross-listings in the United States is associated with the passage of the Sarbanes and Oxley Act. They also document that the cross-listing premium for firms that cross-list in the United States persists, while this is not the case for firms that choose to cross-list on London's Main Market. Doidge *et al.*, therefore, dispute the notion that compliance costs associated with the Sarbanes and Oxley Act are prohibitive.

2.3.5 *Summary of Section 2.3*

Overall, the empirical evidence indicates that the institution of legal protections for minority shareholders decreases the risk of expropriation and is beneficial for stock market valuations. There is also some evidence that internal governance mechanisms, like board independence and the use of debt, may be substitutes for investor protection laws. The empirical evidence further supports the notion that firms from countries with weak investor protection laws can increase individual firm valuations by cross-listing. There is further support for the notion that the decision to cross-list yields positive externalities for the stock market, as a whole, in terms of increased analyst coverage. However, the evidence suggests that firms in countries with weak investor protections which choose to cross-list are those already committed to maximizing total firm value rather than insiders' returns. Given that firm valuations can increase simply because the exchange on which these firms cross-list is more liquid, the increase in firm valuations as a result of the cross-listing decision cannot be interpreted to mean that cross-listing mitigates expropriation risk.

2.4 The Impact of Creditor Protections on Debt Markets

Credit markets are a major source of capital around the world. In fact, Demirgüç-Kunt and Levine (2001) document that banks provide more capital to corporations than any other source in most of the world economies. Since lenders have a fixed claim on the cash flows of the borrowing firm and only hold remedial claims to the firms' assets, their biggest concern is the recovery of capital in the event of default, with recovery rates significantly affected by the rights conferred on lenders within the public domain.

2.4.1 *The Creditor Rights Index*

La Porta *et al.* (1998) examine the legal protection conferred on creditors by constructing a creditor rights index. The creditor rights index is constructed by counting the number of rights, out of the following four, conferred on creditors within each country: creditor's consent is required before going into reorganization; there is no automatic stay preventing secured creditors from possessing the assets of a firm under reorganization; secured creditors have priority of payment when the firm is being liquidated; the court or creditors can replace the management of the firm under reorganization. As discussed, all of these rights are remedial in nature, that is, they relate to the creditors' ability to seize the firms' assets in the event of default. La Porta *et al.* (1998) find that common law countries offer better legal protection to creditors than civil law countries. Among civil law countries, those derived from French law offer the least protection to creditors.

2.4.2 *Creditor Protections, the Cost of Debt, and the Size of Debt Markets*

Similar to the impact of minority shareholder protection on capital markets, differences in investor protection for creditors also have a significant impact on capital markets. Djankov *et al.* (2008) study the efficiency of debt contract enforcement around the world and their impact on capital markets, with the efficiency of debt enforcement measured as the difference between the value of the firm, and the cost incurred during the debt enforcement process. The channels of debt enforcement can be foreclosure, reorganization or liquidation. Using a sample of 88 countries, they find that the efficiency of debt enforcement is higher in developed nations and lower in French law nations where creditors have fewer rights. Inefficient debt enforcement is further associated with relatively small debt markets. In less developed countries, debt enforcement mechanisms that involve more court oversight result in lower efficiency of debt enforcement. Djankov *et al.* (2008), in fact, prescribe less formal debt contract enforcement mechanisms for less developed countries. Djankov *et al.* (2007) show that the supply of private credit increases with the rights conferred on creditors. In addition to creditor rights, they also show the importance of information sharing among creditors as means of promoting private credit.

There exists evidence that lenders, in countries with weak creditor rights, are less likely to monitor debtors and seek enforcement of debt contracts, as the costs associated with enforcement may exceed benefits. Claessens and Klapper (2005) find that bankruptcies are more common in countries with strong creditor rights and judicial systems. Diamond (2004) describes the lack of contract enforcement in countries with weak creditor rights as lender passivity and suggests that debt should be structured as short-term in these countries since short-term debt is more prone to 'debt-runs' (lenders may refuse to renew the maturing debt), thus providing a way to keep a check on management. Consistent with Diamond's argument, Qian and Strahan (2007) show that stronger credit rights are associated with more concentrated loan ownership, longer maturities and lower interest rates on bank loans. Esty and Megginson (2003) also report a similar diffusion of loan ownership in countries with weak creditor rights. They conclude that diffused loan ownership serves to deter strategic bankruptcy filings that enable firms to operate under the protection of the court when the law provides little protection to creditors. Likewise, Bae and Goyal (2009) demonstrate that banks, when faced with weak enforcement of debt contracts, resort to reducing loan size and maturity, and raise loan spreads.

However, structuring debt as short-term also has its downside. Gupta *et al.* (2008) argue that when faced with the possibility of debt-runs, borrowers may take actions to hide bad performance until after the renewal of debt contracts. Consistent with this argument, they show that firms with short-term debt are more likely to manage earnings to hide bad performance, and that this relation is stronger in countries with weak creditor rights.

In addition to structuring debt as short-term, are there other mechanisms that creditors can rely upon when the law provides them with little protection? Brockman and Unlu (2009) report smaller and less probable dividends in countries with weak creditor rights. They conclude that, in the absence of strong legal protection, creditors put greater restrictions on dividends.

Overall, the evidence is consistent with the notion that the legal protections conferred on creditors, which facilitate loan recovery in the event of default, have a significant impact on the size and efficiency of credit markets. Stronger creditor rights are associated with larger debt markets, more concentrated loan ownership, less restrictive protective covenants, and more efficient loan recovery in the event of default.

2.5 Conclusion

The empirical evidence summarized in this chapter shows, very clearly, that the legal protection conferred on outside shareholders affects the availability and cost of equity financing, as well as the size and efficiency of stock markets around the world. Both preemptive and remedial rights conferred on outside shareholders are shown to be significantly associated with the size of stock markets and control premiums. However, insofar as it relates to deterring expropriation, the relative importance of preemptive and remedial rights remains unclear. That is, in countries where outside shareholders have both preemptive and remedial rights, it is unclear whether preemptive rights are more important than remedial rights, and vice-versa. In the same vein, it is unclear whether preemptive or remedial rights are more important deterrents to tunneling by inside or controlling shareholders. The link between legal protection conferred on outside shareholders and the size of debt markets is also somewhat unclear. That is, are debt markets larger and debt less costly than equity in countries where outside investors' rights are primarily remedial?

Although both increased financial disclosure and cross-listing are alternative mechanisms by which controlling shareholders bond themselves to investors, there is no evidence that these mechanisms actually decrease the risk of expropriation. With respect to cross-listing in particular, the evidence suggests that firms which choose to cross-list are exactly the same firms whose controlling shareholders are committed to maximizing total firm value rather than insiders' returns. More detailed examination of the benefits of cross-listing vis-à-vis the reduction of expropriation risk seems to be a fertile area for research.

Chapter 3

GEOGRAPHIC LOCATION AND CORPORATE FINANCE*

CHRISTO A. PIRINSKY[†] AND QINGHAI WANG[‡]

[†]*George Washington University*
[‡]*Georgia Institute of Technology*

3.1 Introduction

There is overwhelming empirical and anecdotal evidence that when it comes to economic decisions, 'near' is better than 'far'. First of all, most economic agents exhibit a strong preference for proximity — investors in their security choices, banks in their loans, financial analysts in their coverage and corporate executives in their capital budgeting decisions. Second, most local choices tend to be rewarded with better outcomes — for investors: higher returns, for banks: better loans, for financial analysts: more precise forecasts and for corporate executives: better investment decisions. Finally, the local choices of economic agents leave a lasting imprint on markets and prices, thus influencing everybody else in the economy.[1]

---

* The authors thank Vladimir Atanasov for helpful comments.
[1] Coval and Moskowitz (1999) show that US institutional investors tend to invest in firms that are headquartered geographically close to them. Ivković and Weisbenner (2005) and Zhu (2002) uncover similar patterns for individual investors. Coval and Moskowitz (2001) find that firm ownership by nearby investors is positively related to the firm's future returns. Ivković and Weisbenner (2005) show that the average household generates higher returns from its local holdings relative to its non-local holdings. Malloy (2005) and Bae *et al.* (2008) show that geographically proximate analysts are more accurate in their earnings estimates than distant analysts. Kang and Kim (2008) and Kedia *et al.* (2008) find that geographic proximity provides an information advantage in acquisitions, while Schultz (2003) shows that in the context of an IPO syndicate. Pirinsky and Wang (2006) show that location affects price formation in capital markets.

In this chapter, we review the importance of geographic location for corporate finance with an emphasis on corporate governance. We summarize the importance of geographic proximity within the context of four theoretical frameworks — agency theory of the firm, asymmetric information, market segmentation, and behavioral finance.

Before elaborating on the above theories, it is important to clarify the concept of firm location. The modern firm has fuzzy boundaries and its operations and management could encompass numerous countries around the globe. The academic literature usually defines a firm's location as the location of its headquarters. Corporate headquarters are usually close to corporate core business activities. More importantly, corporate headquarters are the place where corporate decision makers reside and are the center of information exchange between the firm and its suppliers, service providers, and investors (see Davis and Henderson, 2004, for a detailed discussion on the role of corporate headquarters).

In the review, we focus predominantly on research that looks at a single country. Countries exhibit robust differences with respect to regulation, culture, and language — all of which make it difficult to isolate the impact of distance on economic outcomes. Given that our topic is corporate finance, we review papers that emphasize the distance between the firm and its capital providers (investors). We also pay special attention to some regional issues, such as the overall financial development and strategic interactions of local financial institutions.

We begin our chapter by focusing on articles that discuss geographic location in light of the agency theory of the firm. Agency problems within the firm emanate from the fact that, under conditions of incomplete and asymmetric information, the principal (financier) is at risk of expropriation by the entrepreneur (manager). Such agency problems will be more severe when the entrepreneur's ability is unknown and when the operations of the firm are hard to observe and monitor. One way to deal with these problems is a performance-sensitive contract design (see Milgrom and Roberts, 1992). This approach, however, is limited by the inherent incompleteness of financial contracts (Prendergast, 1999).

We argue that geographic proximity between the principal and the agent could alleviate agency problems as a result of *better monitoring* and *relationship building*. On the one hand, proximity makes actions and, particularly, effort level more observable. This allows the principal (investor) to identify more variables correlated with the effort level of the agent (manager). Proximity also makes it easier to estimate/assess the agent's risk tolerance and the agent's responsiveness to incentives. All of these factors would facilitate the design of more complete compensation contracts.

Another way proximity could alleviate the conflicts of interest between investors and managers is through the development of long-term relationships.

Long-term relationships with firms allow investors to acquire more reliable information about their projects. The repeated game set-up of multiple rounds of financing also allows investors to alleviate potential moral hazard issues. Relationships provide investors with leverage over firms because firms will be favored in future rounds of financing only if they 'behave', i.e. provide correct information and comply with the conditions of existing financing contracts. Firms could also benefit from long-term relationships with their investors as a result of greater financial flexibility and lower cost of capital.

Next, we analyze the impact of geographic location on corporate finance from the perspective of asymmetric information. Even with the advance of technologies for information transmission, distance still inhibits information flows among financial market participants, particularly in the case of 'soft' information (Stein, 2002). The asymmetric information aspect of proximity could affect corporate financing decisions directly in the case of external financing (Myers and Majluf, 1984). It could also affect them indirectly by creating clienteles of local investors. Such clienteles could influence major corporate decisions, such as capital structure and payout policies.

In light of the above clientele effects, we next explore in more detail the implications of geographic segmentation of capital markets for firm corporate financial decisions. There is overwhelming evidence that all major classes of investors exhibit strong preference for local securities in their portfolio choice. Such local preference is largely motivated by the informational advantages of proximity and results in geographic segmentation/fragmentation of the domestic capital market.

The formation of local investor clienteles can have a significant impact on corporate policies. For example, corporate payout policies can cater toward investor preference, and the preference of the local investor base could play a central role in determining a firm's dividend polices. Similarly, a firm's equity issuance and borrowing decisions, as well as capital structure polices, could be affected by local investor preferences and local credit market conditions. In this part of our review, we also discuss the implications of local competition in the financial sector for firms from the region.

In the last section of the chapter, we review recent corporate finance research on various local non-economic factors, such as culture and social interactions. Studies have shown that these non-economic factors underlie all major economic activities (Glaeser and Scheinkman, 2003). These non-economic factors can affect corporate finance through different channels. On the one hand, they could affect investor behavior and stock market participation. On the other hand, they can influence corporate executives directly. Finally, these factors could affect the bonding mechanisms and contracts between investors and corporate decision makers.

The chapter is organized as follows. Section 2 discusses the importance of geographic location for corporate financial decisions from the perspective of agency theories; Section 3 evaluates the implications of asymmetric information; Section 4 studies the importance of geographic segmentation of the capital market; while Section 5 discusses non-economic local interactions. We conclude in Section 6.

3.2 Geographic Location and Agency Theories of the Firm

Agency problems within the firm emerge from the separation of ownership and control (Jensen and Meckling, 1976). As previously mentioned, the geographic proximity between the firm and its investors could alleviate these agency problems by facilitating better *monitoring* and *relationship building*. Given that the agency-risks for investor expropriation increase with distance, we expect that investments in more distant firms would be associated with more detailed contracts between managers and entrepreneurs. Such distant investments would tend to have greater monitoring costs and, as a result, leads to higher yields to compensate investors for covering these costs.

A large literature analyzes the value of lending relationships for firms. A sub-sample of this literature has provided insights on the role of geographic proximity for these relationships.[2] In a recent article, Berger *et al.* (2005) find that small banks provide more local loans, interact more personally with their borrowers and have longer and more exclusive relationships. Small banks which are more likely to operate locally are also more likely to alleviate the credit constraints of their customers than do large banks. The authors also provide evidence consistent with small banks being better able to collect and act on soft information than large banks. In particular, large banks are less willing to lend to firms with greater informational asymmetries, such as firms with no financial records. Overall, their evidence is consistent with the idea that geographic proximity alleviates the agency costs between firms and their lenders.

In public equity markets, Becker *et al.* (2008) observe that individuals tend to hold blocks in public firms located close to where they reside. They show that large local block holders in a firm increase firm profitability,

---

[2] For the United States, James (1987), Lummer and McConnell (1989), and Petersen and Rajan (1994) document the value of relationships for firms, while Dahiya *et al.* (2003) document the same for lenders.

increase dividends, reduce corporate cash holdings, and reduce executive compensation. They conclude that local shareholders are effective monitors.

John *et al.* (2008) investigate the impact of geography on firm dividend policies. If distance is correlated with agency problems, firms in remote areas would have more severe agency problems than firms in urban areas, given that their investor base is expected to be more geographically dispersed. Managers in such remote firms would be more likely to use free cash flow for empire building, resulting in less efficient investment. Agency theory predicts that such firms would be more likely to pay higher dividends, especially when firms have few growth opportunities. Consistent with this conjecture, they find that firms in central locations have lower dividend yields and a preference for repurchases and special dividends. The relationship between location dividends is most strongly pronounced for firms with few growth opportunities.

In a related vein, Gaspar and Massa (2007) show that local ownership improves governance and induces value-enhancing decisions, such as less over-investment and fewer but better acquisitions. They also argue that local ownership tends to reduce the liquidity of the stock by increasing the adverse selection discount required by less informed investors to trade. The latter could partially offset the benefits of local ownership. Nevertheless, proximity promotes better corporate governance.

There is also extensive evidence on the link between geographic location and agency problems from the venture capital industry. The Venture capital market exhibits a large degree of regional fragmentation. VCs often invest locally (Gupta and Sapienza, 1992; Norton and Tenenbaum, 1993; and Sorenson and Stuart, 2001) and also form strong syndication networks with other local VCs Hochberg *et al.* (2007).

The local segmentation of the Venture capital industry is not surprising given the many potential agency problems for start-up firms. It is very likely that entrepreneurs know more about their ability than the VC. In addition, the VC is also facing the risk that the entrepreneur can 'hold-up' the VC by threatening to leave the venture when the entrepreneur's human capital is particularly valuable to the company (Hart and Moore, 1994).

As suggested by previous literature, staging is an effective way to mitigate information and agency problems since VCs retain the option to abandon the project that does not meet stage financial or non-financial targets (see, e.g., Gompers, 1995; Davila *et al.*, 2003; Comelli and Yosha, 2003; and Kaplan and Stromberg, 2004). An implication of the monitoring hypothesis is that VCs may tend to reduce staging when monitoring costs are low. Consistent with the idea that proximity facilitates monitoring and reduces information risk, Tian (2008) finds that firms located closer to their VCs receive fewer financing rounds, have a longer duration between successive investment rounds and receive larger investment amounts per round.

Cumming (2004) explores factors that affect the portfolio size of Canadian venture capital funds. He shows that geographic proximity affects overall portfolio size as well as the rate of portfolio expansion. A 10 percent increase in extra-provincial investment lowers portfolio size by approximately two entrepreneurial firms. Similarly, the rate of investment is lower among funds that invest more frequently in distant entrepreneurs — a 10 percent increase in extra provincial investments decreases the rate of investment by 0.07 entrepreneurial firms per VC per year. The results are consistent with the hypothesis that geographic distance requires extra monitoring, which lowers portfolio size.

3.3 Asymmetric Information

Existing research has shown that the asymmetric information problem between firms and outside investors is very likely to increase with distance.[3] Asymmetric information could have a distinct effect on firm investment and financing decisions beyond the agency considerations discussed in the previous subsection. On the one hand, asymmetric information could be an advantage in product market competition; on the other hand, it could increase the cost of external finance (Myers and Majluf, 1984). In this section, we focus on how geographic distance could interfere with firm financing decisions in light of this asymmetric information problem.

Loughran and Schultz (2006) analyze the financing decisions of rural and urban firms. Rural firms have greater average distance between the firm headquarters and its investor base relative to urban firms. Consistent with greater information asymmetries for rural firms, they find that rural firms are less likely to rely on external equity financing — they wait longer to go public and are less likely to conduct seasoned equity offerings. When they use external financing, rural firms work with lower quality underwriters. In addition, rural firms have more debt in their capital structure than otherwise similar urban firms. The stronger pecking order financing patterns for rural firms relative to urban firms suggest that distance increases the information asymmetry costs for firms.

---

[3] Consistent with this view, Coval and Moskowitz (2001) and Ivković and Weisbenner (2004) find that institutional and individual investors realize better performance in local stocks. Malloy (2005) and Orpurt (2004) further show that financial analysts are more accurate in their earnings forecasts of local firms.

Uysal *et al.* (2008) examine the impact of geographical proximity on the acquisition decisions of US public firms. They find that acquirer returns in local transactions (where the acquirer and target firms are located within 100 km of each other) are more than twice the returns in non-local transactions. They attribute the value premium of local acquisitions to information advantages of bidding firms.

Butler (2008) highlights evidence for the informational advantages of proximity from the municipal bond market. He finds that local investment banks charge lower fees and sell bonds at lower yields relative to non-local banks. These findings suggest that investment banks with a local presence are better able to assess 'soft' information and place bond issues that are more difficult to value. Butler concludes that, as a result of reduced informational asymmetries, local underwriters are able to offer municipal bond issuers more competitive pricing.

3.4 Geographic Segmentation and Corporate Policy

Investors exhibit strong preference for geographic proximity in their portfolio allocation decisions.[4] There are two main explanations for the strong preference for local stocks — information and behavioral bias. The information explanation suggests that the preference for proximity is a preference for more/better information. Consistent with this explanation, Coval and Moskowitz, (2001) and Massa and Simonov (2006) find that local investors are better informed about a company than non-local investors. The behavioral explanation states that the decisions to invest in close-by firms are a result of an availability heuristic, a form of familiarity bias (Kahneman and Tversky, 1973). Huberman (2001) and Zhu (2002) find evidence consistent with this explanation.

We refer to this local preference of investors as segmentation/fragmentation of domestic capital markets. This segmentation extends beyond equity markets. Banks still remain largely local financial intermediaries: they rely heavily on local deposits for funding and much of their lending is also local (Petersen and Rajan, 2002). Becker (2007) uses demographic variation in savings behavior to provide evidence on segmentation in the US bank loan markets. He shows that cities with a large fraction of seniors have higher volumes of bank deposits. Because banks rely heavily on deposit financing, this affects local loan supply.

---

[4] Coval and Moskowitz (1999) show that US professional money managers tend to invest in firms that are headquartered geographically close to them. Ivkovic and Weisbenner (2004) and Zhu (2002) uncover similar patterns for individual investors. Using international data, Massa and Simonov (2006) and Grinblatt and Keloharju (2001) also find that investors prefer stocks located nearby.

The geographic segmentation of capital markets could affect corporate financing and investment policies in a variety of ways. First, if information risk is priced, then geography would influence equilibrium valuations and expected returns, which would affect the firm cost of capital. We elaborate on these possibilities in Subsection A.

Second, the local preference of investors naturally creates a clientele of investors from the same region, which could have an influence on major corporate policies. For example, a company that is headquartered in Boston would have a disproportionately large number of (local) institutional investors, which could affect its corporate governance and pay-out policy. We discuss this local clientele effect in Subsection B.

Finally, the fact that firms are financed locally implies that the overall structure and organization of the local financial industry would affect the corporate financing decisions of the firms from the region. We discuss this industrial organization angle of geographic location in Subsection C.

3.4.1 *Geographic Segmentation and the Cost of Capital*

Hong *et al.* (2008) examine the impact of local bias in equity investing on firm valuation. They show that in the presence of local bias, the price of a stock should be decreasing with the ratio of the aggregate book value of firms in its region to the aggregate risk tolerance of investors in its region. They argue that regions with low population density are home to relatively few firms per capita, which leads to higher stock prices, dubbed as the 'only-game-in-town' effect.

Francis *et al.* (2008), on the other hand, find that firm location significantly affects firm's bondholders. They show that bondholders prefer local firms and firms located in remote rural areas exhibit significantly higher costs of debt capital in comparison to their urban counterparts. Focusing on the municipal bond market, Pirinsky and Wang (2009) find a strong segmentation-driven valuation effect in the municipal bond market — municipal bond yields are highly correlated with local demand and supply.

The geographic segmentation of capital markets could also affect the systematic risks of stocks. Pirinsky and Wang (2006) document strong co-movement in the stock returns of firms headquartered in the same geographic area. The local co-movement of stock returns is not explained by economic fundamentals and is stronger for smaller firms with more individual investors and in regions with less financially sophisticated residents. The evidence suggests that price formation in equity markets has a significant geographic component that is associated with the investment decisions of local investors.

Loughran and Schultz (2005) study the effect of a firm's geographic location on liquidity. Rural firms are likely to have greater cost of information acquisition than firms in large metropolitan areas. Loughran and Schultz (2005) find that rural stocks attract less analyst coverage than urban stocks, institutions own significantly lower proportions of the outstanding shares of rural stocks than urban stocks, and rural stocks trade much less than urban stocks. Furthermore, trading costs for NASDAQ stocks are higher for companies that are located in rural areas. Overall, rural-based firms are less liquid than their urban counterparts, which could adversely affect their cost of capital.

3.4.2 *Geographic Segmentation and Investor Clienteles*

Gao *et al.* (2008) provide comprehensive evidence of the local effects of corporate financial policies. They show that corporate geographic location helps explain the cross-sectional variations of firm capital structure and payout polices. Corporations located in the same metropolitan areas exhibit similar leverage ratios and have a similar level of cash holdings. These firms also tend to follow similar patterns of issuing equity and debt. While corporate headquarter locations have less impact on the amount of payouts made by firms, corporations located in the same metropolitan areas show commonality in decisions on whether to pay dividends and repurchase shares. They argue that a large part of these local effects of corporate policies could be explained by investor preference for local stocks.

Becker *et al.* (2008) examine the effects of local stock preference of investors on corporate dividend policies. Because retail investors tend to hold local stocks and older investors prefer dividend-paying stocks, the study utilizes demographics to identify the effect of geographically varying demand on firm payout policy. The study finds that in locations where seniors constitute a large proportion of the population, firms are more likely to pay and to initiate dividends and, conditional on doing so, they have higher dividend yields. The authors conclude that regional clienteles can explain firm payout policies.

Variations in the local supply of capital affect both local economic outcomes and corporate polices. Becker (2007) uses demographic variation in savings behaviour to provide evidence of segmentation in the US bank loan markets. He shows that cities with a large proportion of seniors have higher volumes of bank deposits, which affects exogenously local loan supply. As a result, Metropolitan Statistical Areas with high levels of deposits have more manufacturing firms and relatively more small and new firms. Furthermore, the effect of the local deposit supply is stronger in industries that are more externally dependent. Loughran (2008) examines the impact of firm location on equity issuance and find that rural firms are less likely to conduct seasoned equity offerings than firms located in urban areas because the costs in generating information are higher for rural firms.

Finally, Landier *et al.* (2008) document the role of geographic location, and particularly geographic dispersion, on a range of corporate decisions. They show that geographically dispersed firms are less employee-friendly. Even within such firms, dismissals of divisional employees are less common in divisions located closer to corporate headquarters than in more distant divisions. Firms also appear to adopt a 'pecking-order' and divest out-of-state entities before in-state entities. Additionally, stock markets respond favorably to divestitures of in-state divisions. Firms are more likely to protect proximate employees in soft information industries (i.e. when information is difficult to transfer over long distances). Their findings suggest that social factors work alongside informational considerations in making geographic dispersion an important factor in corporate decision-making.

3.4.3 *Geographic Segmentation and Local Competition*

A large literature, beginning with Schumpeter (1911), emphasizes the positive role of a country's financial development for economic growth. A large body of empirical research has also shown that a country's level of financial development impacts its ability to grow.[5] Does local financial development and industrial organization of the financial sector matter for growth within regions of the same country? While a positive relationship between local financial development and firm growth is largely expected, the implications of local competitions are not as clear. On the one hand, concentration of market power in banking would generally imply lower equilibrium amounts of credit. On the other hand, it is also possible that banking market power is actually needed for banks to establish valuable lending relationships.

The idea that relationship and competition are not compatible has been addressed in labor economics. According to this literature, a firm would be more reluctant to invest in training workers in a competitive labour market, since workers can threaten to quit and demand a competitive salary once they are trained (Becker, 1975). We note, however, that relationships could interact with labour market competition in an elaborate way over the business cycle.

---

[5] King and Levine (1993) and Rajan and Zingales (1998) are among the first to show that the financial system promotes economic growth internationally.

In the banking area, Becker *et al.* (2009) present international evidence that higher bank concentration is associated with more financing obstacles, especially for smaller firms. Maurer and Haber (2003) find evidence that bank concentration favoured lending to 'connected' borrowers in the domestic textile industry over other competitors, even though these competitors exhibited higher efficiency measures. In contrast, Bonaccorsi di Patti and Dell'Ariccia (2004) find that concentration in banking reduces entry rates for Italian firms in industries with relatively opaque assets.

Cetorelli and Strahan (2006) study whether concentration of market power in banking has an effect on the number of firms in a given sector, on average firm size and on the overall firm-size distribution. They find that more vigorous banking competition — that is, lower concentration and looser restrictions on geographical expansion — is associated with both more firms in operation and with a smaller average firm size. They find, moreover, that the share of firms in the smallest size category (fewer than five employees) increases most dramatically with better bank competition, mostly at the expense of firms with between 100 and 1,000 employees.

Degryse and Ongena (2005) study the effect of geographic distance on bank loan rates, taking into account the distance to both the major bank and its competitors. They find that loan rates decrease with the distance between the firm and its lending bank and increase with the distance between the firm and competing lenders. They observe that increasing distance between the borrower and alternative lenders significantly relaxes price competition and results in substantially higher borrowing costs for the firm.

Finally, Garmaise and Moskowitz (2006) use bank mergers as an instrument for local bank competition and also find negative temporary effects on loan supply and economic activity following a bank merger.

3.5 Local Non-economic Factors and Corporate Finance

Recent studies in economics and finance have provided convincing evidence that non-economic factors such as culture, trust, social interactions and social networks have a significant impact on economic activities and economic outcomes (see Glaeser and Scheinkman, 2003). Physical proximity facilitates social interactions, transmission of sentiment and non-market information. As a result, geographic location plays a central role in the formation of culture and social networks. In this section, we provide a brief review of studies that examine cultural and network effects of corporate policies.

3.5.1 *Culture*

Culture is 'transmission from one generation to the next, via teaching and imitation, of knowledge, values, and other factors that influence behaviour' (Boyd and Richerson, 1985, p. 2). Culture is largely local or regional. The role of culture in economics is well established. The literature can be traced back to Weber (1930) who argues that cultural changes inspired by the Protestant Reformation helped to explain the rise of capitalism in Western Europe and America. Economic research has recently witnessed a renaissance in studies of culture as a determinant of economic activities and outcome (see Guiso *et al.*, 2006, for a review).

Culture is difficult to classify and measure in empirical studies. Guiso *et al.* (2008) view 'trust' as a cultural attribute and study the effect of trust on stock market participation. They find that less trusting individuals are less likely to buy stock and, conditional on buying stock, they will buy less. They find similar evidence both within countries and in cross country data.

Various studies use religion as a proxy for culture and find it is related to government quality across countries (La Porta *et al.*, 1999) and macroeconomic development (Barro and McCleary, 2003). Stulz and Williamson (2003) find that a country's religion, among other cultural attributes, helps explain the cross-sectional variation in creditor rights. They also find that religion is an important predictor of how countries enforce rights.

A few recent studies have examined the impact of culture on corporate polices within a country. A single-country approach can differentiate the impact of culture from differences in the legal and economic environment across countries. Hilary and Hui (2009) examine how religiosity (measured by church attendance and a subjective rating of religion's importance in one's life), influences firms' investment decisions. They find that firms located in counties with higher levels of religiosity display lower degrees of risk exposure as measured by variances in equity returns or in returns on assets. In turn, such firms require a higher internal rate of return before investing. They exhibit a lower rate of investment in both tangible assets and R&D, and their long-term growth is also lower. The authors also document how when CEOs switch employers, they are more likely to join firms with a similar religious environment to that of their last firm. Gao *et al.* (2008) examine capital structure and payout polices in a similar framework and find that some of the documented difference in corporate financial policies is related to local cultural attributes.

3.5.2 *Social Interactions, Networks, and Peer Effect*

Different from culture, social interactions refer to how 'the actions of a reference group affect an individual's preferences' (Scheinkman, 2006 p. 1).

Social interactions can affect the investment decisions of local investors, policy decisions of corporate managers and the formation of networks among providers of capital and financial intermediaries.

Brown *et al.* (2008) investigate the importance of geography in explaining equity market participation. They show that individuals are influenced by the investment behaviour of members of their community. They further find that proximity to publicly-traded firms also increases equity market participation. Hong *et al.* (2004) also show that stock-market participation is influenced by social interaction. Using data from the Health and Retirement Study, they find that social households (those who interact with their neighbours, or attend church) are more likely to invest in the market than non-social households.

Formal and informal networks among investors/managers from the same region could influence their investment/management style. Gompers *et al.* (2005), show that many new venture-backed companies are spawned from local public companies that were once venture-backed. Hochberg *et al.* (2007) examine the performance consequences and the success of the start-up companies of venture capital firms. They find that better-networked VC firms experience significantly better fund performance, as measured by the proportion of investments that are successfully exited through an IPO or a sale to another company. Similarly, the portfolio companies of better-networked VCs are significantly more likely to survive subsequent financing and eventual exit.

Social interactions and peer effects can be particularly important for corporate decision makers. Managers who work in the same geographic area normally have many opportunities to network and build valuable relationships with their peers, exchanging ideas and learning from each others' experience. For example, they may attend the same CEO clubs or meetings, or they may be members of the same regional business leadership associations, such as local charitable organizations and chambers of commerce. Davis and Greve (1997, p. 13) note that '[t]he country club cliché — that much business gossip is traded over golf games — is, in fact, surprisingly accurate, according to discussions with directors.'

Operating in an uncertain environment, corporate managers may look to their peers for ideas about appropriate strategies or mimic one another's behaviour through direct contact. Recent studies have suggested that social interaction with peers has tangible effects on a wide range of firm activities from charitable action (Galaskiewicz and Wasserman, 1989; and Marquis *et al.*, 2009), political contributions (Mizruchi, 1989), acquisition decision (Haunschild, 1993), corporate borrowing (Mizruchi and Stearns, 1994), to adoption of antitakeover procedures (Davis and Greve, 1997).

Kedia and Rajgopal (2009) study the 'neighbourhood effects' in corporate compensation policy where the peer effects are clearly location-based.

They find that firms grant more options when a higher proportion of firms in the local community (firms located within 100 or 250 km of its headquarters) grant more broad based options. The neighbourhood's option granting practices matter most when labor markets are tight and especially when firms want to retain employees by indexing wages to their outside opportunities in the neighbouring area.

Using data on antitakeover provisions and headquarter location for a large sample of US public corporations, John and Knyazeva (2008) document robust evidence of peer effects in corporate governance. They find that good governance breeds good governance locally; and good governance matters the most when peers have good governance.

3.6 Conclusion and Implications for Future Research

The geographic location of firms and financiers plays an important role in financial decision making. In this chapter, we review recent research on the link between location and corporate finance. Many of the studies included in this review are relatively new papers, which reflects the fact that most of the progress towards understanding the implications of location for finance has been made only recently. It also suggests that future research in this direction is potentially worthwhile and in order.

Existing research has established a strong link between the geographical proximity to firms and the degree of asymmetric information and agency costs of these firms. Generally, both information asymmetries and agency costs tend to decrease when capital providers reside closer to the firm. On the information side, proximity facilitates information acquisition through personal communications, social interactions and access to 'soft' information sources. On the agency side, proximity reduces agency conflicts as a result of higher transparency, lower costs of monitoring and a better ability to build personal relationships.

The informational and monitoring advantages of geographic proximity tend to benefit all parties involved — firms and various capital providers. Proximity enriches firms through a lower cost of external financing and financial flexibility — the option to raise capital later in sufficient amount and at reasonable costs. Proximity benefits financiers through the possibility of eliminating excessive information- and moral hazard-risks.

Given all the benefits of proximity, it is not surprising that both firms and investors exhibit strong preference for local transactions — all things equal, 'near' is better than 'far'. In economic systems, however, everything is interrelated. Systematic behaviour in one direction inevitably interacts with all other aspects of reality and these interactions could trigger a series of positive and negative feedbacks on the parties involved. Local preference is not an exception.

To clarify, the local preference of investors creates (partial) geographic segmentation of capital markets. In this segmentation, firms from a particular locale are largely financed and serviced by local investors and financial institutions. This segmentation creates value on the grounds of information production and monitoring but it also exposes the firm to a wide variety of individual and institutional characteristics from the region. Such exposure could interact with the firm in a variety of ways.

For example, regions with a greater proportion of young residents could have smaller aggregate savings than regions with a predominantly older population. This could have an impact on the regional supply of credit and, as a result, on the cost of debt capital. Next, consider a company that is headquartered in an area with a large number of institutional investors. Such a company would naturally have a lower cost of equity capital. Institutional investors, however, are different from individual investors and even institutional investors could differ among themselves. As a result, the mentality of institutional investors from the region could affect the behaviour of local firms in a unique way. If these institutional investors are active in corporate governance, the overall value of the firm could be higher. If these investors have long-term investment horizons, the firm would be more likely to invest long-term, while if these investors chase short-term returns, the firm would feel pressured to deliver short-term performance. In sum, local segmentation brings a rich set of attributes which could profoundly affect the behaviour of firms.

In our view this aspect of locality, namely the side-effects associated with local regional, demographic, cultural, and investor characteristics, is a promising direction for future research. On one hand, it could explain some general trends in regional economic development. On the other hand, it could have some useful policy implications, given that most countries exhibit some form of legal pluralism, i.e. coexistence of both national (federal) and local (state) level legislative branches.

The issue of geographic location naturally touches upon some fundamental questions of economics, such as the boundaries of the firm. For example, if locality is an advantage then geography imposes limits on the growth of firms. This may be the reason why some organizational forms, such as franchises, exist in the first place. Such forms allow the firm to have some level of centralized control, while at the same time maintaining sufficient local autonomy. Investigating how the organizational form of firms interacts with spatial composition is, in our view, another promising direction for future research.

Finally, the advantages of geographic proximity impose natural limits to financial globalization. It seems that even in the absence of strong regulatory and cultural differences across countries and regions, certain levels of segmentation would be always present in the market place. This suggests that the benefits of integration could have been significantly overstated in the academic literature.

Chapter 4

TUNNELING TECHNIQUES AND THEIR EFFECT ON FIRM VALUE AROUND THE WORLD

VLADIMIR ATANASOV

College of William and Mary

4.1 Introduction

Expropriation of firm value by insiders (managers and controlling share-holders), is perhaps the dominant agency problem in corporations and other joint companies around the world. Simply organizing the large number of possible transactions or activities that transfer wealth from minority investors to controllers remains a daunting task. Johnson *et al.* (2000b) advance the literature with a description of three case studies of large-scale wealth expropriation in European companies. They coin the term 'tunneling' to label such wealth transfers. Since Johnson *et al.* (2000b), research on tunneling has exploded into several different lines of literature encompassing economics, finance, and law.

Johnson *et al.* (2000b) define tunneling as the 'transfer of resources out of a company to its controlling shareholder (who is typically also a top manager).' They divide tunneling into two categories: (1) self-dealing transactions, which include transfer pricing, excessive compensation, taking of corporate opportunities, and asset sales; and (2) financial transactions that 'discriminate against minorities,' such as dilutive equity offerings and minority freeze-outs. Gilson and Gordon (2003) argue that the latter category is more damaging to minority shareholder value because it extracts the full present value of a future stream of income, rather than just this year's flow. Similar to Gilson and Gordon (2003), a number of other studies rely on the Johnson *et al.*'s (2000b) parsing of tunneling.

This chapter adopts a more refined taxonomy of tunneling developed by Atanasov, Black and Ciccotello (2008, ABC hereafter). Based on what is being tunneled, ABC divide tunneling techniques into three categories: equity tunneling, asset tunneling, and cash flow tunneling. Similar to Johnson *et al.* (2000), equity tunneling increases the controller's share of the firm's value but does not directly change the firm's productive assets. Asset tunneling involves the transfer of productive, long-term assets from the firm for less than market value, such that the transfer has a permanent effect on firm operations. Cash flow tunneling removes a portion of current year's cash flow, but does not affect the remaining stock of productive assets.

Borrowing a metaphor from ABC, if one describes a firm as an apple orchard, equity tunneling steals claims to ownership of the orchard; asset tunneling steals some of the trees (potentially making the remaining trees less valuable); and cash flow tunneling steals some of this year's crop of apples. Equity and asset tunneling involve the transfer of the stock of firm value; cash flow tunneling captures the flow. The stock versus flow logic builds on the intuition of Gilson and Gordon (2003). The distinction is also useful in thinking about the operational impact of tunneling. In ABC's taxonomy, cash flow and equity tunneling do not directly affect the company's future operations and profitability, while asset tunneling does.

Within the context of ABC's tunneling taxonomy, the chapter summarizes much of the existing empirical studies documenting various tunneling techniques around the world ranging from dual-class recapitalizations in Italy (Bigelli *et al.*, 2006) to inter-firm loans in China (Berkman *et al.*, 2008). The review of the literature shows that insiders in both emerging and developed markets use similar transactions to engage in tunneling, but the magnitude of wealth expropriation may vary widely across markets.

Several robust conclusions and policy implications arise from the review of the literature. First, tunneling has a large negative impact on firm value and capital market development. Limiting tunneling with regulations or other institutional mechanisms is a necessary condition for an emerging market to materialize. Second, legal and other institutions affect the occurrence of tunneling techniques and their magnitude. Effective anti-tunneling protections should reside in securities, corporate or tax law, and policy makers have to carefully take into account the interactions among legal statutes and evaluate the possible consequences from adopting any new rules on tunneling techniques. Lastly, strong securities regulators are necessary to enforce anti-tunneling statutes, at least during the early years of market development. Non-legal mechanisms are also important. Mechanisms like reputational concerns, independent directors, outside block ownership, or the media have been shown to limit the extent of tunneling.

The chapter identifies the following promising areas for future research on tunneling — (1) an economic analysis of legal protections against tunneling with the intent to evaluate the effectiveness of current anti-tunneling regulations and, where necessary, design more effective ones; (2) documenting the effect of tunneling using a more refined set of diagnostic tools as developed by ABC and complementing the Law and Finance literature with a series of Law–Tunneling–Finance studies similar to Atanasov *et al.* (2010a); (3) studying tunneling in public versus private companies and documenting the effectiveness of laws generally designed for publicly-traded companies on tunneling in private companies; and (4) adding tunneling to theoretical and empirical asset pricing models.

The chapter proceeds as follows. Section 3.2 describes the unbundling of tunneling. Section 3.3 then summarizes existing empirical studies of tunneling around the world and outlines several policy implications. Section 3.4 discusses areas for future research on tunneling. Section 3.5 concludes the chapter.

4.2 Taxonomy of Tunneling Techniques

This section classifies the types of tunneling by what is being tunneled — cash flow, assets, or equity using the model developed by ABC. This is followed by a table listing different types of transactions and activities by tunneling type (cash flow, asset, or equity).

4.2.1 *Cash Flow Tunneling*

Cash flow tunneling involves ongoing self-dealing transactions which divert cash flow from the firm to the controlling shareholder and/or manager. The central attributes of cash flow tunneling are: (1) it can potentially recur indefinitely; (2) it leaves the firm's long-term productive assets unchanged; (3) it leaves ownership claims over the firm's assets unchanged; and (4) if limited in extent, it may not significantly affect the firm's future cash-generating ability. Extensive cash flow tunneling may affect the firm's long-term ability to generate cash, by making it harder for the firm to attract employees, to raise capital, or obtain trust from counterparties (Black *et al.*, 2000), or by attracting the attention of tax collectors (Desai *et al.*, 2007).

Specific examples of cash flow tunneling include transfer pricing arrangements where the controlling shareholder (directly or through a controlled company) sells inputs to the firm at above-market prices or purchases firm outputs at below-market prices, excessive cash compensation for insiders, and loans to insiders at below-market rates. Outright theft of replaceable assets, including cash and equivalents, inventory, or receivables can also be classified as cash flow tunneling. Table 4.1 (Panel A) lists examples of cash flow tunneling transactions.

4.2.2 Asset Tunneling

Asset tunneling involves one-time self-dealing transactions that remove productive assets from the firm for less than fair value, to the favor of the controlling shareholder and/or manager. Johnson et al. (2000b) bundle asset tunneling together with cash flow tunneling into a category they label 'self-dealing transactions.' The difference in ABC's framework relates to the distinction between cash or cash equivalents, which are fungible (replaceable) assets, and other productive assets, which are firm-specific.

Asset tunneling is separate from cash flow tunneling for two main reasons. First, tunneling from the productive stock of assets diverts all future cash flows associated with the asset in a single transaction, while diverting cash flows is an ongoing process, which can be modified in the future. Second, diverting a productive asset may reduce the value of the firm's remaining assets and thus lower the overall profitability of the firm, while diverting firm free cash flow is purely redistributive and does not affect a firm's operating performance. Table 4.1 (Panel B) provides examples of cash flow tunneling transactions.

4.2.3 Equity Tunneling

The core characteristic of equity tunneling is that it rearranges stock ownership claims without directly affecting the firm's operations. Two important examples of equity tunneling transactions are stock offerings to insiders at below fair value and going-private transactions (freezeouts). Similarly, (jumbo) stock option or stock grants which award a large proportion of stock ownership to executives can be considered equity tunneling. Target share repurchases ('greenmail') and dual-class share recapitalizations are also forms of equity tunneling, as well as market timing and late trading in mutual funds. Table 4.1 (Panel C) provides examples of equity tunneling transactions.

4.3 Review of the Tunneling Literature

Since Johnson et al. (2000b) introduced the term "tunneling", dozens of papers have documented the prevalence of certain tunneling techniques

Table 4.1　Tunneling Transactions Classified by What is Being Tunneled.

Tunneling Type	Description
Panel A. Cash Flow Tunneling	
Transfer Pricing	Overpaying for inputs provided by related parties or undercharging for outputs sold to related parties
Cash compensation, perks and other personal consumption	Excessive salaries, pension benefits and other perks extended to insiders at the expense of the firm
Personal or intercompany loans	Interest rate charged on loan set at zero or below market interest rates. In some cases, loans are not expected to be repaid.
Panel B. Asset Tunneling	
Sales of long-term assets	Assets are sold to related party at a discount
Purchases of long-term assets	Assets are purchased from related party at a premium
Asset swaps	Firm exchanges assets with a related party at unfair terms
Granting use of firm assets	Assets are used by related party for reduced rent/lease
Transfer of intellectual property	Common with venture capitalists and other private equity investors. Venture capitalists transfers know-how and other intellectual property from company to other firms that the VC has invested in
Diverting business opportunities	Business opportunities are given to related parties for no compensation.
Panel C. Equity Tunneling	
Seasoned equity offerings or private placements for less than fair value	Controlling shareholder initiates a share offering at a price well below the current market price, which makes it difficult for minority shareholders to participate, and buys all unsubscribed shares
Targeted repurchases (greenmail)	Shares of related party are repurchased by the company at a premium to market price
Debt-, Assets- or Equity-for-Equity exchanges	Controller exchanges debt, assets, or equity in another firm for equity in company at non-market terms
Freeze-out via tender offer	Minority shares are bought by controller or company at a discount to intrinsic value. Company is then brought private

(Continued)

Table 4.1   (*Continued*).

Tunneling Type	Description
Going dark/delisting	Controlling shareholder causes company to delist. Trading ceases, minority shareholders retain illiquid, often worthless or nearly worthless shares
Sale of control at preferential terms for controlling shareholder	Controller sells company to an acquirer and receives a higher price for his shares than the price paid to minority shares
Market timing and late trading of open-end mutual funds	Excessive trading at stale mutual fund NAVs by selected informed investors dilutes the shares of buy-and-hold mutual fund investors
Dilution via excessive equity-based executive compensation	Insiders receive large restricted stock or option packages at zero cost that, when exercised, dilute remaining shareholders
Dual-class share recapitalizations	When converting to a single-class of shares, the low-voting shares are purchased by company at non-market prices

around the world, analyzed the impact of tunneling on firm value, financing, and profitability, or looked at the interactions between law and tunneling. I summarize this extensive literature in the following three sub-sections. In the last sub-section, I outline three major policy implications stemming from the extant tunneling literature.

4.3.1 *Studies Documenting Tunneling Methods*

4.3.1.1 *Cash Flow Tunneling*

Cash flow tunneling techniques are common around the world. Controllers in many companies have both the incentive and ability to divert a portion of the firm cash flow to themselves or related parties and there are plenty of opportunities to do so even in well regulated and developed markets. Of all cash flow tunneling techniques, transfer pricing is perhaps the most common. One of the three case studies presented in Johnson *et al.* (2000b) — concerning the Italian machine-maker Marcilli — is a classic transfer pricing case. The controlling shareholder set up another company that purchased all the output of Marcilli at below-market prices and then sold the output at a high markup. Other studies of transfer pricing include Deng *et al.* (2008) and Cheung, *et al.* (2006). Liu and Lu (2004) and Ming and Wong (2003) analyze transfer pricing transactions that are used to manage the earnings of listed Chinese companies. Finally, Bertrand *et al.* (2002) indirectly detect transfer pricing in Indian corporate pyramids by measuring the sensitivity of companies in the pyramid to shocks to the earnings of another company in the pyramid.

Other cash flow tunneling techniques investigated by academic studies include inter-corporate and executive loans (Berkman *et al.*, 2008; Jiang *et al.*, 2005) and dividend policy (Faccio *et al.*, 2001; Chen *et al.*, 2008). Lastly, Crystal (1991) presents many examples of excessive executive compensation in the US.

4.3.1.2 *Asset Tunneling*

In many cases cash flow tunneling is accompanied by large-scale asset tunneling (asset stripping). Asset tunneling, as argued by ABC, is much more destructive than cash flow tunneling, because it affects the future profitability of the company and, in the extreme, can leave only a corporate shell owning no productive assets. The third case covered by Johnson *et al.* (2000b) — the Italian company Barro — involves several asset tunneling transactions including pledging all assets as collateral for a loan and diverting future business opportunities to a related party.

China (mainland and Hong Kong) has been a fertile ground for studying asset tunneling. Prominent studies of asset tunneling in Chinese and Hong Kong companies include Cheung *et al.* (2008) who examine asset sales, purchases and swaps between related parties, and Deng *et al.* (2008) and Gao and Kling (2008) who focus on asset sales (asset stripping).

4.3.1.3 *Studies of Equity Tunneling*

Equity tunneling has received the most attention in the academic literature. Because equity tunneling is often associated with mergers, equity offerings or other major corporate events, researchers can observe the exact date of the equity tunneling event and obtain a lot more detail about the transaction compared to occurrences of cash flow or asset tunneling. The outcomes of equity tunneling are also easier to measure as equity tunneling, by definition, changes the ownership structure of the firm, which is observable on at least an annual basis in many countries.

Several recent studies have documented equity tunneling in countries from the former Soviet Bloc. For example, Atanasov *et al.* (2010a) show that before 2002, minority shareholders did not participate in equity issues initiated by companies listed on the Bulgarian Stock Exchange. Some of the controlling shareholders thus manage to increase their ownership stake from

50 to above 90 percent without expending much effort or resources in the process. Atanasov *et al.* (2010a) also document that the controllers of more than 60 percent of firms listed on the Bulgarian Stock Exchange either delist their firms (at no compensation for minority shareholders) or freeze out minority shareholders at large discounts to fair value.

Black (1998) analyzes a case in Russia, where the controlling shareholder places an "astounding 196,300 percent" of newly-issued shares into the hands of four related parties at a price more than 50 percent lower than the prevalent market price at the time of the placement. Given the size of the privately-placed blocks, non-participating shareholders lost more than 50 percent of their wealth following the transaction. The case described in Black (1998) was not an isolated event in the Russian market during the 1990s. Goldman (2003) reports at least five more cases of shareholder dilution, all in major Russian companies.

The transactions leading to the largest wealth expropriation via equity tunneling so far are the debt-for-equity swaps in post-Soviet Russia. Based on Goldman (2003), debt-for-equity swaps were an effective way for a handful of oligarchs to expropriate the government equity stake in many of the prized Russian corporations. Tunneled wealth is estimated to equal hundreds of billions, if not trillions, of dollars. In these debt-for-equity swaps, a modest loan to a state-owned company was converted into a private majority equity stake relying on artificially low equity valuations, well below fair value.

Equity tunneling does not occur only in ex-Socialist countries. Baek *et al.* (2006) investigate a large sample of private placements at non-market prices among companies in Korean chaebols and find evidence of shareholder dilution. Examples of equity tunneling in other East Asian countries are discussed in Backman (2002). Bigelli *et al.* (2006) analyze shareholder dilution following dual-class shares recapitalizations in Italian companies, while Kirchmaier and Grant (2005) present several case studies involving German and Italian companies that involve control transfers and mergers harmful to minority investors.

The common perception among academic scholars is that equity tunneling in the US is rare. Perhaps this is true in large publicly-traded companies. In contrast, investors in privately-held corporations often suffer from equity tunneling by controlling shareholders. The seminal work of O'Neal and Thompson (2004) presents, among other examples, the egregious case of Doll vs. James Martin Associates, in which the majority shareholder increases capital by half a million shares priced at $1 and dilutes the value of the minority shareholder from $90 per share to $1.78.

There is another set of privately-held corporations where potential dilution of company founders is part of the contract — venture capitalist backed startups. VCs often negotiate anti-dilution provisions in their contracts with entrepreneurs. These anti-dilution provisions are an effective way to dilute entrepreneurs if firm value declines in subsequent investment rounds. The problem of equity tunneling via such down-rounds is investigated in Leavitt (2005) and Atanasov *et al.* (2006).

Although classic equity tunneling in US publicly traded companies is arguably rare, many companies suffer from a more subtle form of equity tunneling — excessive stock or option-based executive compensation. Crystal (1991) includes several examples of egregiously large stock-option executive grants. In the case of Fairchild Corporation, the CEO, Jeffrey Steiner, increased his holdings in the company from 24 percent in 1985 to 66 percent in 1990 by granting himself options and other bonuses notwithstanding the subpar stock price performance of his company. Many large option grants are also backdated to choose the most attractive stock price in a past period (Lie, 2005). Backdating increases the shareholder dilution resulting from the large option grants.

Bates *et al.* (2006) look at short-form mergers that result in freezeouts of minority shareholders and do not find significant harm to minority share-holders, although such mergers are at smaller premiums to conventional mergers. Leuz *et al.* (2008) and Marosi and Massoud (2007) study going dark transactions and the resulting drop in liquidity and valuations affecting the shareholders of delisted companies. Another equity tunneling technique used in the US is targeted repurchases at a premium to market value. Such transactions were common in the 1980s and were denoted by the term 'greenmail' (Peyer and Vermaelen, 2005).

The last setting for equity tunneling in the US is the practice of mutual fund market timing and late trading (Bhargava *et al.*, 1998; Chalmers *et al.*, 2002; Zitzewitz, 2003). Greene and Ciccotello (2006) argue that, in essence, the market timers are buying undervalued shares at a net asset value, which does not reflect the market price of these shares. Zitzewitz (2003) estimates that the total transfer of wealth from buy-and-hold mutual fund investors to market timers equals $4.9 Billion in 2001.

4.3.2 *Tunneling and Equity Valuations*

The three categories of tunneling separately or in combination can affect equity valuations significantly. There are three types of studies that document the effect of tunneling on equity valuations — studies of private benefits of control, studies looking at the Tobin's q of firms around tunneling transactions, and studies measuring the announcement effect of disclosed tunneling transactions. The large and now well-established literature focusing on the value of voting rights documents that large investors enjoy private benefits of control. In particular, studies of large block transactions and dual-class share companies report a substantial control premium (Dyck and Zingales, 2004; Nenova, 2003; Atanasov, 2005), which is consistent with expected tunneling by controlling shareholders. Dyck and Zingales (2004) and Nenova (2003) estimate that the private benefits of control (alternatively expected tunneling transfers) equal between 0 and 50 percent of firm value depending on the country, while Atanasov (2005) shows that controlling shareholders of firms participating in the Bulgarian mass privatization expect to tunnel on average 85 percent of firm value.

Among the studies looking at the effects of tunneling on Tobin's q, Atanasov et al. (2010a) follow publicly-traded firms on the Bulgarian Stock Exchange and show that during a period of inadequate anti-tunneling legal protections equity tunneling was so rampant that Tobin's q was severely depressed. Following a strengthening of regulations against equity tunneling in 2002, average Tobin's q increased by more than 50 percent. Other studies looking at Tobin's q include Atanasov, et al. (2010b), who show that the combined effect of cash flow and asset tunneling results in a 20 percent discount of the Tobin's q of US companies with a large corporate blockholder; Gordon et al. (2004), who look at the effects of related party transactions on Tobin's q of US firms and find that executive loans are associated with the largest discounts; and Black et al. (2008), who show an increase in Tobin's q following regulations that improve anti-tunneling rules in large Korean firms.

There are much fewer studies measuring the short-term announcement effects of disclosed tunneling transactions due to the disclosure rules in most countries. Hong Kong has one of the strongest disclosure rules for related-party transactions. These disclosures are used by Cheung et al. (2006) to study the announcement effects of various tunneling transactions. This study finds as much as a 22 percent decline in firm value following announced asset sales to related parties. Bae et al. (2002) look at the announcement effects of mergers involving a company in a Korean chaebol on other companies in the same chaebol and find large negative valuation effects of suspected tunneling mergers.

4.3.3 Tunneling and Laws and Other Institutional Mechanisms

The literature that looks at how laws and regulations affect the extent of tunneling is relatively limited. Johnson et al. (2000b) discuss briefly the main legal principles in common law that limit widespread tunneling and a few statutes in Continental European law that may serve the same purpose. Gilson and Gordon (2003) and Black (2001, 2001a) discuss extensively anti-tunneling statutes, but do not conduct any empirical analysis of actual tunneling. Djankov *et al.* (2008) develop a comprehensive economic model of various legal statutes regulating related-party transactions and use their model to evaluate the quality of anti-tunneling laws around the world. They indirectly show that these laws are associated with more developed equity markets and higher valuations. In a similar vein, Atanasov *et al.* (2008) present a model of preemptive rights and other anti-dilution protections and classify the approaches against equity tunneling via dilution taken by various countries around the world.

Perhaps the first studies that analyze equity tunneling transactions pre and post-legal change are Atanasov *et al.* (2006 and 2010a). These studies document that dilutive equity issues and freezeouts at large discounts cease following the changes to Bulgarian securities law in 2002. Other studies of legal changes that indirectly document changes in expected tunneling are Nenova (2005) and Carvalhal-da-Silva and Subrahmanyam (2007) which look at the dual-class shares premia around a suspension of a mandatory bid rule in Brazil.

Besides laws on the books, studies have shown that other mechanisms can modify or limit tunneling. These include — (1) a strong securities regulator (Atanasov *et al.*, 2010a; Pistor and Xu, 2005; Glaeser *et al.*, 2001); (2) media coverage, especially from established business outlets like the Wall Street Journal and the Financial Times (Dyck *et al.*, 2008); (3) reputational concerns, especially when courts provide little remedy against tunneling in privately held companies (Atanasov *et al.*, 2007); and (4) outside activist blockholders (see the case study of SK Telecom in Atanasov *et al.*, 2008).

4.3.4 *Policy Implications*

The following conclusions stem from the analysis of the tunneling literature. First, tunneling has large negative effects on firm value and capital market development. If tunneling is left unregulated, trillions of dollars can be tunneled (Goldman, 2003) and as much as 85 percent of a firms value can be diverted on average by controlling shareholders (Atanasov, 2005). All studies of the effects of tunneling on firm value document significant discounts due to tunneling risk. Limiting tunneling risk is a necessary condition for an emerging market to eventuate and should be the main focus of regulators seeking to improve equity market performance (Glaeser *et al.*, 2001). Atanasov *et al.* (2010a) show that uncontrolled equity tunneling via dilution and freezeout almost destroyed the Bulgarian stock market until, in 2002, new government reforms limited equity tunneling and dramatically increased equity valuations and liquidity.

Second, legal and other institutions affect the occurrence of tunneling techniques and their magnitude. The extant evidence on tunneling suggests that tunneling transactions tend to be relatively more complex in developed markets. Efforts by insiders in developed markets to disguise tunneling transactions are made rationally in response to stricter legal protection and enforcement mechanisms present in the developed market. Depending on the type of tunneling technique that needs to be regulated, effective anti-tunneling protections can reside in securities, corporate or tax law. Policy makers have to carefully take into account the interactions among legal statutes and evaluate the possible consequences from adopting any new rules on tunneling techniques. For example, the adoption of the Private Securities Litigation Reform Act (PSLRA) in the US has unintentionally made litigation of tunneling in privately-held companies much harder (Atanasov *et al.*, 2007).

Third, strong securities regulators are necessary to enforce anti-tunneling statutes, at least during the early years of market development. Non-legal mechanisms are also important. Mechanisms like controller reputation concerns, independent directors, outside block ownership, and the media have been shown to limit the extent of tunneling. Any analysis of the quality of anti-tunneling protections in a country has to take into account enforcement and the above-listed non-legal mechanisms as complements or substitutes to the written laws.

4.4 Areas for Future Research

The existing literature on tunneling is already large and growing fast. Yet, there are still promising areas that have not been extensively studied. This section identifies four such areas for future research on tunneling.

4.4.1 *Economic Analysis of Law and Tunneling*

There are only a handful of studies that rigorously analyze the effect of legal statutes on tunneling techniques. Notable examples include Djankov *et al.* (2008) and Atanasov *et al.* (2010a). Most existing studies do not model in sufficient detail the mechanisms through which laws and regulations limit the magnitude or likelihood of tunneling (Bebchuk and Jolls, 1999; Burkart *et al.*, 1998; Shleifer and Wolfenzon, 2002; Durnev and Kim, 2005). Theoretical analysis of these anti-tunneling legal mechanisms is a promising area of research that requires the collaboration of experts in law, economics (especially game theory) and finance. Detailed theoretical models can enable the *ex ante* economic analysis of proposed legal changes and their interactions with existing statutes across different bodies of law and provide policy recommendations for the design of optimal anti-tunneling rules.

The empirical literature on the effect of rules and regulations on tunneling is also scant. With more advanced modeling in place, empiricists will have a large number of specific predictions to test, or conversely, empirical research can stimulate the design of more realistic theoretical models that explain the documented empirical findings. There are many countries that have implemented changes in their anti-tunneling laws which provide natural experiments for pre- versus post-law changes analysis of tunneling in the spirit of Atanasov *et al.* (2009a).

4.4.2 *Measuring the Impact of Tunneling in a Law–Tunneling–Finance Framework*

ABC show that different types of tunneling have differing effects on valuation and profitability metrics. These differences provide an opportunity for empirical research to separate the effects of each tunneling type. Cash flow tunneling, which is expected to continue indefinitely, directly impacts firm market capitalization, Tobin's *q*, and ROA, but does not directly affect Price/Observable Earnings, because it affects both the numerator and denominator similarly. Anticipated asset tunneling will reduce Tobin's *q* because the risk of tunneling affects market value (the numerator), but the book value of assets (the denominator) remains unaffected. The risk of equity tunneling directly affects all market-based measures but does not impact profitability metrics like ROA or operating margin.

An effort to document more precisely the effects of different forms of tunneling on valuation and profitability metrics could help to more tightly link law to finance. The law-to-finance link has been established at a country level in La Porta *et al.* (1997, 1998) and the now large body of related literature. One way that law affects finance is by affecting tunneling — the channel is law to tunneling to finance. To establish this link, one needs to show two main connections — between law and tunneling and between tunneling and observed financial metrics. ABC's tunneling taxonomy would assist the development of the law and tunneling literature by allowing researchers to classify different statutes based on their expected impact on different types of tunneling, and to then study how these statutes affect financial metrics, either in cross-country analysis or single-country time-series studies.

4.4.3 *Tunneling in Private vs. Public Companies*

Many of the tunneling examples in the seminal work of O'Neal and Thompson (2004) involve private companies. The lack of adequate disclosure or any external governance pressures and the frequent dual-role of investors as employees make privately-held companies more susceptible to large-scale tunneling. The legal system is also likely to less effectively protect minority investors in privately-held companies (for example, private companies are not monitored by securities regulators). Yet, the majority of tunneling studies focus on publicly-traded companies. This imbalance is perhaps due to data availability, but some data on private companies is available, at least in developed markets. Bureau van Dijk collects accounting and ownership data for more than one million privately-held companies in Europe. Many Scandinavian countries have extensive data on all joint companies regardless of listing status. Any study of the tunneling techniques used in private companies and the economic effects of tunneling on small businesses and entrepreneurship will be an important addition to the academic literature. Such a study can document the relative importance of laws on the books that apply to both public and private companies versus public enforcement, media attention, and other external corporate governance mechanisms that are available only in public companies.

4.4.4 *Tunneling and Asset Pricing*

ABC argue that asset and equity tunneling can be decomposed into a probability of a tunneling event (e.g. freezeout) and a total loss of wealth for minority shareholders conditional on the tunneling event occurring (e.g. freezeout discount), similar to models of debt default risk (e.g. Merton, 1974). The advantage of separating these parameters is that they can be estimated separately using data on the incidence of tunneling transactions and the average wealth transfers suffered by minority investors in such transactions. Compared with the extensive literature on default risk, there is very little research on what firm characteristics predict the likelihood of tunneling to occur and what the average tunneling discounts are. Considering the importance of tunneling risk for equity investors (similar to the importance of default risk for bond investors), it is likely that such research will not only have an academic impact, but will receive plenty of interest from practitioners.

Tunneling risk directly affects firm valuation and firm implied cost of capital/expected return. Firms at high risk of tunneling will have depressed valuations. Equivalently, their cost of capital will appear higher than the cost of capital of low-tunneling-risk firms. This apparent cost of capital surcharge will derive partly from country-wide tunneling risk and partly from firm-level risk. The impact of tunneling risk on firm cost of capital appears similar to a conventional asset pricing factor like firm size of book-to-market.

If one estimates total cost of capital using only standard asset pricing factors as independent variables and omits the impact of tunneling risk, omitted variable bias could affect coefficient estimates. For example, tunneling risk is likely to be correlated with firm size (Atanasov *et al.*, 2010a). Book/market is directly related to market value of equity, which is related to tunneling risk. Hence, firm expected returns may appear driven by size and book/market, while in fact these apparent effects are entirely due to tunneling risk. All of these concerns warrant a whole new research area that combines tunneling and asset pricing.

4.5 Conclusion

Tunneling in its various forms is pervasive in both developed and emerging markets. Not surprisingly, a large number of recent papers study tunneling and its interactions with laws and regulations on one hand, and finance on the other hand. This chapter summarizes the extensive tunneling literature and outlines several important policy implications stemming from this literature. The chapter then identifies four promising venues for future research on tunneling and its impact on capital markets.

Tunneling is likely to continue being a major factor deterring equity market development and firm performance in the long run. Going forward, I believe research on tunneling will maintain its strong growth and not only contribute to the academic literature, but will also improve the decision making of government regulators, foreign and domestic investors, fundamental analysts and other financial intermediaries. Research on tunneling can be valuable even to controlling shareholders by showing them the long-term impact of tunneling on firm value and the trade-offs involved.

Chapter 5

INSIDER TRADING REGULATIONS: A THEORETICAL AND EMPIRICAL REVIEW

BART FRIJNS, AARON GILBERT
AND ALIREZA TOURANI-RAD

Auckland University of Technology

5.1 Introduction

Investors nowadays have unprecedented and increasing access to a vast multitude of investment opportunities in a variety of financial markets around the world. Hence, it is vital that countries make investing in their domestic markets as appealing to local and international investors as possible. One area of focus for policy makers should be improving the regulatory and governance setting, allowing investors to feel assured that they face minimal risk of expropriation via unsavoury practices. In recent years, a growing body of academic literature in finance and law has examined the impact of regulation on the development of financial markets. In particular, insider trading, as a subset of this field and the focus of this chapter, has received considerable attention. Insiders have an informational advantage, due to their relationship with the issuing company, over other investors. Access to unpublished information allows insiders to earn excess returns when they trade their companies' shares. Academic studies examining insider profitability has established that insiders do earn significant abnormal returns almost irrespective of the country or period examined (see among others, Jaffe, 1974; Finnerty, 1976; Seyhun, 1986, 1998; Rozeff and Zaman, 1988; and Lakonishok and Lee, 2001, for the US; Baesel and Stein, 1979, for Canada; Del Brio *et al.*, 2002, for Spain; Etebari *et al.*, 2004, for New Zealand; and Pope *et al.*, 1990; Friederich *et al.*, 2002, for the UK).

55

While insiders win, it is outside investors who are perceived, accurately or inaccurately, to lose. The perception of playing in a 'rigged' game has been argued as contributing to a loss of confidence in the market as a whole, resulting in investors limiting their investments in such markets or withdrawing completely, requiring higher returns, and seeking investments with a low risk of expropriation (Bernhadt *et al.*, 1995). Therefore, markets which do not effectively regulate insider trading will find themselves at a distinct disadvantage compared to better regulated markets. While the negative evidence regarding insiders' impact on the market has generally been accepted, the most useful schemes to prevent, or at least limit, insider trading has been scarcely studied to date.

This chapter provides an overview of the debate on the positive and negative aspects of insider trading in general and moves on to discuss regulating insider trading in particular. We attempt to provide evidence on the structure of insider trading laws that are most effective in limiting the harm from insiders. To date, enacting laws to control insiders has been on a somewhat ad-hoc basis with little guidance from the literature as to what is and is not important for an effective regime. This has led to several unsuccessful situations around the world including New Zealand's private enforcement and the Netherlands' criminal-only regime, both of which failed to effectively address the problem. The main concern is that the ad-hoc nature of the regulations has the potential to do more harm than good if they are not effective. In most cases, the insider trading laws that have been implemented have been designed without specific thought or understanding of the potential impacts on financial markets. It also appears that much of the evidence cited when regulatory changes are made relates to anecdotal examination of the performance of specific definitions, rules and punishments in other markets. As such, there has been a lack of detailed evidence used in the construction of these regulations despite the potential for significant harm where poorly designed regulations are implemented. Specific blame for this cannot be laid at the feet of regulators. The absence of academic literature, at least until recently, on the performance of specific insider trading regimes and the lack of guidance on what constitutes good insider trading rules has given regulators little assistance in policy making.

5.2 The Debate on Insider Trading Laws

5.2.1 *The Case for Insider Trading*

Manne (1966) is largely credited with originating the debate on insider trading. He argues that insider trading is not only beneficial, but vital, for the development of financial markets based on two arguments. First, insider trading improves price accuracy, and second, insider trading is the best way to compensate managers. These assertions have been challenged and counter-arguments for why insiders should be prohibited from trading have been developed as a result.

5.2.1.1 *Price Accuracy*

Price accuracy is widely accepted as being an important component in developing efficient capital markets. More accurate pricing of securities allows the market to more effectively evaluate the prospects of companies and so, improves allocation decisions within the economy (Fishman and Hagerty, 1992; Khanna and Slezak, 1994). Bainbridge (2000) points out that price accuracy reduces share price volatility, which in turn reduces individual windfall gains, making the capital markets more attractive for risk-adverse investors. Price accuracy is also important in monitoring managers as it allows prices to more accurately measure firm performance.

However, the goal of promoting price accuracy is considered less important than a firms' need to withhold material information from the market and its competitors to function effectively. Developing and undertaking new projects are all functions of a company that require the company to be able to delay informing the market until they are ready. However, it is also vital for the market to possess this information to allow it to accurately put a value on the firm. What Manne (1966) argued is that insider trading can provide a bridge between the need for corporate privacy and the markets' need for information. When an insider initiates a trade in the market, their presence is detected, and while the specific details of the information the insider is trading on remains undisclosed, the price impact of the information can be inferred based on the insider's trades. This allows the market to incorporate the price impact of the undisclosed information into the price and maintain accurate prices. In this fashion, insider trading effectively acts as a substitute for public disclosure.

The price accuracy argument made by Manne (1966) has been questioned on several grounds. The first argument questions whether insider trading does, in fact, provide an effective process by which material information can be presented to the market. A number of studies have examined the price effects of insider trading to see whether insider trades convey information to the market, with mixed results. Meulbroek (1992) examined the impact on the daily prices of illegal insider trades that were detected and prosecuted by the SEC in the US. She concluded that the presence of insiders in the market resulted in price movements consistent with the market correcting for the insider's information.

Cornell and Sirri (1992) and Chakravarty and McConnell (1997), using datasets of illegal insider transactions, also found similar evidence of price movements consistent with price correction. However, Chakravarty and McConnell (1999) recanted their early positive evidence by comparing the market's price reaction to informed and uninformed trading, and found no significant difference. More concerning is the finding of Chung and Charoenwong (1998) who argued that insider trading cannot be observed accurately by the market based on the reactions of bid-ask spreads on days with insider trading. Chang and Suk (1998) show that, even after trades are disclosed to the market, secondary disclosures in the Wall Street Journal result in price adjustments. This adds further evidence to the argument that the process by which insider trading informs the market of the price effect of information is slow, sporadic and not efficient, calling into question the price accuracy basis for allowing insider trading (Bainbridge, 2000).

The other major critique of Manne's (1966) price accuracy argument came from those who question whether the net effect of insider trading would be positive. Brudney (1979) and Esterbrook (1981) both pointed out that allowing insiders to profit from inside information may result in significant agency problems. In particular, it may encourage insiders to delay disclosure of that information to the market via an announcement for as long as possible to preserve the possibility of trading profits. This argument gains support from evidence showing that insiders attempt to hide their presence by splitting up trades to preserve their informational advantage for as long as possible (Kraakman, 1991). Further, Fishman and Hagerty (1992) suggested that the presence of insiders may discourage private information gathering activities by investors and analysts. Bushman *et al.* (2005) examined the relationship between insiders and analysts by studying analyst following for companies in 103 markets after the introduction and first enforcement of insider trading laws. They found that actions that limit insider trading resulted in increased analyst following suggesting that information production is negatively affected by insiders. Gilbert *et al.* (2006) further show that this relationship also holds at the firm level based on actual levels of disclosed insider trading within the firm. Despite the criticisms for the basis of insider trading, it is widely acknowledged that insider trading does improve price accuracy.

5.2.1.2 *Efficient Compensation*

Manne (1966) contended that the strongest argument in favour of allowing insider trading was the idea that it represented the most efficient way of compensating managers. Manne (1966) and Carlton and Fischel (1983) argued that innovators are encouraged to produce valuable information only when they have the ability to share in the rewards, namely the firm's increase in value. Rather than attempting to renegotiate after the creation of valuable information, which is both extremely costly and difficult, allowing innovators to trade on their information which has not been released offers an alternative, cheaper form of compensation. Manne (1966) argued that contractual and bonus compensation is inadequate largely because it fails to accurately reflect the added value of the innovation to the firm. This means that the innovators will likely be under-rewarded for their contribution, and will therefore be less likely to innovate.

This line of reasoning has run into criticism for a number of reasons. First, while it is arguably right to compensate the innovator, due to the nature of such information and the fact that it is often necessary for the information to be shared, it is virtually impossible to limit its use simply to those who created it (Bainbridge, 2000). In essence, those who have contributed little to the increase in firm value can also benefit equally. As Ausubel (1990) noted, much of the modern insider trading activity is not being conducted by traditional corporate insiders but, instead, by market professionals involved with the company, such as investment bankers. Preventing information-based trading by those not directly involved with its creation, the majority of those defined as insiders, would have little effect on information creation. The other concern raised by Bainbridge (2000) is that it is also difficult to limit insiders simply to profiting when they have produced valuable information. The availability of trading mechanisms that allow insiders to benefit from price declines, through short selling and put options, undermine the disincentive component of risky compensation as insiders can benefit regardless of the performance of the firm. Ausubel (1990) further suggested that as insiders can profit from either good or bad news, there may even be an incentive for managers to intentionally perform poorly because bad news is easier to create.

Another concern regarding insider trading as a source of compensation is the incentives it gives to insiders. Carlton and Fischel (1983) argues that insider trading as a portion of compensation will discourage high quality management as risky compensation tends to attract less competent and less risk-adverse managers. They even go so far as to suggest that the possibility of trading on bad news is justified as it may induce insiders to take on risky projects while still being compensated. Esterbrook (1981) and Bebchuk and Fershtman (1994) both note that while insider trading may reduce the problem of risk-adverse managers who turn down risky projects, there was no guarantee that the projects selected by managers will earn sufficient returns to compensate for the extra risk. As the insider's compensation is based on stock price volatility in either direction, positive or negative, the key factor for the insider becomes volatility (Beny, 1999; Manove, 1989).

Finally, it has also been noted that contracts involving insider trading are difficult to enforce. While an agreement may be worked out between the insider and the company, difficulties in assessing the trading returns in advance make selecting the most cost-effective compensation package problematic (Esterbrook, 1981). Further, even where the agreement allows for a level of insider trading, it is easy for the insider to overstep these boundaries. Only careful monitoring, therefore, will allow the company to maintain the contracted levels of compensation, and, given the possibility of an insider hiding their trading, it is possible for an insider to circumvent and expropriate unearned compensation (Kraakman, 1991).

Given the development of a variety of new techniques for compensating managers and the identification of a number of serious issues surrounding the use of insider trading as a compensation mechanism, Manne's (1966) argument that insider trading is an efficient form of compensation has been largely dismissed. As a result, the only reason still used to justify a stance allowing any insider trading is to some extent the idea of price accuracy.

5.2.2 *The Case Against Insider Trading*

A number of arguments have been put forward for prohibiting insider trading. Reasons offered for rejecting insider trading revolve around several concepts, including the property rights of information and the impact this has on the actions of insiders, and arguments around the inequity of insider trading and the effect it has on the markets. Both arguments appear to have found some favour: property rights for the legal justification it gives for prohibiting insider trading and unfairness arguments as an explanation for why insider trading may not promote market efficiency.

5.2.2.1 *Property Rights*

The property rights argument has largely resulted from the rationale used in US cases to justify federal prosecution of insider trading (Bainbridge, 2000). This is based on the belief that the property right created to undisclosed information should be vested in the company. This opens up two causes of action against insiders: a breach of a fiduciary duty to the company itself, and an argument for misappropriation. Bainbridge (2000) argued that the property rights argument had a great deal of appeal as the concept of creating and vesting a property right to the company is both relatively straight forward and has precedents in other areas of law. Property rights in intangibles like information are a well established principle in areas of law such as patent and copyright. The creation of such a right is justified on the basis that property rights should be given where there is a significant risk of the creator of valuable information being denied the opportunity to benefit from their efforts (Bainbridge, 2000). Bainbridge (2000) argued that there is a possibility that premature disclosure of information or alerting of the market to valuable opportunities for a firm before the firm is in a position to exploit them, can reduce the value of any information created. The investment of the property right with insiders may even have an effect on firm plans such as the timing of revenues, depreciation or dividend payments in an attempt to offer profitable situations for insiders (Brudney, 1979), again affecting the value of information to the company. Bainbridge (2000) also argued that the mere possibility, however remote, of a reduction in value to the creating company is enough to warrant vesting the property rights with the company as opposed to insiders.

The view that the company should possess any property rights to information created by the firm has found favour with the US courts and opens up two legal justifications for prosecuting insiders. The first of these is the breach of a fiduciary duty owed by the insider to the company which the US Supreme Court in *Chiarella v United States* was deemed to be necessary for rule 10b-5, the section of the law in the US that prohibits insider trading, to be breached. In particular, the courts have ruled that the insider must have a duty to refrain from trading based on confidential information. It was stated by the court in *Chiarella* that three situations give rise to such a fiduciary duty: (1) where the insider is an employee of the company such as a director or executive, (2) where the insider is not an employee but works in a capacity which lends an obligation to the shareholders such as investment bankers or lawyers working for the firm, and (3) where the insider receives information from someone who breached a duty in giving them that information, that is, a tippee of a corporate insider. These situations effectively cover most occasions in which a person will receive material information, and therefore present little problem in establishing a fiduciary duty.

The concept of misappropriation offers an alternative in the situation where there is no direct fiduciary duty between the trader and the company producing the information. The US Supreme Court in *US v O'Hagan*, and earlier in the dissenting opinion in *Chiarella v US*, ruled that an individual can breach the necessary duty when they misappropriate the source of the information. For instance, where an individual works in a firm with a duty to the issuing company and receives information as a result of that employment, they may be held to have breached their duty to their employers. That breach was deemed to be sufficient in *O'Hagan* to constitute the breach of fiduciary duty required for a prosecution.

5.2.2.2 *Unfairness*

The other major argument against insider trading is the concept that insider trading is fundamentally unfair and the harm caused to the investor damages the market as a whole. The outside investor is principally harmed by the insider being able to sell or buy at the most advantageous times as a result of their superior knowledge, ensuring that the outsider is at a disadvantage. This is not without its detractors. Manne (1966) and Carlton and Fischel (1983) both disputed the basic assumption that outsiders are actually harmed by the actions of insiders. As they pointed out, the other party to the trade was a willing participant having come to the market to trade because they believed, based on their assessment of the company, that it was either under or overvalued. Had there not been a better informed party in the market, and it is mere bad luck that they traded against such a party, the trade would still have been conducted at the same price. Bainbridge (2000) went so far as to suggest that the perception that outsiders are harmed is merely envy on the part of those harmed rather than an actual economic harm. This argument does have some appeal but is flawed due to the nature of the information. It is information that is unavailable to anyone except someone associated with the firm, and, therefore, regardless of the efforts of the outsider is an information gap they cannot bridge, unlike other informed parties such as analysts.

Bainbridge (2000) and Macey (1991) both offered some anecdotal evidence to suggest that the predicted effects on the market have not occurred. Bainbridge (2000) noted that despite major scandals of the mid-1980s, the performance on the US markets since had been excellent. He argued that it is hard to accept that investor confidence had been diminished when, in spite of new evidence that insider trading is prevalent, the market has performed so well. Likewise, Macey (1991) argued that the depth and health of the stock markets of Japan, Hong Kong and India, where insider trading had either only just been regulated or insider trading regulations had been repealed, implies investor confidence is not overly harmed by insider trading.

There is empirical evidence, however, indicating that the harm to the market from reduced investor confidence is both real and does impact markets. Ausubel (1990) modelled the effects of insider trading on outside investor's confidence in the market and concluded that when investors feel that they will be taken advantage of, they reduce their investment in that market. This results in a decrease in the liquidity of the market. Bernhadt *et al.*

(1995) likewise theorised that investors will be attracted to investments where there is a lower chance of being exploited. While measuring investor confidence directly has so far proven difficult, Beny (2005) concluded that liquidity is lower in markets with weaker insider trading laws, in line with the predictions of Ausubel (1990) and Bernhardt *et al.* (1995). Further, weaker regimes are also associated with reduced price accuracy and more concentrated share ownership (Beny, 2005), lower analyst following (Bushman *et al.*, 2005) and higher costs of capital (Bhattacharya and Daouk, 2002). Copeland and Galai (1988), Glosten and Milgrom (1985) and Kyle (1985) also argued that insider trading adds to the transaction costs within a market, an outcome that inherently makes the markets less efficient.

Regardless of the issue of whether the profits earned by insiders represent an actual harm to the other party in the trade, both theoretically and empirically, there is a strong acceptance that insider trading undermines confidence in the market. At its most basic level, insider trading does represent an inherently unfair advantage. The evidence also suggested that insider trading is related to a number of factors that affect the development and efficacy of the market as a whole, such as the liquidity and cost of capital of the market (Beny, 2005; Bhattacharya and Daouk, 2002). Whether this is an acknowledgement of the risk associated by trading in a market with more prevalent insider trading or a result of insiders' actions undermining the market, is an open question. The net effect, however, remains the same — the market is made less efficient and its development is retarded. This suggests a strong reason for prohibiting the actions of insiders.

5.3 Insider Trading Laws in Practice

The debate so far appears to have stalled as both those advocating for and against insider trading have valid arguments backing their position. However, regulation covering insider trading has become far more common. Prior to the mid-1980s relatively few countries had regulations covering insiders, but since that time, the absence of such laws has become the exception. Bhattacharya and Daouk (2002) noted that, by 1998, 87 countries had laws including all the world's developed markets, in contrast to just 34 before 1990. Whether these laws are correctly aligned and, indeed, whether the various arguments for and against insider trading are valid, are empirical questions (Carlton and Fischel, 1983). However, empirical studies providing some clues have been slow in coming. Only with further empirical study of the various impacts of insider trading, both positive and negative, can the debate regarding the regulation or total prohibition of insider trading be concluded.

Given the potentially serious consequences of unrestricted insider trading on investor confidence in the market, some restrictions are justified. However, at the same time, insider trading does offer a useful source of unpriced information that results in more accurate prices. What is also apparent is the fact that insider trading is difficult, if not impossible, to resolve via private contracting. Monitoring to ensure breaches of the contract do not occur is extremely costly and outside the means and abilities of most private individuals, while the ability to benefit from both good and bad news undermines many of the incentives that insider trading might have otherwise offered. As a result, insider trading meets the requirements laid out by La Porta *et al.* (2000) for public regulation and enforcement.

Regulators, however, need to develop regulations that can prevent the worst harm of insider trading while promoting trading in situations where it benefits the market. The solution in many markets has been to ban trading on certain information and allow it on other information. Many markets delineate legal from illegal based on the information used by the insider such that the use of ***material*** or price sensitive information is prohibited. Material information covers specific information that has not yet been released to the market and that which, if released, would have an impact on the price, such as merger announcements, earnings information or new product developments. The basis of this prohibition seems to be that the information could be better released via a company announcement with a limited delay (Manove, 1989). In these cases, a small delay in getting specific information into the price is less harmful than the impact of allowing insiders to profit at the expense of other market participants. In essence, this leaves insiders to act in a similar fashion to analysts, processing all publically available information and using that information to identify situations where the market price is wrong and so profit from the corrections. In this sense, they act to improve price accuracy without using knowledge of upcoming events and so minimises the harm from their trading.

5.4 Empirical Evidence on the Impact of Insider Trading Regulations

Just as La Porta *et al.* (1997, 1999, 2000, 2002, 2006) in a series of studies have started to examine the impact of investor protection laws in general, studies have begun to examine the impact of insider trading laws, particularly with an emphasis on trying to identify the features of a good insider trading law regime. To date, the literature is incomplete and more work is needed to assist lawmakers in developing effective rules.

The first paper to examine the issue of the effectiveness of insider trading rules was one that looked at the impact of the enactment and enforcement of insider trading laws on the cost of capital within a market by Bhattacharya and Daouk (2002). They examined changes in the cost of capital within a country for 103 countries around the first enactment and the first enforcement of insider trading laws. Their results show that, for developing countries, it was enforcement, not enactment, which resulted in a significant reduction in the country risk premium. They argued this as evidence that, irrespective of what was included in laws, the laws had to be enforceable to be effective. Developed markets, on the other hand, saw an improvement following the enactment, likely an acknowledgement of the generally superior legal systems making enforcement a more certain outcome. In a follow up paper, Bhattacharya and Daouk (2009) also found that in countries where laws had been enacted but not enforced, the risk premium was actually higher than if they had not enacted laws in the first place.

Bris (2005), examining insider trading in the lead up to a takeover announcement in a sample of 51 countries and 4541 acquisitions, found that the enforcement of insider trading laws actually increased insider trading. In addition, Bris (2005) found that in countries with weaker insider trading laws, the introduction of the laws also increased the profits earned from illegal insider trading. Greater penalties, rather than enforcement, reduced the profitability of insider trading. What Bris (2005) concludes, therefore, is that it is the potential penalty, not the risk of being prosecuted, which has the deterrence value in relation to insider trading. Durnev and Nain (2004) also find that insider trading laws are a mixed blessing: while they do find that stricter insider trading laws reduce private information trading, they find evidence to suggest that where agency costs are high, controlling shareholders simply use other methods of expropriating returns, resulting in more opaque earnings.

Teen *et al.* (2008) examine the impact of a person-connected versus information-connected approach to the prohibition of insider trading. Under a person-connected approach, the prosecution needs to establish a fiduciary relationship with the company in addition to establishing trading on material non-public information. An information-connected approach, however, ignores the connection to the company and focuses purely on the possession and use of non-public price-sensitive information. This makes it an easier test for the prosecution and, therefore, was argued as being the stricter law. The US, for instance, requires the insider to have a connection to the company in which the trading occurs. Given that the US was the first to regulate against insider trading, many countries have followed this approach. However, when Teen *et al.* (2008) tested the switch from person-connected to information-connected rules in Singapore, Malaysia and Australia, they found mixed outcomes. Illegal insider trading decreased in Singapore after the enactment of the rules, and in Malaysia after the first enforcement, supporting the findings from Bhattacharya and Daouk (2002) regarding developed and emerging markets. However, there was no reaction in Australia to the change in legal regime.

Frijns *et al.* (2008) also considered the effect of a regulatory change that was argued as tightening the insider trading laws in New Zealand in 2002. Rather than looking at measures of insider trading surrounding takeover announcements as Teen *et al.* (2008) does, however, Frijns *et al.* (2008) used the Madhaven *et al.* (1997) bid-ask spread decomposition model. Spread decomposition, using this model, separates spreads into two components: inventory and order processing costs, and information asymmetry costs. As the model looks at changes in spreads as a result of trades only, the information asymmetry component does not include the arrival of new public information which will result in spread changes without causing trades. Rather the information asymmetry component measures information arriving as a result of unexpected trade volume. This represents informed traders exploiting unpriced information. The information asymmetry component is useful in examining insider trading as spreads are set so that market makers cover their costs. As a result, the information asymmetry component represents the likelihood of the market maker trading against an informed trader and the losses they expect to incur. Changes in this measure, therefore, represents the market's perception of the impact of regulatory changes. This also allows quick evaluation of the impact of laws.

Frijns *et al.* (2008) found that the law changes in NZ, which included the introduction of a public watchdog and a significant reduction in the time between an insider's trade and its disclosure to the market, did strengthen the insider trading regime. The proportion of the spread attributable to information asymmetry declined, driven primarily by illiquid companies and by those with high information asymmetry prior to the law change, as did the price volatility. These findings suggest that the structure of laws do affect the market outcomes of insider trading regimes and that regulation appears to assist those companies who suffer the most from information asymmetry.

Beny (2005) went into some depth in examining the structure of the insider trading regime within a country to see the impact on the market. Beny (2005) looked at a number of specific aspects of the laws. The first is the breadth of coverage, measured by examining whether tipping information to outsiders was covered and if those tipped were then counted as insiders. The second is the sanctions available, measured as the presence of criminal sanctions and a dummy if monetary sanctions are greater than the profits made or the loss avoided. The paper also expanded on the Bhattacharya enforcement measure by looking at actual enforcement as well as potential enforcement based on the strength of public and private enforcement systems. The scope and sanction variables were then combined into an overall measure of the strength of the laws in a country. The paper concluded that more prescriptive laws result in wider share ownership and greater share market turnover, suggesting more liquidity and more accurate prices. When scope and sanctions were considered individually, the results indicated that it was the potential penalties, and not the scope of the law, that was important in improving liquidity and price accuracy. Enforcement was also shown to be important, but only in relation to public enforcement, however, private enforcement and past enforcement did not have a significant impact on the majority of the market variables.

One issue with the Beny (2005) paper is the market variables upon which the insider trading regulations were tested. Specifically, three were examined: stock market turnover, concentrated share ownership and stock price synchronicity. Market turnover relates to liquidity which should improve if insiders are less prevalent in the market. Likewise, share ownership should be more widespread with more market participants who are prepared to invest if insiders are regulated appropriately. Stock price synchronicity measures the degree of co-movement between stocks. More co-movement suggests that stocks are driven by more macroeconomic and industry-based factors than firm-specific factors. The use of this variable, therefore, relates to the belief that less insiders will promote more analyst activity — an argument put forward by Fishman and Hagerty (1995). However, these are indirect measures and, while the differences between countries may be caused by the insider trading regulations, it may be other factors not controlled for that are the cause.

A recent paper by Frijns *et al.* (2009) expanded on the work by Beny to explore the issue of specific aspects of insider trading laws which reduce information asymmetry. The study employed a more detailed list of sanction variables, including aspects like whether financial sanctions are for a fixed sum, a sum that scales in direct proportion to the insiders profits or the losses avoided, whether they are required to give back their profits, and the maximum criminal penalty that can be imposed. Equally, the paper expanded on the enforcement variables in order to explore the potential role of not only past enforcement but also past criminal enforcement, the ability of shareholders to sue, the transparency of related party transactions and aspects of the public regulator such as their budget and staffing. These variables were explored in relation to a sample of 30 countries.

The results show that different legal origins tend to cluster in terms of their approaches to insider trading regimes. The different legal origins have taken quite different approaches to the regulations. The most notable differences exist between the different types of civil laws, particularly German and French Civil Laws. Germanic civil law countries rely heavily on criminal sanctions: all German civil law countries have criminal sanctions, and on average, they are stricter than other countries. Their financial sanctions, on the other hand, are relatively light. French civil law countries, by contrast, rely more heavily on financial sanctions, having the stiffest financial penalties. On the other hand, they have, on average, the lightest criminal sanctions and also have relatively weak enforcement measures with considerably less powers and resources given to public regulators and the lowest rate of criminal enforcement. Common law countries, on average, run relatively strong financial penalties and also have, on average, the strictest enforcement with both the strongest private and public enforcement measures in addition to the highest level of resourcing for the regulators.

These dependent variables were regressed by Frijns *et al.* (2009) at a firm level and at the country level against the insider trading law variables and a number of control variables. The results were broadly supportive of Beny's (2005) earlier work but added further insights into the makeup of a good insider trading regime. In particular, the scope of the laws was found to be ineffective. What did have an impact were sanctions and, more specifically, financial sanctions were more effective than criminal sanctions. Longer prison sentences also failed to effectively deter insiders. The smaller impact of criminal sanctions is likely related to the much higher burden of proof required for a criminal conviction (required for a jail sentence) as opposed to a civil conviction (typically associated with financial-only sanctions). Given the inferential nature of insider trading, we see an insider had information and traded, and infer they traded upon their information, it can be hard to satisfy the criminal burden of proof. This suggests that law makers might have been potentially lured down the wrong path by the belief that criminal sanctions represent the greatest potential deterrent to insiders. What the authors find is that it is financial penalties that have the greatest deterrence value and, more specifically, financial penalties that scale in relation to the profit made or the loss avoided. For instance, some countries run systems that allow for a scaling penalty such as three times the profit made or the loss avoided. This ensures that when an insider is caught, they will lose more than what they gained from the trading.

In terms of enforcement, none of the variables tested were shown to be effective. This could indicate that, as Bris (2005) concludes, enforcement is ineffective in deterring insiders or it may be that the variables used are missing the key element of enforcement. Becker (1968) suggests that deterrence is a function of the probability of prosecution and the potential penalties that will be imposed. While the enforcement variables were designed to capture the probability of enforcement, past success and the resources available to regulators are not perfect proxies for likely enforcement, a better variable would be a measure of the actual prosecutions for insider trading in various countries. This would better quantify the likelihood of prosecution given differences in legal regimes. However, this data is not readily available and offers avenues for future research.

5.5 Conclusions and Implications

What the literature shows is that there are still significant gaps in our understanding of the impact of insider trading regulations and the specific aspects of insider trading laws that impact insiders' behaviour. Given the potentially negative consequences of untamed insiders in terms of investor confidence, liquidity and stock market development, it is important that their behaviour be restrained. But the literature's advice to policy makers is still incomplete and rudimentary. Research on the reason why enforcement has such a mixed effect on insiders is required, especially given the considerable cost of prosecuting insiders. Also, more detail on the definitions and coverage of insider trading laws could help to clarify what should and should not be considered insider trading. Finally, research on the way the various aspects inter-relate, such as how enforcement and the sanctions work together, needs to be considered in terms of determining a complete set of rules.

Chapter 6

CORPORATE GOVERNANCE AND THE GLOBAL FINANCIAL CRISIS: THE REGULATORY RESPONSES

THOMAS CLARKE AND ALICE KLETTNER

University of Technology, Sydney

6.1 Introduction

It has been suggested that the financial crisis was caused essentially by opportunistic behaviour permitted by poor regulation, weak corporate governance and inadequate risk management. The consequences of the crisis will be a sea-change in how corporations are regulated in the finance sector, in the standards of corporate governance demanded, and in the effectiveness of the application of risk management. This chapter highlights the corporate governance causes of the financial crisis, and analyses the international corporate governance reforms resulting from this experience.

A brief overview is offered in this chapter of some of the causes of the crisis, focusing on the failures in corporate governance in the context of inadequate risk management and weak regulation. This is followed by a summary of the regulatory reforms proposed in international forums and in three countries: the US, UK and Australia. These proposals are extremely wide-ranging and, thus, our focus is on the corporate governance reforms proposed in the immediate aftermath of the crisis. As the crisis originated in the financial sector, many of these proposals are finance-specific, but not all, and the tighter regulatory and risk management standards will undoubtedly impact the governance of all corporations in the post-crisis period. Although regulatory reform will be applied most urgently to the financial sector, it should be expected that any corporate governance reforms will ultimately become best practice for all corporations. The two issues considered paramount in almost every forum are risk management and how the remuneration policy influences the willingness to take excessive risks.

There has been considerable debate in the US and the UK over potential changes to the overall supervisory framework. The various regulatory bodies have been vying for power which does not assist the development of effective regulatory systems. However, the emerging regulatory response to the crisis is likely to include:

- improvements in the governance of risk management and related disclosure;
- supervisory focus on executive remuneration and its alignment with corporate risk;
- specific prudential regulation and accounting standards for complex financial products;
- expanding the scope of regulatory oversight to include credit rating agencies and hedge funds;
- new focus on systemic risk and cooperation between supervisory bodies.

6.2 Causes of the Financial Crisis

The beginnings of the financial crisis occurred early in 2007 as the limits of the credit explosion were reached. By 2008, with a seemingly endless sequence of collapses of financial institutions, it became clear that there would be a severe impact on the wider global economy with a serious global recession inescapable:

> "Starting in the summer of 2007, accumulating losses on US subprime mortgages triggered widespread disruption to the global financial system. Large losses were sustained on complex structured securities. Institutions reduced leverage and increased demand for liquid assets. Many credit markets became illiquid, hindering credit extension" (Financial Stability Forum, 2008).

The Organisation for Economic Co-operation and Development (OECD) was one of the more influential international organisations examining the causes of the crisis. It provides a setting for governments to "compare policy experiences, seek answers to common problems, identify good practice and coordinate domestic and international policies" (OECD website, 2009). Falling squarely within this remit is the search for solutions to the financial crisis.

An OECD report on the causes of the crisis explained that it was instigated at two levels:

"...by global macro policies affecting liquidity and by a very poor regulatory framework that, far from acting as a second line of defence, actually contributed to the crisis in important ways" (Blundell-Wignall *et al.*, 2008).

Central to the regulatory framework criticised here is the Basel Capital Accord, introduced by the Basel Committee on Banking Supervision. The 1988 Accord, commonly known as Basel I, was revised and re-issued in June 2004 as Basel II. Blundell-Wignall and Atkinson (2008) identify the transition to Basel II as one of the triggers of the crisis because the revised capital standards favoured mortgages and freed up bank capital. Alone this may not have triggered a crisis; however a series of other de-regulatory policies implemented in 2004 combined to set the scene for the disaster to come:

- the Bush administration's 'American Dream' legislation that facilitated zero equity mortgages, extending loans to those without the means to repay them;
- the imposition of greater capital requirements on Fannie Mae and Freddie Mac, the two government sponsored mortgage giants which opened a gap in the market for other banks to provide sub-prime mortgages; and
- Securities and Exchange Commission ("SEC") rule changes that allowed investment banks to increase their leverage ratio (Blundell-Wignall *et al.*, 2008).

This de-regulated environment encouraged a new banking business model, particularly in the US, with the number of residential mortgage-backed securities (RMBS) rising exponentially. A newly developed and risky banking business model was then accommodated by a less-than-perfect financial system. As Blundell-Wignall *et al.* (2008) explain:

"Many of the reforms underway focus on securitisation, credit rating agencies, poor risk modelling and underwriting standards, as well as corporate governance lapses, amongst others, as though they were causal... but in the most part these are only aspects of the financial system that accommodated a new banking business model..."

More robust corporate governance may have counteracted or, at least, mitigated the excessive risk-taking being encouraged by the prevailing business model, perhaps curtailing to a degree the willingness to engage in excessive leveraging and to invest in the most exotic securities. However, the basic cause of the crisis was the enthusiastic attraction to the new banking business model of many US and European banks, and the fact that many fringe financial companies were entirely committed to this model.

Compounding the problem was the consistent failure of the credit ratings agencies to adequately assess the risk associated with particular financial institutions and financial instruments, in order to give investors a better understanding of the risks they face. The question asked by many when the financial crisis erupted was how could asset-backed securities containing subprime mortgages and other high-risk debt possibly be given AA credit ratings by Standard and Poor's or Moody's? The answer is, again, that financial innovation has outpaced regulatory prowess.

The ratings agencies, instead of rigorously monitoring the growth of financial markets and instruments, have become junior partners in this enterprise. Coffee (2006), in his critique of the failure of the gatekeeper professions in US corporate governance including auditors, corporate lawyers, and securities analysts, raises serious issues regarding rating agencies: their entrenched market oligopoly; the conflict of interest in the agencies receiving their revenue for the issuers of debt products; their capacity to understand the underlying assets and cash flows involved in complexly structured finance products; and the fact that ratings agencies do not review how the risk profile of debt products may change in different market conditions.

Blundell-Wignell *et al.* (2008) note that it was the investment banks that performed particularly badly, and put forward four hypotheses that might explain the deficiencies of corporate governance in such firms:

- the culture of investment banking is hard to control from the board room;
- the business is complex, and the products are inherently more difficult to understand than simple banking products, making risk control practices much more difficult;
- there was a lack of ownership of long-term strategic risk, perhaps associated with board structure and the independence of the directors;
- remuneration incentives were part of the business model drivers, with bonuses linked to up-front revenue and the current share price.

In testing these hypotheses against the banks that failed, Blundell-Wignall *et al.* (2008) found "no simple indicator of good governance linked to independence, compensation and remuneration" concluding that good governance "is likely to be complex and idiosyncratic to the firm". However, research by RiskMetrics (2009) reveals some fundamental problems in the governance of the Wall Street investment banks. The Wall Street banks were a bastion used to retain the combined CEO/Chairman (at Morgan Stanley, Citigroup, Merril Lynch, Bank of America, Washington Mutual, Bear Stearns, Wachovia, JP Morgan, Lehman Brothers, Wells Fargo and Goldman Sachs, the roles were combined in 2006–2008).

This meant that dominant figures, such as Richard Fuld at Lehman Brothers, could be autocratic about strategic objectives, performance targets and reward systems (whether they understood what was really happening in their banks or not). In 2008 when it was too late to avert disaster, Bear Stearns and Citigroup made some effort at splitting the roles, in both cases appointing an executive or former executive of the bank to the chairman's role. The other banks' CEOs resolutely insisted on retaining both roles despite the international trend of separating the roles to ensure a more balanced board direction. (In April 2009, Ken Lewis, the CEO/Chairman of Bank of America, was stripped of his Chairman's role after a shareholder vote following the Bank's takeover of Merril Lynch, the loss of 75 percent of its market value and the US$45 billion rescue by the US government).

A second weakness of Wall Street banks revealed in the RiskMetrics survey was a lack of finance experts on the boards of directors of the banks. Morgan Stanley, Merril Lynch, Bank of America, and JP Morgan only had two or three financial experts on their boards during the critical years from 2006–2008, while Washington Mutual, Wachovia and Lehman Brothers only had one financial expert on the board. This suggests that the investment banks' boards involved were critically disabled in the effort to independently understand and monitor complex financial transactions.

In another report for the OECD, Kirkpatrick (2009) looks more specifically at the corporate governance issues revealed by the crisis, concluding that:

> "The financial crisis can be, to an important extent, attributed to failures and weaknesses in corporate governance arrangements which did not serve their purpose to safeguard against excessive risk-taking in a number of financial services companies. Accounting standards and regulatory requirements have also proved insufficient in some areas. Last but not least, remuneration systems have, in a number of cases, not been closely related to the strategy and risk appetite of the company and its longer term interests" (2009).

Kirkpatrick (2009) explains that:

> "Risk management systems have failed in many cases due to corporate governance procedures rather than the inadequacy of computer models alone: information about exposures in a number of cases did not reach the board or even senior levels of management, while risk management was often activity rather than enterprise-based."

Financial businesses innovation in financial products had far exceeded the capacity of risk management measurement and monitoring tools to gauge risk, with undue reliance on the VaR (value at risk) measure which did not evaluate risk in the most extreme circumstances. As the report on the reasons for the $44 billion writedowns at UBS reveals:

> "The investment bank was focused on the maximisation of revenue. There appears to have been a lack of challenge on the risk and reward to business area plans within the investment bank at a senior level. UBS's review suggests an asymmetric focus in the investment bank senior management meetings on revenue and profit and loss, especially when compared to discussion of risk issues" (UBS, 2008).

As with many other US, UK and European banks, UBS sailed towards the iceberg of the subprime mortgage crisis in a state of profound ignorance:

> "Presentations of Market Risk Control to UBS's senior governance bodies did not provide adequate granularity of subprime positions UBS held in its various businesses. No warnings were given to senior management about the limitations of the presented numbers or the need to look at the broader contextual framework and the findings were not challenged with perseverance" (UBS, 2008).

The corporate governance aspect of risk management focuses on the way in which risk information is used within a corporation, including its transmission to the board. The crisis has revealed that some boards had no knowledge of strategic decisions regarding risk management and, therefore, no control mechanisms to oversee overall risk appetite. The firms that fared better were those that had a comprehensive approach to sharing risk information and more effective stress-testing using scenario analysis (Kirkpatrick, 2009).

Remuneration policies have also been identified as a potential cause of the crisis:

> "Remuneration and incentive systems have played a key role in influencing financial institutions' sensitivity to shocks and causing the development of unsustainable balance sheet positions" (Kirkpatrick, 2009).

The same report goes on to suggest that the problem was not restricted to the financial sector:

> "This reflects a general concern about incentive systems that are in operation in non-financial firms and whether they lead to excessive short-term management actions and to 'rewards for failure'" (Kirkpatrick, 2009).

The issue of corporate governance here is that firms' remuneration policies have not been stress-tested for varying economic conditions. Kirkpatrick's (2009) conclusion is that both the deficiencies in risk management and distorted incentive systems point to deficient board oversight — a clear corporate governance issue.

6.3 International Reforms

Undoubtedly, the most serious financial crisis since the 1930s Great Depression will elicit the most comprehensive and robust international regulatory response, comparable to the influence of the Glass-Steagall Act of 1932, and the Securities Acts of 1933 and 1934. After more than a decade of sustained de-regulation of financial institutions and markets across the world, the essential role of regulation in ensuring stability and balance is being re-discovered and the lessons of the past re-learned. For example, illustrative of the power of regulation is the remarkable reduction in bank failures following the passing of the Glass-Steagall Act which lasted for nearly five decades until deregulation occurred in 1980 (Figure 6.1). Although the current financial crisis originated in US investment banks, it has impacts across the world, and the regulatory response requires international coordination. This regulatory response is still emerging and will take several years to complete. However, substantial policy foundations are already in place.

Reports and recommendations are fast emerging from a multitude of influential organisations both at the international and national level. Navigating through this maze of information and initiatives is one of the first

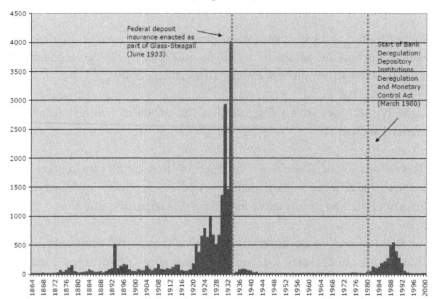

Figure 6.1 The Impact of the Glass-Steagall Act on the Level of Bank Failures in the United States

Source: Historical Statistics of the United States: Colonial Times to 1970 (Washington, D.C.: Government Printing Office, 1975), Series X-741 (p. 1038). "Failures and Assistance Transactions." Table BF02, FDIC website (http://www2.fdic.gov/hsob/index.asp).

hurdles in understanding the likely outcomes. Appendix 1 sets out some of the key publications that are likely to shape the decisions of relevant authorities. Bearing in mind that the process is only in its early stages, we include in our timeline scheduled future developments.

One of the early reports responding to the crisis was the Report of the Financial Stability Forum (FSF) on Enhancing Market and Institutional Resilience. The FSF was set up by the G-7 in 1999 and brings together senior representatives of national financial authorities from 12 countries (for example, central banks, supervisory authorities and treasury departments), international financial institutions, international regulatory and supervisory groupings, committees of central bank experts and the European Central Bank. Its membership was soon expanded to include all of the G-20 members (Financial Stability Forum, 2009a). The FSF's role is to improve co-ordination and information flow and oversee "a broad-based multilateral agenda for strengthening financial systems and the stability of international financial markets" (Financial Stability Forum, 2009b).

In October 2007, the G-7 requested that the FSF undertake an analysis of the causes and weaknesses underlying the emerging financial turmoil. The FSF's report was published in April 2008 and proposed concrete action in five areas:

1. Strengthened prudential oversight of capital, liquidity and risk management.
2. Enhancing transparency and valuation, particularly in relation to the risk exposures of complex investments and financial products.
3. Changes in the role and uses of credit ratings.
4. Strengthening the authorities' responsiveness to risks.
5. Robust arrangements for dealing with stress in the financial system.

Of relevance to the field of corporate governance is the focus on risk which is likely to result in increased supervisory attention, regulation and disclosure. Closely connected to the general question of risk management is the issue of remuneration policy. The FSF report identifies various incentive distortions at the heart of the crisis including the fact that:

"Compensation schemes in financial institutions encouraged disproportionate risk-taking with insufficient regard to longer-term risks. This risk-taking was not always subject to adequate checks and balances in firms' risk management systems."

Thus, the FSF report recommends that compensation models be aligned more closely with long-term, firm-wide profitability (2008). In discussing areas for policy action, the FSF report notes:

"A striking aspect of the turmoil has been the extent of risk management weaknesses and failings at regulated and sophisticated firms. While it is the responsibility of the firms' boards and senior management to manage the risk they bear, supervisors and regulators can give incentives to management so that risk control frameworks keep pace with the innovation and changes in business models."

The report identifies the fact that, although some of the issues were known or suspected before the turmoil began, regulatory and supervisory responses were:

• not fast enough to keep up with the pace of innovation in financial markets;

- not followed up to ensure implementation; and/or
- not successful in changing behavior.

On this basis, the report recommends much more proactivity on the part of supervisors and regulators. This would include monitoring the skills of risk managers and communicating any concerns directly to the firm's board.

The FSF's recommendations will ultimately have to be translated to fit national supervisory bodies and implemented appropriately. However, regulatory inadequacy, rather than over-regulation, was the new focus of world attention. Australia's *twin peaks* regulation with the Australia Securities and Investment Commission (ASIC) responsible for corporate governance and the Australian Prudential Regulation Authority (APRA) for prudential regulation appeared, to some, a more effective system than the hopelessly fragmented and competitive approach of the US regulators, or the heavily integrated Financial Services Authority in the UK (Table 6.1). In contrast, the *institutional* approach, as employed in countries like China and Mexico, focuses regulation on different business sectors, but becomes complex when firms diversify into other businesses. Similarly the *functional* approach, as used by Italy and France, focuses on particular business activities (such as security trading), and can readily lead to a single business facing multiple regulators. All of the regulatory systems are under review presently, though the possibility of arriving at a more coherent and effective system in each jurisdiction has been limited to a degree by competition between existing regulators as was witnessed in 2009 in both the UK and the US. It is possible that the results of the reform process will be mechanisms to ensure greater cooperation between regulators, and a move towards the *twin peaks* approach with separate regulators concentrating on prudential regulation for capital adequacy, and another regulator focusing on market and business conduct (World Economic Forum, 2009).

The need for a global solution to a global crisis is clear, and thus the FSF is intensifying its co-operation with the International Monetary Fund (IMF). The two bodies already work closely together in the area of standards-setting, particularly with respect to the joint IMF/World Bank assessment of countries'

Table 6.1 Examples of Regulatory Models.

Institutional	Functional	Integrated	Twinpeaks	Fragmented
China	Italy	United Kingdom	Australia	United States
Mexico	France	Germany	Netherlands	

compliance with the 12 international standards that the FSF has designated as necessary for sound financial systems and worthy of priority implementation. As an example, these include the IMF's Code of Good Practices on Fiscal Transparency, the International Accounting Standards Board's International Accounting Standards, the Basel Committee's Principles for Effective Banking Supervision, and the OECD's Principles of Corporate Governance.

The flow-on from the FSF's recommendations for the financial sector is likely to include changes to the OECD's Principles of Governance. On 18 March 2009, the OECD held a conference in Paris to discuss monitoring, implementation and enforcement of corporate governance as well as possible reforms and improvements to the OECD Principles in light of the crisis. Priority areas for reform were listed as including "board practices, implementation of risk management, governance of the remuneration process and the exercise of shareholder rights." The conference provided input to a set of key findings and main messages published in June 2009.

However, the body to emerge with the greatest impact on the regulatory response to the financial crisis was the G-20. The G-20 is made up of the Finance Ministers and Central Bank Governors of 20 systemically important industrialised and developing economies. It is an informal forum designed to promote open and constructive discussion on global economic stability, and was created as a response to the financial crises of the late 1990s and a growing recognition that the G-7 did not adequately represent emerging market countries (G-20, 2009). The increasing prominence of the G-20 is a further recognition of the multi-polarity of the emerging global economy as one of the consequences of the global financial crisis. The G-20 was institutionalised as a constant set of partners in 1999 and includes the three nations that we focus upon in this chapter: Australia, the United States of America and the United Kingdom. The common principles established by the G-20 have guided the regulatory reform process in the individual states (Table 6.2).

The April 2009 London meeting of the G-20 made various pledges aimed at repairing the financial system and restoring confidence. They agreed to strengthen the financial system and a timetable was set for the implementation of a series of regulatory measures. Importantly, it was agreed to set up a new Financial Stability Board (a stronger successor to the FSF) which, together with the IMF, will monitor progress and provide reports to future meetings of the G-20 Finance Ministers. The regulatory measures agreed upon can be summarised as follows:

- To reshape regulatory systems so that authorities can identify and take account of macro-prudential risks. The Financial Stability Board (FSB)

Table 6.2   G-20 Common Principles and Actions for Reform of Financial Markets.

Common Principle for Reform	Immediate Actions by 31 March 2009	Medium Term Actions
Strengthening transparency and accountability: Enhance disclosure on complex financial products and align incentives to avoid excessive risk-taking	• Enhance guidance for disclosing the valuation of complex, illiquid securities • Enhance governance of international accounting standard-setting bodies • Assess private sector best practices for private pools of capital and/or hedge funds	• Create single, high-quality global accounting standards • Ensure that regulators, supervisors, accounting standard-setters and the private sector work more closely together on consistent application and enforcement of standards • Enhance financial institution risk and loss disclosures including off-balance sheet activities
Enhancing sound regulation: Strengthen regulatory regimes, prudential oversight and risk management	• *Regulatory regimes:* Review pro-cyclicality, including the ways that valuation, leverage, bank capital, executive compensation and loss provisioning exacerbate cyclicality • *Prudential Oversight:* Enhance international standards and minimize conflicts for ratings agencies; ensure maintenance of adequate capital, speed efforts to implement central counterparty services • *Risk management:* Re-examine bank risk management and internal controls, in particular relating to liquidity and counterparty risk, stress testing, incentive alignment and development of structured products.	• *Regulatory Regimes:* Undertake Financial Sector Assessment Program with view to ensure that all systematically important institutions are appropriately regulated • *Prudential oversight:* Register credit rating agencies; develop robust international framework for bank liquidity management and central bank intervention • *Risk management:* Ensure awareness and ability to respond to evolving financial markets and products; monitor substantial changes in assets prices and their implications for the macro-economy/financial system

(Continued)

Table 6.2 (*Continued*).

Common Principle for Reform	Immediate Actions by March 31, 2009	Medium Term Actions
Promoting integrity in financial markets; Protect integrity of financial markets and promote information sharing	• Enhance regional/international regulatory cooperation • Promote information sharing on threats to market stability; ensure legal provisions to address threats • Review business conduct rules to protect markets and investors against market manipulation and fraud	• Implement measures that protect against uncooperative and/or non-transparent jurisdictions posing systematic risks • Continue work against money laundering and terrorist financing • Promote international tax information exchange
Reinforcing international cooperation: Formulate consistent global regulations	• Establish supervisory colleges for all major cross-border financial institutions to strengthen surveillance • Strengthen cross-border crisis management procedures and conduct simulation exercises	• Collect information on areas of convergence in regulatory practices (e.g. accounting, auditing, deposit insurance) to accelerate progress where necessary • Ensure that temporary measures to restore stability and confidence create minimal distortions
Reforming international financial institutions: Advance the reform of *Bretton Woods* institutions to reflect changing economic weight	• Add emerging economies to *Financial Stability Forum* • Strengthen *IMF* and *FSF* collaboration on surveillance and standard-setting, respectively • Review resource adequacy of development banks • Review ways to restore access to credit and resume private capital flows to emerging economies	• Comprehensively reform *Bretton Woods* institutions so they can more adequately reflect changing international economic weights and effectively respond to future challenges • *IMF* should conduct surveillance reviews of all countries • Provide capacity-building programs for emerging economies on the formulation of effective regulation

Source: US Executive Office of the President, 2009.

was requested to work with the Bank for International Settlements (BIS) to develop macro-prudential tools and provide a report by Autumn 2009.

- To extend regulation and oversight to all systemically important financial institutions, instruments and markets, including, for the first time, hedge funds. The IMF and FSB were asked to produce guidelines on whether a financial institution, instrument or market is "systemically important" by the next G-20 meeting. Hedge funds or their managers are to be registered and will be required to disclose appropriate information on an ongoing basis to supervisors or regulators.
- To endorse and implement the FSF's principles on pay and compensation and to support the corporate social responsibility of all firms. National supervisors are to ensure significant progress in the implementation of the principles by the 2009 remuneration round. The principles, published in April 2009 are intended to be applied to significant financial institutions. They require:

  o boards of directors to play an active role in the design, operation and evaluation of compensation schemes;
  o compensation arrangements including bonuses to properly reflect risk such that the timing and composition of payments are sensitive to the time horizon of risks; and
  o firms to publicly disclose clear, comprehensive and timely information about compensation.

The objectives of the G-20 were improve the quality, quantity and international consistency of capital in the banking system; improve accounting standards on valuation and provisioning and achieve a single set of high-quality global accounting standards; and extend regulatory oversight to credit rating agencies. This regulatory oversight regime was to be established by the end of 2009 and should assure the transparency and quality of the ratings process (G-20, 2009). The main corporate governance aspect of the G-20 plan is the focus on remuneration policy. This has already resulted in activity at the national level which is likely to crystallize into legal and regulatory changes.

There are three further international reports worthy of mention. The first two are industry-based initiatives by the International Institute of Finance (IIF) and the Counterparty Risk Management Policy Group (CRMPG). Both are proactive attempts at influencing and perhaps limiting the scope of regulatory reform. Wehinger (2009), in his report for the OECD, labels them as the most pertinent proposals by the industry and certainly some of their recommendations, discussed below, are likely to be reflected in future regulation. The third report is by the Bank for International Settlements and deals specifically with the governance of central banks, however, Chapter 8 on risk management contains some useful ideas on strengthening non-financial risk management.

The IIF is a global association of financial institutions. Its members include large banks, insurance and investment firms from over 70 countries. On 17 July 2008, the IIF published its Final Report of the Committee on Market Best Practices. This sets out what it calls the financial industry's response to the market turmoil of 2007–2008, including proposed principles of conduct and best practice recommendations. It covers the areas of:

> "…risk management; compensation policies; liquidity risk, conduit, and securitization issues; valuation issues; credit underwriting, ratings, and investor due diligence in securitization markets; and transparency and disclosure issues."

Three of these areas could be said to fall within the ambit of corporate governance: risk management, compensation policies and disclosure issues. The IIF report sets out very clear recommendations as to how governance could be improved in these areas and it is highly likely that these will become best practice not only in financial companies but across all industries. Within risk management, suggestions include:

- the promotion of appropriate risk culture;
- defining risk appetite;
- clarifying the role of the chief risk officer;
- integrating different risk management areas; and
- stress-testing outcomes.

In redesigning compensation policies, it is suggested that firms should:

- base compensation on risk-adjusted performance, and align incentives with shareholder interests and long-term, firm-wide profitability;
- ensure that compensation incentives do not induce risk-taking in excess of the firm's risk appetite;
- align payout with the timing of related risk-adjusted profit;
- take into account realised performance for shareholders over time in determining severance pay; and

- make the approach, principles, and objectives of each firm's compensation policies transparent to stakeholders.

The report goes on to give some examples of compensation techniques that could achieve these aims.

The CRMPG is made up of senior executives from major international banks. Their report entitled, *Containing Systemic Risk: The Road to Reform*, was published in August 2008 and was provided to the FSF and the US President's Working Group on Financial Markets. Also known as the "Corrigan Report" after the co-chair Gerald Corrigan, this report puts forward "core precepts" and recommendations with the objective of forming "a private initiative that will complement official oversight by insisting on industry practices that will help mitigate systemic risk" (Counterparty Risk Management Policy Group, 2008). The five core precepts are aimed at large, integrated financial intermediaries and comprise:

1. Regular reviews of corporate governance
2. Development of risk management
3. Defining risk appetite
4. Identifying potential contagion "hot spots"
5. Enhanced oversight with regular meetings between supervisory officials and boards of directors.

Most of the recommendations of the report are specific to the finance industry, such as those relating to accounting standards, high risk complex instruments and the credit market. However, some of the suggestions regarding risk management have much wider relevance. These include recommendations dealing with chief risk officers, staffing of risk management functions, information flow, approval of risk appetite, integration of risk management and the composition of risk committees (Counterparty Risk Management Policy Group, 2008).

In conclusion, at an international level, the reform agenda was fully engaged in 2009. The G-20 members agreed to implement the recommendations of the FSF on remuneration policy and individual countries began the process of implementing reforms into their domestic regulatory frameworks. The OECD Principles of Corporate Governance were reviewed and it was concluded that there was no urgent need to revise the Principles, rather more guidance was required to assist companies in more effective implementation of the Principles (OECD, 2010). These will gradually filter its way into domestic frameworks. Within the finance sector, private associations have been proactive in putting forward recommendations for reform, particularly in the areas of risk management and remuneration policy. These regulatory reforms are likely to be influential in crystallising changes to national regulatory systems. We now examine national reforms in three countries — the US, the UK and Australia.

6.4 United States

In response to the crisis, the US Administration put forward a four part regulatory reform strategy: (1) addressing systemic risk; (2) protecting consumers and investors; (3) eliminating gaps in the regulatory structure; and (4) fostering international cooperation (US Treasury, 2009). In March 2009, the House Committee on Financial Services received details of the Administration's plan to regulate systemic risk and protect the broader economy from the potential failure of large financial institutions. This plan included:

- the formation of a single independent regulator with responsibility over systemically important firms;
- higher standards on capital and risk management for systemically important firms;
- registration of all hedge fund advisors with assets under management above a certain threshold;
- a comprehensive oversight system for the over the counter (OTC) derivatives market; and
- new requirements for money market funds to reduce the risk of rapid withdrawals (US Treasury, 2009).

Legislation put forward by the Treasury in March 2009, if passed, will give the government power to put systemically significant firms into receivership. This addresses gaps in the current regime which only allows the government to take control of depositary banks. The crisis made it clear that other financial institutions, outside of current US government powers, can destabilise the system, in particular, bank holding companies. Citigroup Inc. which has received billions of dollars in government aid, is a prime example of such an event.

Essentially, the complex historical development of the US regulatory structure has resulted in the fragmentation of a complex pattern of competing regulatory authorities, including the Securities and Exchange Commission (SEC), the Commodity and Futures Trading Commission (CFTC), the Office of Thrift Supervision, among the many Federal agencies, as well as the involvement of individual states in corporate law and other specific matters. However, some officials want to see larger reform proposals considered by the House Financial Services Committee in July 2009. These wider reform proposals include:

> "vastly expanding the Federal Reserve's power to oversee the health of the entire financial system, creating a single banking overlord, merging the Securities and Exchange Commission (SEC) with the Commodity Futures Trading Commission (CFTC), and launching a new consumer protection agency" (Rucker and Younglai, 2009).

However, though the US Treasury's proposal to give the SEC a key role (including membership of the Financial Services Oversight Council (FSOC), a body that includes the Chairmen of key US financial regulators) was designed to ensure proper coordination among regulators, it appears that competition between the US regulators might undermine this goal. Furthermore, resistance from the banks was likely to delay the effective implementation of the new regulatory regime (Rucker and Younglai, 2009).

On 20 May 2009, the Fraud Enforcement and Recovery Act 2009 was signed by President Obama. It approved the creation of a commission of inquiry into the financial crisis (Phillips, 2009). This commission is modeled after the Pecora Commission which studied the 1929 stock market crash. The Pecora Commission eventually helped pave the way for the Securities Act of 1933, the Securities Exchange Act of 1934 and the creation of the Securities and Exchange Commission in 1935. The current commission has been given a wide-ranging remit to examine the role of US regulators and the prudential legal framework, along with companies' accounting practices, corporate governance, executive pay schemes and the use of exotic investment tools. Possible fraud, the controversial role of credit risk agencies and short-selling on the markets are also listed in the legislation for investigation (Section 5(c), Fraud Enforcement and Recovery Act). Thus, it is unlikely that any comprehensive reform of US financial regulation will be finalised before the commission reports its findings on 15 December 2010. The Sarbanes Oxley Act of 2004 was widely criticised as a knee-jerk reaction to the corporate collapses of 2001 and thus any regulatory response to the 2008 crisis is likely to be more considered.

Nevertheless, on 17 June 2009, the US Treasury released its white paper on financial regulatory reform. The paper's key proposals included:

- the setting up of a Financial Services Oversight Council to oversee systemic risk and improve co-operation between the many existing supervisory agencies;

- new authority for the Federal Reserve to supervise all firms that could threaten financial stability;
- registration of hedge fund advisors with the SEC;
- stronger regulation of financial markets, in particular, credit rating agencies, securitization markets and OTC derivatives;
- the setting up of a Consumer Financial Protection Agency and stronger regulation to protect consumers and investors;
- providing the government with power to deal with the failure of non-bank institutions;
- promoting stronger international regulation and cooperation.

In pursuit of these aims, several pieces of draft legislation were proposed:

- On 30 June 2009, a bill that would create the Consumer Financial Protection Agency.
- On 10 July 2009, investor protection legislation with the aim of establishing "consistent standards for all those who provide investment advice about securities, to improve the timing and the quality of disclosures and to require accountability from securities professionals." It would also make the recently constituted SEC Investor Advisory Committee permanent. This group of well-respected investors will advise on the SEC's regulatory policies.
- On 15 July 2009, legislation that would require all advisers to hedge funds and other private pools of capital, including private equity and venture capital funds, to register with the SEC.
- On 16 July 2009, legislation that would ensure compensation committees meet strict independence standards.
- Also, on 16 July 2009, "say-on-pay" legislation that would require all publicly-traded companies to give shareholders a non-binding vote on executive compensation packages, similar to those mandated in the UK since 2002.

Interestingly, the introduction of better compensation practices comes under the white paper's "improve international cooperation" section and is clearly a matter that may not have been included were it not for US involvement in the G-20:

> "In line with G-20 commitments, we urge each national authority to put guidelines in place to align compensation with long-term shareholder value and to promote compensation structures that do not provide incentives for excessive risk-taking. We recommend that the BCBS expediently integrate the FSB principles on compensation into its risk management guidance by the end of 2009" (US Treasury, 2009).

A Congressional research paper states that "a large question for Congress may be how US regulations might be changed and how closely any changes are harmonized with international norms and standards" (Nanto, 2009).

6.5 United Kingdom

In March 2009, the Financial Services Authority (FSA) published the Turner Review of global banking regulation together with a Discussion Paper that explored some of the key policy issues (Financial Services Authority, 2009). Most of the report discusses necessary changes to bank capital and liquidity regulations and to bank published accounts. Of relevance, more generally, are the recommendations regarding:

- increased reporting requirements for unregulated financial institutions such as hedge funds;
- regulation of Credit Rating Agencies to limit conflicts of interest and inappropriate application of rating techniques;
- national and international action to ensure that remuneration policies are designed to discourage excessive risk-taking; and
- major changes in the FSA's supervisory approach, with a focus on business strategies and system-wide risks, rather than internal processes and structures.

The change in regulatory philosophy is an interesting one that may reverberate more widely. The crisis has invalidated the belief that markets are, in general, rational and self-correcting and, on this basis, the FSA is to abandon its 'light touch' approach in favour of what it terms 'intensive supervision' (Turner, 2009). However, Turner considers that even this more aggressive approach will fall short of what is deemed the 'bank examiner' model of the US. The FSA is also re-considering the best division of regulatory responsibility:

"Effective regulation and supervision of financial services needs to encompass the full range of firms, sectors and markets, and to cover both prudential issues (e.g. capital adequacy) and the conduct of business issues (e.g. fair sales practices or insider trading). Different countries have made different choices as to how to divide or combine these functions. There are three key choices to be made: (i) whether to combine the prudential supervision of all financial sectors (e.g. banking or insurance) or to supervise them separately; (ii) whether the prudential supervision of banks should be combined with central bank functions; (iii) whether prudential and conduct of business supervision should be combined or separate" (Turner, 2009).

Relevant to corporate governance, the Turner Review identifies many cases where internal risk management in financial institutions was ineffective with boards of directors failing to adequately identify and constrain excessive risk-taking (2009). Recommendations to combat these failings include:

- a more direct relationship between senior risk management and board risk committees;
- remuneration policy to take account of risk management considerations;
- improvements in the skill level and time commitment of non-executive directors; and
- more effective communication of shareholder views to non-executives.

The Turner Review does not probe these issues in depth because, in February 2009, the UK government announced a review of bank governance led by Sir David Walker, and the FSA intended to take this review into account and issue specific proposals by the end of 2009.

The FSA also was active in the area of remuneration policy. Action commenced with a letter dated 13 October 2008 from the FSA to the CEOs of major financial institutions. This letter set out the FSA's concerns on remuneration policies and put forward some basic criteria for good and bad remuneration practice. The message was to encourage financial institutions to eliminate anything in the 'bad' list and move towards the practices included in the 'good' list. The letter was followed by a review of remuneration practices in a group of major banks and building societies.

In February 2009, the FSA published a draft Code on Remuneration Practices. The Code will ultimately apply to large banks and broker dealers but the FSA encouraged all firms to review their compensation policies in accordance with the Code. The general requirement of the Code is that "remuneration policies must be consistent with effective risk management." In order to demonstrate compliance with this general requirement, it is recommended that firms show that they have adopted the Code's ten principles. The principles are described as follows:

1. The role of bodies responsible for remuneration policies and their members — the independence and skill of remuneration committees.
2. Procedures and input of risk and compliance functions — clear, documented procedures for setting remuneration with significant input from the risk management function.
3. Risk and compliance function remuneration — should be determined independently of other business areas.
4. Profit-based measurement and risk-adjustment — bonus pool calculations to be based principally on profits with an adjustment for risk.

5. Long-term performance measurement.
6. Non-financial performance metrics — should form a significant part of the performance assessment process.
7. Measurement of performance for long-term incentive plans — should be risk adjusted.
8. Fully flexible bonus policies — to be enabled by ensuring fixed remuneration is a sufficient proportion of total remuneration.
9. Deferment of the majority of any significant bonus.
10. Linking deferred elements to the firm's future performance.

The draft Code was updated in March 2009 — from this point it was to be regarded as a benchmark for good practice. A consultation paper on the draft Code was published in March 2009. The paper consults on the proposal that the draft Code is included in the FSA Handbook which would enable the general requirement to be enforced. The FSA's aim is to bring the Code into effect from early November in time for the firms' 2009 remuneration reviews. Initially, the Code would only apply to large financial institutions (approximately 48 firms) but the paper also proposes that it should be extended to all FSA-authorised firms. This would include all financial services firms.

The Financial Reporting Council is the UK's independent regulator in the area of corporate governance. It monitors the operation of the Combined Code on Corporate Governance and, in March 2009, announced that the Combined Code would be subject to review. A consultation paper was published with responses requested by May 2009. On 28 July 2009, the FRC published a progress report and a second consultation paper inviting views on the main issues to emerge from the first phase of the review. The intention was to publish a final report at the end of 2009 with further consultation in the event of proposed changes to the Combined Code which, if deemed necessary, would take effect in mid-2010. The FRC's review of the Combined Code was conducted in parallel with the Walker Review of bank governance, and the two were committed to share relevant research and other evidence. Sir Walker released a consultation paper on 16 July 2009 which was taken into account in the second FRC consultation paper.

While respondents were welcome to comment on any aspect of the Combined Code, the first consultation paper stated that views would be particularly welcome on:

- the composition and effectiveness of the board as a whole;
- the respective roles of the chairman, the executive leadership of the company and the non-executive directors;
- the board's role in relation to risk management;

- the role of the remuneration committee;
- the quality of support and information available to the board and its committees; and
- the content and effectiveness of Section 2 of the Code, which is addressed to institutional shareholders and encourages them to enter into a dialogue with companies based on a mutual understanding of objectives and to make considered use of their votes (Financial Reporting Council, 2009).

This list reflects some of the issues raised in previous reviews as well as the issues emerging from the financial crisis. The second consultation paper takes into account both the submissions to the first consultation plus the recommendations of the Walker Review in terms of whether they would be applicable outside the financial sector. Issues raised include:

- the time commitments of chairmen and non-executive directors;
- balancing the requirements of independence and relevant experience across non-executive directors;
- the possibility of annual (as opposed to 3-yearly) director re-election;
- director education and performance evaluation;
- the possibility of separate risk committees.

In July 2009, the UK government released a big-picture white paper on financial regulation. The paper described the steps already taken by the government towards better regulation:

- the new Banking Act 2009 which gives the Bank of England powers to deal with failing banks;
- the Turner Review of the UK regulatory regime;
- the Walker Review of remuneration practices;
- reform of the overall regulatory framework by giving the Bank of England a clear statutory objective to protect the stability of the financial system and supporting the FSA's internal reorganisation.

The white paper went on to describe proposals for further reform. These included providing the FSA with a formal, statutory objective for financial stability and extending its rule-making and enforcement powers.

What the paper did not do, to the disappointment of many, was to recommend a more radical shake up of the UK's tripartite supervisory framework. The existing system involves a sharing of regulatory duties between the Treasury, the Financial Services Authority and the Bank of England.

Regulatory and supervisory functions for all sectors, including both prudential and conduct of business issues, are combined in the FSA while the Bank has overall responsibility for financial stability. However, each of the three bodies has been accused of failing to do their job properly and communication between them has been reportedly poor (Conway, 2009).

In a speech on 17 June 2009, the Governor of the Bank of England, Mervyn King, sparked a row between himself and the Chancellor, Alistair Darling. He stated in fairly blunt terms that the Bank had been given responsibility for keeping the financial system in good health but without the powers to actually do the job. Despite this criticism, the white paper failed to recommend significant changes, only going so far as to propose a new Council for Financial Stability to assist in bringing together the work of the three organisations and to oversee overall systemic risk.

6.6 Australia

Australia experienced the impact of the financial crisis largely in its fringe finance sector, where seriously over-leveraged institutions quickly collapsed when the global credit crisis cut off their access to funds, leading to a fire-sale of their assets. At the United Nations on 25 September 2008, the Australian Prime Minister neatly summarised Australia's likely response to the financial crisis:

- First, systemically important financial institutions should be licensed to operate in major economies only under the condition that they make full disclosure and analysis of balance sheet and off-balance sheet exposures.
- Second, we need to ensure that banks and other financial institutions build up capital in good times as a buffer for the bad times, using predictable rules.
- Third, financial institutions need to have clear incentives which promote responsible behaviour, rather than unrestrained greed.
- Fourth, supervisory systems must be compatible with accounting principles that reflect reasonable assessments of the value of assets over time.
- And, lastly, the IMF should be given a strengthened mandate for prudential analysis (Rudd, 2008).

Australia's regulatory system weathered the crisis better than other industrial countries, with all four major banks retaining an AA credit rating. There were a number of reasons for the more cautious approach of the Australian banks, including their experiences with earlier overseas adventures, their absorption in the resources boom in Australia and their close prudential regulation by the Australian Prudential Regulation Authority. The division of

Table 6.3 Regulating the Financial System.

Agency	Government	Central Bank	Prudential Regulator	Market Conduct Regulator
RESPONSIBILITY	Fiscal Policy	Monetary Policy	**Prudential Regulation & Supervision**	**Product Distribution Integrity**
		Economy		
		System Stability		
IMPACT		Institutional Stability		
			Customer Fairness	

Source: Trowbridge (2009).

roles, with the APRA responsible for prudential regulation of the banks and the ASIC for corporate and market regulation, was the essential logic of the Australian regulatory system (Table 6.3). However, gaps in this regulatory shield were exposed when Allco Finance, Babcock and Brown, ABC Learning, Opes Prime and a host of other finance and property companies collapsed as they were not subject to prudential regulation by the APRA. In addition, in the securities and investments industries regulated by the ASIC, it was believed that disclosure and transparency would allow the market to enforce proper conduct, and thus, the ASIC was not equipped to enforce capital adequacy or to regulate business models (even if, as in this case, these models could be said to represent systemic risk) (D'Aloisio, 2009).

In terms of domestic regulatory reforms, significant activity was focused on the area of executive remuneration. The APRA was asked to explore the issue of executive remuneration and excessive risk-taking in October 2008. The APRA announced its approach in December 2008 and, in May 2009, released a discussion paper on its proposed extensions to the governance requirements for regulated institutions (Australian Prudential Regulation Authority, 2009a). The proposed governance standards are based on the FSF's Principles of Sound Compensation Practices. They would require regulated institutions to:

- Have a board remuneration committee comprised of independent directors with appropriate expertise that would review the remuneration policy at least every three years;
- Have a remuneration policy that covers all employees and agents "whose actions could put the institution's financial soundness at risk." Guidance

is provided on the categories of personnel likely to fall within the scope of this provision;

- Arrange for input from risk management personnel in the design and operation of remuneration arrangements;
- Design remuneration policy to encourage behavior that supports the firm's risk management framework.

The proposed Prudential Practice Guide gives guidance on techniques for measuring performance and for adjusting these measures to take risk into account (Australian Prudential Regulation Authority, 2009b). APRA's intends to have the extended standards come into effect in January 2010.

Also relating to executive remuneration, in March 2009, the Australian Treasurer and the Minister for Superannuation and Corporate Law made a joint announcement proposing the reform of the *Corporations Act 2001* (Cth) in respect of termination payments. The draft of the Corporations Amendment (Improving Accountability on Termination Payments) Bill 2009 was released on 5 May 2009. The amendments would:

- Reduce the cap on termination payments to one year's average base pay unless shareholder approval is obtained. Currently, they can reach up to seven times a recipient's total annual remuneration before shareholder approval is required.
- Extend these shareholder approval requirements to cover termination payments made to any 'key management personnel.' Currently, section 200B of the Corporations Act only imposes the shareholder approval requirement on payments made to directors.
- Expand the definition of 'termination benefit' to comprise of all types of payments, benefits and rewards given on termination.

Also, in March 2009, the Government referred the broader issue of executive remuneration to its independent advisory body, the Productivity Commission. In April, the Productivity Commission published its issues paper on executive remuneration. The inquiry, led by Allan Fels and scheduled to release a final report in December 2009, was to examine:

- Trends in director and executive remuneration in Australia and internationally;
- The effectiveness of the existing framework for the oversight, accountability and transparency of director and executive remuneration practices;
- The role of institutional and retail shareholders in the development, setting, reporting and consideration of remuneration practices;

- Any mechanisms that would better align the interests of boards and executives with those of shareholders and the wider community;
- The effectiveness of the international responses to remuneration issues arising from the global financial crisis (Productivity Commission, 2009).

Allan Fels is widely expected to recommend that the government ban the practice of executives voting in favour of their own remuneration packages (Mayne, 2009). Another outcome deemed likely is for shareholder approval to be required for all equity grants to directors.

In the meantime, both the Australian Institute of Company Directors (AICD) and the Australian Shareholders Association (ASA) have released guidelines on corporate remuneration policy, clearly demonstrating that reform is not limited to the financial sector. The AICD issued its *Executive Remuneration Guidelines for Listed Company Boards* in February 2009, designed to assist large publicly-listed companies negotiate and set executive remuneration (Australian Institute of Company Directors, 2009). The guidelines reflect the AICD's view that executive remuneration should remain a matter for boards, and that further regulation in this area is unnecessary and may be counterproductive to the outcomes sought. The ASA's policy statement, released on 23 March 2009, condemns large termination payments and suggests the deferment of any equity awards (Australian Shareholders Association, 2009).

Outside of the topic of executive remuneration, on 19 November 2008, the Australian Government requested the independent Corporations and Markets Advisory Committee (CAMAC) to provide advice in relation to the effect of various market practices on the integrity of the Australian financial market. The Minister's letter to CAMAC states that "[a]s a result of the global financial crisis and the related turbulence in Australian financial markets, the effect on the market of a number of practices has given rise to a significant degree of concern in the business, and broader, community." CAMAC released an issues paper entitled *Aspects of market integrity* on 19 February 2009 and published its final report in July 2009. The report deals with the following issues:

- directors entering into margin loans over shares in their company;
- trading by company directors in 'blackout' periods;
- spreading false or misleading information; and
- corporate briefing of analysts.

It recommends the implementation of clearance processes and restrictions on dealings by corporate officers by way of governance requirements set by the ASX Corporate Governance Council or in the ASX Listing Rules.

6.7 Conclusion

The causes of the financial crisis are complex and multidimensional. A combination of many factors, including low interest rates, highly complex financial products, poor risk management and excessive bonus schemes, have led many banks to ruin and set the scene for widespread corporate failure. As a result, nations around the world are reassessing their prudential and corporate governance regulation. The aim of this chapter is to highlight likely changes in the field of corporate governance.

A report for the OECD places a good deal of blame on the boards of directors for failing to properly supervise risk management and incentive systems (Kirkpatrick, 2009). It identifies credit rating agencies, disclosure regimes and accounting standards as contributing to the problem but considers that a good board ought to have been able to overcome these weaknesses:

> "[There were] significant failures of risk management systems in some major financial institutions made worse by incentive systems that encouraged and rewarded high levels of risk-taking. Since reviewing and guiding risk policy is a key function of the board, these deficiencies point to ineffective board oversight" (Kirkpatrick, 2009).

As we have seen, the international policy foundations for reform in these areas have already been laid and more concrete reforms are underway at a domestic level. At a practical level within corporations, this will require the reformulation of both remuneration policy and risk management with increased involvement at the board level. With regard to risk management, Wehinger's OECD report suggests that:

> "To increase the weight of risk management in corporate decisions, risk managers should be placed at the board, or equivalent level, of an enterprise. The board will also have to establish and enforce clear lines of responsibility and accountability throughout the organisation to ensure the integrity of the essential reporting and monitoring systems" (2008).

This will be particularly important for companies that have international activities spanning different jurisdictions where internal cross-border communication can be quite a challenge. The independence versus competence debate has again arisen with some suggestions that placing independence above suitable qualifications have led some banks to have boards that lacked appropriate risk management expertise (Kirkpatrick, 2009). The IIF has suggested that:

"...boards need to be educated on risk issues and to be given the means to understand risk appetite and the firm's performance against it. A number of members of the risk committee (or equivalent) should be individuals with technical financial sophistication in risk disciplines or with solid business experience giving clear perspectives on risk issues" (Kirkpatrick, 2009).

Board remuneration committees are also going to find themselves with an increased workload. Recommendations as to the board's role in deciding remuneration policy have already been drafted in the UK and Australia. Directors' skills will be under scrutiny and policies will have to be thoroughly stress-tested.

The overall aim will be to put safeguards in place against the human tendency towards greed when times are good. In their report for the OECD, Blundell-Wignell and Atkinson (2008) cut to the heart of the difficulties in regulating in this area:

"The key regulatory issue that still confronts policy makers... is one of understanding the business model and corporate culture that always pushes risk-taking too far and results in periodic crises" (2008).

The global crisis was triggered by a particularly tempting environment for risk-taking. The aim of regulatory reforms will be to reduce the incentives for this occurring again. Excessive restraints in any area are generally not good for the economy and thus the overall challenge will be in finding the right balance. As Wehinger puts it:

"...Regulators and policy makers have to keep in mind that no regulatory system can ever be fail-safe, and 'good' regulation has to strike a balance between stability and growth, in supporting and maintaining financial stability without stifling financial innovation and growth" (2008).

Nonetheless, the financial crisis has reminded the world of the importance of transparency, disclosure, risk management, prudent and competent governance and effective regulation.

Appendix 1 International Regulatory and Governance Reform 2008–2009.

Date	International	USA	UK	Australia
04/08	Financial Stability Forum report on enhancing market and institutional resilience released			
07/08	Final Report of the International Institute of Finance's Committee on Market Best practices released			
08/08	Counterparty Risk Management Group report on Systemic Risk released			
10/08			FSA letter to CEOs on Remuneration Practices	
02/09		American Recovery and Reinvestment Act signed	Review of bank governance to be led by Sir David Walker announced FSA Draft Code on Remuneration Practices released	AICD Guidelines on executive remuneration released

(Continued)

Appendix 1 (*Continued*).

Date	International	USA	UK	Australia
03/09		Legislative proposals on resolution authority proposed 25 March	Turner Review of global banking regulation published together with FSA discussion paper	Legislation on termination payments announced
			FRC issued consultation paper on review of Combined Code	ASA Guidelines on executive remuneration released
				Productivity Commission Issues Paper on executive remuneration published
04/09	G-20 agree on Action Plan			
	FSF Compensation Principles published			
05/09	Bank for International Settlements Report on Issues in the Governance of Central Banks	Fraud Enforcement and Recovery Act signed 20 May, setting up Commission of Inquiry into the Financial Crisis		Exposure draft of Corporations Amendment (Improving Accountability on Termination Payments) Bill 2009 released
				APRA discussion paper on remuneration released
06/09		White paper on financial regulatory reform published 17 June		

(*Continued*)

Appendix 1 (*Continued*).

Date	International	USA	UK	Australia
07/09		Draft legislation delivered to Congress (consumer protection; investor protection; hedge fund registration; independent compensation committees; say-on-pay)	White paper on financial regulation published 8 July FRC second consultation paper on review of Combined Code Walker consultation paper on bank governance released	CAMAC report on market integrity published
10/09				
11/09	G-20 follow up meeting			
12/09	OECD Recommendations to be published by end 2009		FSA to make specific proposals based on Walker Review by fourth quarter 2009 FRC review of Combined Code to report late 2009	Productivity Commission report on executive remuneration due 19 December
01/10				APRA requirements on remuneration to come into force
06/10			Any changes to the Combined Code likely to come into force mid-2010	
12/10		Commission of Inquiry to report 15 December		

Chapter 7

AUDIT COMMITTEE INDEPENDENCE: REGULATORY DEVELOPMENTS, THE EMPIRICAL LITERATURE AND DIRECTIONS FOR FUTURE RESEARCH

DIVESH S. SHARMA AND VINEETA D. SHARMA

Florida International University

7.1 Introduction

Regulators around the world have converged on the view that director independence is the apex of strong corporate governance. The independence of the directors has been heralded as one of the most critical factors for effective corporate governance. Although such views are not novel, they came into the limelight following the Enron-led string of scandals that rocked the US and other capital markets wiping out billions of dollars of stockholder value. The prevailing fraudulent accounting and related practices at Enron, Global Crossing, Tyco, Sunbeam, WorldCom, and Xerox, to name a few, shattered market confidence and consequently led to the US Congress taking swift action to restore investors' confidence in the world's largest capital market. The US Congress enacted unprecedented laws and regulations aimed at improving investors' confidence in the processes responsible for ensuring the integrity of the information filed with regulators such as the Securities and Exchange Commission (SEC), and ultimately, released to the capital market. The Sarbanes-Oxley Act of 2002 (SOX), and various listing rules of the New York Stock Exchange (NYSE) and National Association of Securities Dealers (NASDAQ), introduced new regulations, including director independence rules, to promote good corporate governance.

The sorry state of director independence was most evident from the scandal at Enron. Congressional inquiry into Enron revealed that seemingly independent directors on the board of Enron, and the audit committee that was responsible for monitoring the financial reporting process, were not independent at all. The US Senate report on Enron (US Senate, 2002) found that independent directors at Enron were paid compensation in excess of $350,000 which, at that time, far exceeded the norm. Such enormous compensation raised doubts about the willingness of independent directors to exercise objective due diligence. In addition, the US Senate report identified that some independent directors had served on Enron's board for at least 10 years, suggesting that independent directors developed some sort of relationship with the management. The Senate inquiry also brought to the attention of the regulators the business affiliations some directors had with Enron. Many other corporate governance "shortcomings" (e.g. auditor independence) were identified through the Enron inquiry, which is beyond the scope of this chapter.

It appears that the scandals and associated governance defects are not isolated to the US. Similar defects have been reported in fraudulent financial reporting in Asia, Australia, and Europe. The scandals at China Aviation and Oil in Singapore, Satyam Computers in India, HIH and One.tel in Australia, and Parmalat in Italy, are often referred to as the international 'siblings' of Enron. The differences between the fraudulent activities in the US and other nations are more in degree than in kind. The governance defects can be considered identical, with the chief among them being the failure of corporate boards and their sub-committees, such as the audit committee, to comprise independent directors willing to perform independent and effective monitoring of management.

Given that director independence is paramount to effective monitoring of the financial reporting process, three issues are pertinent to our discussion. First, we survey the most recent corporate governance regulations on director independence from around the world. Second, we review selected empirical literature on director independence, and finally, we provide directions for future research. As the ambit of the oversight of the financial reporting process rests primarily with the audit committee, but is an issue for which the board of directors is ultimately responsible, we address these issues mainly in the context of the audit committee. Furthermore, since the concept of director independence is not limited to the US, we also address each of these issues from a global perspective. We make no attempt to conduct an exhaustive global analysis or literature review. Our selected countries are for illustrative purposes and generally represent the nature of governance practices in non-US countries spanning the UK, Europe, Asia and the Pacific.

It is important to understand the rules or guidelines issued to assist boards of directors in evaluating a director's independence for several reasons.

First, independence is a state of mind which is difficult, if not, impossible to assess. Rules or guidelines are, therefore, necessary to determine whether a director is likely to be independent. Second, there may be circumstances that create perceptions that independence is threatened although, in fact, there is no loss of independence. To placate market participants that a director's independence is not tainted, boards of directors require acceptable standards for assessing whether a director is independent or not. These standards should be consistently applied. Third, knowledge of these standards will allow market participants to make their own determination of a director's independence. Finally, as the stock markets break cross-national trading barriers, it is useful to conduct a comparative analysis of corporate governance practices with reference to director independence.

7.2 Defining Director Independence

7.2.1 *USA*

Following the enactment of SOX, the SEC approved several definitions of an independent director adopted by the NYSE and NASDAQ. Listing rule 303A of the NYSE as at September 11, 2008 states that:

(a) No director qualifies as 'independent' unless the board of directors affirmatively determines that the director has no material relationship with the listed company (either directly or as a partner, shareholder or officer of an organization that has a relationship with the company). Companies must identify which directors are independent and disclose the basis for that determination.

    The NYSE requires majority independent directors on the board. To provide further clarification, the director independence rules (303A) impose the following conditions in determining independence:

(b) In addition, a director is not independent if:

    (i) The director is, or has been within the last three years, an employee of the listed company, or an immediate family member is, or has been within the last three years, an executive officer, of the listed company.

    (ii) The director has received, or has an immediate family member who has received, during any twelve-month period within the last three years, more than $120,000 in direct compensation from the listed company, other than director and committee fees and pension or other forms of deferred compensation for prior service (provided such compensation is not contingent in any way on continued service).

(iii) (A) The director is a current partner or employee of a firm that is the company's internal or external auditor; (B) the director has an immediate family member who is a current partner of such a firm; (C) the director has an immediate family member who is a current employee of such a firm and personally works on the listed company's audit; or (D) the director or an immediate family member was, within the last three years, a partner or employee of such a firm and personally worked on the listed company's audit within that time.

(iv) The director or an immediate family member is, or has been within the last three years, employed as an executive officer of another company where any of the listed company's present executive officers at the same time serves or served on that company's compensation committee.

(v) The director is a current employee, or an immediate family member is a current executive officer, of a company that has made payments to, or received payments from, the listed company for property or services in an amount which, in any of the last three fiscal years, exceeds the greater of $1 million, or 2 percent of such other company's consolidated gross revenues.

The determining factor in the definition above appears to be 'material relationship' and in its commentary, the NYSE acknowledges, rightfully so, that it is difficult to anticipate circumstances that could give rise to or affect a director exercising independent judgment. As directors normally have other positions or have had such positions, the NYSE rules suggest that when assessing the materiality of a director's relationship with the listed company, the board should consider the issue not merely from the standpoint of the director, but also from that of persons or organizations with which the director has an affiliation. Some examples of material relationships or affiliation given by the NYSE include commercial, industrial, banking, consulting, legal, accounting, charitable and familial relationships. The NYSE does not view significant ownership of stock, in itself, as a factor undermining independence.

Since determining whether a director is independent is not trivial and involves judgment, the NYSE empowers the board of directors to determine, considering all relevant facts and circumstances, if a director meets the independence standards. The identity of the independent directors and the basis for a board determination that a relationship is not material must be disclosed in the listed company's annual proxy statement or, if the company does not file an annual proxy statement, in the company's annual report on Form 10-K filed with the SEC. The board must disclose and specifically explain why a director with a material or other relationship is deemed to be independent, including the listed company's standards for determining independence.

The most recent director independence rules of NASDAQ at the time of writing were adopted on March 12, 2009. The director independence rules of the NASDAQ are quite similar to the rules adopted by the NYSE except that the NASDAQ rules specifically spell out circumstances that may disqualify a director as independent. Like the NYSE, NASDAQ also requires majority independent directors on a listed issuer's board. Listing rule 5605 (a) (2) defines an independent director as:

> "a person other than an Executive Officer or employee of the Company or any other individual having a relationship which, in the opinion of the Company's board of directors, would interfere with the exercise of independent judgment in carrying out the responsibilities of a director. For purposes of this rule, 'Family Member' means a person's spouse, parents, children and siblings, whether by blood, marriage or adoption, or anyone residing in such person's home."

To provide guidance to the board of directors in determining who specifically would or would not qualify as an independent director, the listing rule specifies that the following persons shall not be considered independent:

(A) a director who is, or at any time during the past three years was, employed by the Company;

(B) a director who accepted or who has a Family Member who accepted any compensation from the Company in excess of $120,000 during any period of twelve consecutive months within the three years preceding the determination of independence, other than the following:

  (i) compensation for board or board committee service;
  (ii) compensation paid to a Family Member who is an employee (other than an Executive Officer) of the Company; or
  (iii) benefits under a tax-qualified retirement plan, or non-discretionary compensation.

(C) a director who is a Family Member of an individual who is, or at any time during the past three years was, employed by the company as an Executive Officer;

(D) a director who is, or has a Family Member who is, a partner in, or a controlling Shareholder or an Executive Officer of, any organization to which the Company made, or from which the Company received, payments for property or services in the current or any of the past three fiscal years that exceed 5 percent of the recipient's consolidated gross revenues for that year, or $200,000, whichever is more, other than the following:

(i) payments arising solely from investments in the Company's securities; or

(ii) payments under non-discretionary charitable contribution matching programs.

(E) a director of the Company who is, or has a Family Member who is, employed as an Executive Officer of another entity where at any time during the past three years any of the Executive Officers of the Company serve on the compensation committee of such other entity; or

(F) a director who is, or has a Family Member who is, a current partner of the Company's outside auditor, or was a partner or employee of the Company's outside auditor who worked on the Company's audit at any time during any of the past three years.

In addition to compensation for other than board service, both the NYSE and NASDAQ director independence rules identify family members and affiliations as threats to independence. Three examples of affiliations relate to 'business relationships', 'interlocking' directorships at the compensation committee level, and 'revolving-door' appointments. Business relationships refer to economic transactions exceeding $1,000,000 or 2 percent (NYSE) and $200,000 or 5 percent (NASDAQ) of the supplier's consolidated gross revenues, whichever is the greater. The NASDAQ applies a lower threshold, either because of the smaller size of listed entities or because it takes a more conservative approach. Both stock exchanges state that director 'interlocks' pertaining to service on the compensation committee, with a look back period of three years, will preclude such directors from being independent. The idea here is that when directors are involved in setting the compensation of each other, and that of executives, then some form of economic interest that could be created threatens the director's independence.

'Revolving-door' appointments to the board refers to a director or his/her family member who currently is, or was in the past three years, an employee or partner of the company's external auditor who worked on the audit. Being an employee or partner of the external auditor is perceived to threaten a director's independence because the fees paid to the audit firm arguably creates some form of economic dependence. The current or former audit firm employee/partner would be overseeing the work of his/her own audit firm which is not conducive to independent judgment, or the affiliated director may be able to influence the outcome of the audit, thus undermining the quality of the external audit, amongst other reasons. Later in the chapter, we discuss the research findings related to the merits of the rule on 'revolving-door' appointments to the board.

7.2.2 UK

Unlike the US, the most recent UK corporate governance practices, known as The Combined Code issued by the Financial Reporting Council in 2008, are not mandated by law; 'compliance' is voluntary but deviations should be explained. The Code recommends at least 50 percent of the board members, excluding the chairman, comprise independent directors. These independent directors should be identified in the annual report. Provision A.3 of The Code recommends that the board determine:

> ...whether the director is independent in character and judgement and whether there are relationships or circumstances which are likely to affect, or could appear to affect, the director's judgement. The board should state its reasons if it determines that a director is independent notwithstanding the existence of relationships or circumstances which may appear relevant to its determination, including if the director:
>
> 1. has been an employee of the company or group within the last five years;
> 2. has, or has had within the last three years, a material business relationship with the company either directly, or as a partner, shareholder, director or senior employee of a body that has such a relationship with the company;
> 3. has received or receives additional remuneration from the company apart from a director's fee, participates in the company's share option or a performance-related pay scheme, or is a member of the company's pension scheme;
> 4. has close family ties with any of the company's advisers, directors or senior employees;
> 5. holds cross-directorships or has significant links with other directors through involvement in other companies or bodies;
> 6. represents a significant shareholder; or
> 7. has served on the board for more than nine years from the date of their first election.

The UK concept of independence has three dimensions — independence of character, independence of judgment, and independence in appearance.

To determine whether a director qualifies as independent, the Code lists specific circumstances that may disqualify a director from being independent. There are some commonalities between the UK and the US in that both countries refer to past employee, business relationships, affiliated persons, family ties and board-interlocks as potential threats to a director's independence. However, there are some significant differences. First, a former employee will not be deemed independent in the UK until a five-year cooling-off period; in the US this period is three years. Second, the Code includes board-interlocks as a threat to independence whereas in the US, such interlocks are limited to the compensation committee. Finally, directors with more than nine years tenure on a UK board are deemed to have breached the independence criteria. There is no such criterion in the US.

The preceding differences suggest that the UK independence criteria are more stringent than the US. However, the UK criteria are recommendations and deviations are permitted provided they are disclosed in the annual report to the shareholders. Furthermore, the UK Code leaves some terms undefined such as 'material business relationship', whereas the US provides thresholds beyond which a transaction becomes material.

7.2.3 *Australia*

In 2007, the Australian Securities Exchange (ASX) Council of Corporate Governance issued the most recent recommendations on good corporate governance for companies listed on the ASX. The Australian recommendations appear to have drawn on both the US and UK independence criteria. The ASX recommends that boards comprise one-third, 50 percent, or a majority of independent or non-executive directors. The report titled 'Corporate Governance Principles and Recommendations' defines an independent director as:

> "a non-executive director who is not a member of management and who is free of any business or other relationship that could materially interfere with — or could reasonably be perceived to materially interfere with — the independent exercise of their judgement."

In spirit, this definition is consistent with the independence definitions of the US. However, similar to the UK, the Australian definition specifically refers to *perceptions* of a director's independence. Interestingly, unlike the US rules but similar to the UK, the commercial or economic affiliation does not have a recommended threshold but provides discretion to the board of directors in determining what constitutes 'materially' interfere with. To assist listed companies make this determination, the ASX recommends that they identify the following business or other relationships that could affect a director's independence or perceived independence. The director is not independent if s/he:

1. is a substantial shareholder of the company or an officer of, or otherwise associated directly with, a substantial shareholder of the company;
2. is employed, or has previously been employed in an executive capacity by the company or another group member, and there has not been a period of at least three years between ceasing such employment and serving on the board;
3. has within the last three years been a principal of a material professional adviser or a material consultant to the company or another group member, or an employee materially associated with the service provided;
4. is a material supplier or customer of the company or other group member, or an officer of or otherwise associated directly or indirectly with a material supplier or customer;
5. has a material contractual relationship with the company or another group member other than as a director.

The conditions listed above are consistent with those in the listing rules of the NYSE and NASDAQ except that the Australian conditions are couched in more general terms, and refer to material relationships rather than providing thresholds such as $1,000,000 or 2 percent (NYSE) and $200,000 or 5 percent (NASDAQ). Again, the term material is left to the discretion of the board of directors and, as such, opens the scope for greater flexibility. The three-year 'look back' or 'cooling-off' period relating to former executives or business affiliates is similar to those in the US. While the US rules refer specifically to affiliated persons with the listed company's auditor, the Australian recommendations refer to a professional adviser or consultant which, in practical terms, would include employees of the audit firm and could include a legal or financial adviser. In this respect, the Australian recommendations appear to be much broader. The ASX recommendations suggest that the board consider family relationships when determining whether a director meets the independence criteria.

7.2.4 *New Zealand*

The definition of an independent director in New Zealand is quite similar to Australia except that the New Zealand definition is less specific and creates room for the board to exercise considerable discretion. In its 2004 principles of corporate governance the Securities Commission in New Zealand (NZSEC) defines an independent director as someone:

> "who is not an employee of the entity and who does not represent a substantial shareholder and who has no other direct or indirect interest or relationship that could reasonably influence their judgement and decision making as a director."

Because New Zealand has a limited and small supply of eligible directors, the NZSEC takes the view that director independence should not be limited by a set of defining criteria but is best determined by the board. However, a substantial shareholder (5 percent or more voting equity in the entity) is deemed to not meet the independence criterion. The NZSEC also does not specify what constitutes 'direct or indirect interest or relationship' but the New Zealand Stock Exchange states that a financial transaction in excess of $100,000 will be construed as an economic interest that bars a director from being deemed independent.

7.2.5 *Singapore*

The Singapore Code of Corporate Governance (2005) recommends boards of directors comprise at least one-third independent directors. The Code is not mandatory but highly recommends listed issuers to follow the recommendations. The Singapore Code defines an independent director as someone:

> "who has no relationship with the company, its related companies or its officers that could interfere, or be reasonably perceived to interfere, with the exercise of the director's independent business judgement with a view to the best interests of the company."

Examples of such relationships provided in the Singapore Code are similar to those in the US and UK with the following finer differences. A director or immediate family member cannot accept any form of compensation other than for service on the board. Also, a director or immediate family member cannot be a substantial shareholder in a for-profit business with which the company has a transaction greater than $200,000 in the current or past financial year. Notice here that the business relationship is limited to for-profit organizations and thus excludes not-for-profit entities. If a board decides to deem a director independent even if the director does not meet the guidelines, then full disclosure of the nature of the director's relationship is required, with the Code specifying that the company and board will be fully responsible for any ramifications.

7.2.6 *Germany*

Germany, like most other European nations, has a unique dual-board structure. The German Corporate Governance Code (the 'Code') as of June 6, 2008 governs the Management board and Supervisory board of listed companies. The Supervisory board is akin to the board of directors in non-European countries. In the spirit of international convergence, Germany does permit companies to adopt a single board system of governance. The Management board is responsible for managing the enterprise and the Supervisory board appoints, supervises and advises the members of the Management board and is directly involved in decisions of fundamental importance to the enterprise. The members of the Supervisory board, like director appointments in the US, UK, Australia and other countries, are elected by the shareholders at the General Meeting.

Since the Supervisory board monitors the Management board, the German Code requires that the Supervisory board comprise 'an adequate number of independent members.' It is not clear from the Code what determines 'an adequate number.' A Supervisory board member is 'considered independent if he/she has no business or personal relations with the company or its Management board which could cause a conflict of interests.' In this vein, the Code specifies that not more than two former members of the Management board shall be members of the Supervisory board. To maintain their independence and avoid conflict of interest, each member of the Supervisory board is required to 'inform the Supervisory Board of any conflicts of interest which may result from a consultant or directorship function with clients, suppliers, lenders or other business partners.' Such business relationships are consistent with international best practices. However, the Supervisory board members 'shall not exercise directorships or similar positions or advisory tasks for important competitors of the enterprise.' This is a unique requirement not seen in the US, UK, Australia and in most other governance regulations. Interestingly, the German Code permits Members of the Supervisory board to 'receive fixed as well as performance-related compensation.' Performance-related compensation should also contain components based on the long-term performance of the enterprise.

7.2.7 *Spain*

The Spanish corporate governance code adopted on January 16, 2006 titled 'Unified Code of Recommendations for the Good Governance of Companies quoted on the Spanish Stock Exchange' has several distinguishing features. An obvious distinction is that the Code specifically states that it does not provide discretion to the company or its board of directors to determine who qualifies as an independent director. The Code requires companies to prove a director's independence and business integrity. Independent directors are considered as those who are not influenced by past, present or future ties with the company, shareholders or any director. Past and present affiliations potentially affecting independence are similar to other governance requirements but future ties that may or may not be foreseen is unique and aims to prevent potential conflicts of interest. In some ways, it is an appropriate criterion but, in practice, it may be difficult to implement. The Spanish Code applies the following criteria for determining who would not meet the independence standards:

(a) Past employees or executive directors of the group, unless 3 or 5 years have elapsed, respectively, from the end of the relation.

(b) They receive some payment or other form of compensation from the company or any other company within its group on top of their directors' fees, unless the amount involved is not significant.

(c) They are a partner or employee of the external auditor or the auditor of any other company in the same group, or have been in the past three years.

(d) They are executive directors or senior officers of another company where an executive director or senior officer of the company is an external director.

(e) They have material business dealings with the company or some other in its group or have had such dealings in the preceding year, either on their own account or as the shareholder, director or senior officer of a company that has or has had such dealings.
'Business dealings' will include the provision of goods or services, including financial services, as well as advisory or consultancy relationships. Business dealings will be deemed to be material when billing or payment flows come to over 1 percent of either party's annual revenues.

(f) They are shareholders, directors or senior officers of an entity that receives significant donations from the company or some other company in the same group, or has done so in the past 3 years.

(g) They are the spouse or maintain an analogous affective relationship or are relatives to the second degree of one of the company's executive directors or senior officers.

(h) They have served as independent directors without interruption for a period of over 12 years.

Most of the criteria above are similar to those in the US and elsewhere with the following exceptions. First, directors with more than 12 consecutive years of service on the board are considered not independent. There currently is no such criterion in the US but the UK has a threshold of nine years. Second, former employees or executive directors who stay on or are appointed as directors in any company within the group shall be considered as executive directors. They will not, therefore, qualify as independent unless they leave the board for a period of five years, even though three or five years have elapsed since they ceased to be employees or executive directors, respectively. Third, material business transactions have a lower threshold than the US; 1 percent of revenues compared to 2 percent and 5 percent in the US. Fourth, the Spanish Code appears to include extra-marital affairs as a threat to a director's independence. Finally, like the UK, any interlocking directorships where either one of the interlocked directors is an executive will disqualify both directors from being independent. In the US, this criterion is applied to the compensation committee only. Although the Spanish Code has some unique and stringent recommendations, compliance with the Code is not mandatory.

7.3 Empirical Research

We now turn to empirical research that examines independent directors as one of its primary effects on financial reporting quality. We focus on financial reporting quality because the response by regulators worldwide to renew confidence in the stock market was due to the devastating accounting scandals. As the body of literature on independent directors is extensive, we restrict our review to independent directors on the audit committee because this is the committee primarily responsible for overseeing the quality of financial reporting. We exclude studies that do not focus on audit committee director independence but include it as a control variable because such studies do not draw inferences about director independence. We define financial reporting quality generally as managerial discretion that consists of three empirical indicators widely studied: some form of earnings management (e.g. discretionary accruals), financial statement fraud and financial restatements. Our review is structured according to these three empirical indicators of financial reporting quality.

7.3.1 *Earnings Management and Independent Directors on the Audit Committee*

The study by Klein (2002) is regarded as the seminal study on independent directors on the audit committee and earnings management. Klein (2002) examined the association between various thresholds of independent director composition on the audit committee and abnormal accruals. She defines independent directors as outsiders who have no ties to the firm beyond being a board member and any business relationship that could impair the director's independence as per the then Item 404(a) of Regulation S-K of the Securities and Exchange Act. The threshold at that time was $60,000. Using data for the fiscal years 1992–1993, she finds that (1) complete independence on the audit committee is not related to abnormal accruals; (2) majority independent directors on the audit committee is negatively associated with abnormal accruals; and (3) as the percentage of independent directors on the audit committee increases, abnormal accruals decrease. However, a significant limitation of Klein's (2002) study is that it does not control for audit committee financial expertise and audit committee meetings. These two variables are critical indicators of audit committee effectiveness. An interesting observation in Klein (2002) is that the presence of a 5 percent block-holder on the audit committee is negatively associated with abnormal accruals. This finding is interesting in the context of current criteria in the fact that some governance regulations appear to disqualify a director as independent if that director is a substantial shareholder. Klein's (2002) results suggest that a substantial shareholder may act more like a shareholder, thus enhancing the alignment between directors and stockholders.

Xie *et al.* (2003) examine the characteristics of the board, the audit committee and the executive committee and earnings management. They use discretionary current accruals (using the Jones 1991 model) as a proxy for earnings management for a sample of 282 firms for the years 1992, 1994 and 1996. Based on simple and multiple OLS, their results indicate that earnings management is not related to the independence of the audit committee. Two notable limitations of their study are the use of only two control variables (firm size and year dummies) and the use of largely simple regression to test the hypotheses. Therefore, the results of Xie *et al.* (2003) are not considered robust.

Bedard *et al.* (2004) investigate the relationship between audit committee characteristics and the extent of corporate earnings management as measured by the level of income-increasing and income-decreasing abnormal accruals using the modified Jones (1991) cross-sectional model for a sample of 300 firms in 1996. They define an independent director using the SOX determination which states that in order for a director to be considered independent, the director cannot accept *any* form of compensation from the company other than for service on the board. They develop two independence measures: majority independence (between 50 percent and 99 percent independence) and complete independence (100 percent independence).

An additional proxy for independence employed by Bedard *et al.* (2004) is the value of short-term stock options held by independent audit committee directors. Specifically, the variable, StockOptions, is measured as the ratio of stock options that can be exercised in the 60 days following the fiscal year end to the sum of options and stocks held by non-related outside committee members. Bedard *et al.* (2004) report that only a 100 percent independent audit committee is significant in dampening aggressive earnings management. These results are inconsistent with Klein (2002) and are probably due to the measure of earnings management, model specification (Klein estimates separate regressions for majority (>50 percent) and 100 percent independent audit committees but Bedard *et al.* (2004) include these together in a single regression) and time period. Further, they find that StockOptions are positively associated with aggressive earnings management, suggesting that greater short-term incentives in the form of stock options motivate directors to be less vigilant, thus compromising their independence.

The preceding studies examine data for US-listed companies. Some studies situated elsewhere include Bradbury *et al.* (2004) in Singapore/Malaysia, Rahman and Ali (2006) in Malaysia, Davidson *et al.* (2005) in Australia, and Sharma and Kuang (2008) in New Zealand. These studies define director independence using the regulations in their home country. Bradbury *et al.* (2004) find that 100 percent independent audit committees are associated with lower abnormal accruals but Rahman and Ali (2006) find no significant effect in their sample. Davidson *et al.* (2005) report that a completely independent audit committee is not related to earnings management but a majority independent audit committee is marginally so. When they define independence as directors without any business or other relationship with the company, they find that audit committee independence is not related to earnings management. In the New Zealand study, Sharma and Kuang (2008) find that non-executive directors are not related to earnings management but majority independent directors are negatively related to earnings management.

7.3.2 *Financial Statement Fraud and Independent Directors on the Audit Committee*

Abbott *et al.* (2000) investigate the relationship between audit committees and corporate fraud. They examine audit committee characteristics of 78 firms subject to SEC sanctions and 78 matched on size and industry non-SEC sanctioned firms over the period of 1980 to 1996. Their independent variable of interest is the audit committee's effectiveness (ACENOEMP) that is set to 1 if the audit committee comprises entirely of outsiders (non-employees of the firm) and the number of meetings is greater than two per year, 0 otherwise. They find that ACENOEMP is negative and significantly related to the likelihood of sanction by the SEC. Thus, Abbott *et al.* (2000) conclude that the effectiveness of the audit committee is a function of the presence of outside members on the audit committee and the frequency of audit committee meetings.

Beasley *et al.* (2000) conduct a descriptive study of fraud and corporate governance mechanisms by industry. Generally, they find that the nature of fraud differs by industry. They find that fraud firms are less likely to have an audit committee, and such committees are comprised largely of insiders and meet less frequently than those of non-fraud firms. Interestingly, this study defines director independence by implication using inside employee directors. By definition, it considers non-employee directors as outside directors which does not equate to independent directors.

7.3.3 *Financial Restatements and Independent Directors on the Audit Committee*

Abbott *et al.* (2004) investigate the impact of certain audit committee characteristics identified by the Blue Ribbon Committee (BRC) on the likelihood of financial restatements. They examine audit committee characteristics for 44 firms which issued fraudulent reports and 88 firms which restated annual results without allegations of fraud between 1991 to 1999. They use a sample of 132 control firms matched on the basis of industry, size, exchange and auditor type (Big 5, non-Big 5).[1] For the full sample (fraud, restatement and control firms combined), Abbott *et al.* (2004) find that the presence of a completely independent audit committee (100 percent independent directors on the audit committee where independence is defined according to the BRC) and higher levels of committee activity (at least four meetings per annum) significantly reduce the likelihood of restatements. For the fraud and no-fraud sub-sample, they find that only audit committee independence and the absence of a financial expert are related to the likelihood of fraud.

Among other variables, Agrawal and Chadha (2005) investigate the association between audit committee independence and earnings restatements of US-listed companies in fiscal years 2000 and 2001. Using logistic regression, they find that several important governance characteristics are not related to the likelihood of a company restating its earnings. This includes the independence of the audit committee where independence is defined similar to the

---

[1] Big 5 are the largest public accounting firms such as KPMG, Deloitte, PWC, E&Y, and Arthur Anderson. The remaining public accounting firms comprise the non-Big 5.

current NYSE definitions. However, they find a significant negative relationship between an independent director with financial expertise on the audit committee and the likelihood of financial restatements. This result suggests that independent directors with financial expertise can better equip the audit committee and facilitate oversight of potential financial reporting problems.

Sharma and Iselin (2006) attempt to reconcile the results of Abbott *et al.* (2004) and Agrawal and Chadha (2005) by introducing other factors that could affect a director's independence. Drawing on the management friendliness/social network framework and economic theory, they posit that outside independent directors may not be independent "in fact" if they have a developed relationship with management. Such relationships can develop with a director's longer tenure on the board and through lucrative director compensation. Sharma and Iselin (2006) investigate these factors in a sample of US-listed companies that misstated their financial statements in 1999, 2000 or 2001 with a matched sample of non-restating companies. They define an independent director as someone without any ties or association with management other than as a board member. Sharma and Iselin (2006) find that directors with longer tenure (greater than nine or 15 years) are not related to restatements. Contrary to concerns about cronyism, they find that higher fixed cash compensation is negatively related to financial restatements. In the context of Bedard *et al.* (2004) who find stock options are positively related to aggressive earnings management, the results in Sharma and Iselin (2006) suggest that fixed cash compensation may not have the effect of motivating directors to focus on short-term stock gains.

In a related study, Archambeault *et al.* (2008) examine how the structure of compensation paid to independent audit committee directors is related to financial restatements. They define independence as a director without any ties to the firm other than as a director. Archambeault *et al.* (2008) focus on short and long-term compensation structures. Short-term incentive compensation includes stock options that can be exercised within 60 days and long-term options are those that cannot be exercised within 60 days. They derive values for stock options and construct a quotient measure where the denominator is the total value of compensation that includes all equity compensation, fixed cash compensation and meeting fees. Contrary to expectations, Archambeault *et al.* (2008) find that long-term stock options are positively related to restatements and so are short-term stock options. These results suggest that greater stock option compensation relative to cash compensation motivates directors to support management's engagement in financial misreporting. In addition, these results echo the findings in Sharma and Iselin (2006) that fixed cash compensation is a better motivator for independent directors on the audit committee.

Three major inferences can be made from the sample of the literature reviewed. First, the literature on audit committee independence and financial reporting quality does not provide consistent results. Some studies show that a 100 percent independent audit committee enhances the quality of financial reporting while others show that it does not. Furthermore, some results indicate that majority independence is sufficient and that 100 percent independence is not necessary while others show that the opposite is true. These divergent results suggest that there is more room for research in this area and one could productively begin with a meta-analysis to identify causes of differences in the results. While that is beyond the scope of this chapter, two major contributing factors to the divergent results are model specification and the definition of financial reporting quality. For instance, Klein (2002) examines independent directors only and does not control for financial expertise or audit committee meetings in her empirical analysis. In contrast, Bedard *et al.* (2004), who report results contrary to Klein (2002), include such control variables. In addition, Klein's (2002) dependent variable is abnormal accruals while Bedard *et al.* (2004) use a dichotomy of aggressive or non-aggressive earnings management. Yet others use other measures of financial reporting quality including fraud and restatements. Clearly, replication studies are needed to substantiate prior results and a more critical view of assumptions and inferences of prior studies are called for so as to productively advance research and assist policy makers.

The second inference we can draw from the literature reviewed is that the definition of independent director varies. Most studies define an independent director as an outside director and rely on proxy or annual report disclosures to determine who qualifies as an outside director. Political visibility theory would suggest that it is in the best interests of a firm to not attenuate a director who may not be independent, so relying on corporate disclosures is not error-free. For instance, the directors on the audit committee of Enron were listed as independent in the proxy statements and annual reports issued to shareholders. Upon scrutiny, and a simple perusal of the related party transaction, it was discovered that these directors did not meet the independence requirements! Very few studies acknowledge that the reliance on corporate disclosures about directors is a limitation. As the above definitions of independence show, an outside director is not the same as an independent director. It is important to make this distinction because outside directors include 'gray' directors. Gray directors are non-employee directors who may have some financial or other affiliation with the firm. Such directors face economic or other threats to their exercise of independent judgment and thus ought not to be considered independent.

The third noteworthy inference we make from the literature review is that most studies focus on a simple view of director independence, however defined.

The literature appears to simply take some quantitative measure of independence and run with it. Independence is not a simple concept that can be reduced to a number. It is a complex phenomenon and various forces shape a person's independence. Recognizing other determinants of independence, three studies seem to diverge from the mainstream view: Bedard *et al.* (2004), Sharma and Iselin (2006) and Archambeault *et al.* (2008). All three studies introduced some form of economic incentive effect that could either enhance or impair a director's independence. The common finding across these three studies is that stock options as a form of compensation for independent directors may have introduced unintended consequences; greater stock option compensation appears to undermine a director's independence. The implication is that cash may be a more appropriate form of compensation for directors on the audit committee. In addition, Sharma and Iselin (2006) introduced the effect of audit committee director tenure on independence and, based on their results, there is no compelling evidence to suggest that directors with longer tenure develop social ties with management and thus may compromise their independence. However, there are opportunities for refining the constructs in Bedard *et al.* (2004), Sharma and Iselin (2006) and Archambeault *et al.* (2008), and more importantly for proposing new directions in audit committee research that aims to address the cornerstone characteristic of independence.

7.4 Future Research Directions

Clearly, the inconsistencies in the literature on audit committee independence and financial reporting quality suggest that there is much scope for further work in this paradigm. Notwithstanding the limitations of the research method (e.g. model specification, definition of independence), the inconsistent results suggest that some independent directors appear to be more vigilant in their monitoring of management than others. A relevant and interesting question is to ask why this may be so. A clue to this puzzle is provided by the three somewhat radical studies noted above (e.g. Bedard *et al.*, 2004; Sharma and Iselin, 2006; Archambeault *et al.*, 2008). These studies illustrate that economic incentives and other affiliations can affect a director's independence. We now discuss where we see fruitful areas of future research with reference to incentives affecting a director's independence.

7.4.1 *Economic Incentives*

We do not need rocket science to postulate that economic or monetary incentives can influence a director's independence. It is clear from the CEO compensation literature that independent directors receiving greater compensation approve greater CEO compensation (e.g. Core *et al.*, 1999). What is not so clear is how this applies to directors on the audit committee. Bedard *et al.* (2004) and Archambeault *et al.* (2008) show that greater stock option compensation in the compensation structure of independent directors on the audit committee is associated with greater financial misreporting. In addition, contrary to expectations, Archambeault *et al.* (2008) show that even greater long-term stock option compensation is associated with increased financial misreporting. The implication is that cash may be a better form of compensation for independent directors on the audit committee; an inference that is consistent with Sharma and Iselin (2006) who find that fixed cash compensation appears to reduce the likelihood of financial misstatements.

However, economic incentives are a complex issue. All three studies above assume a linear effect of compensation with Sharma and Iselin (2006) showing some evidence of a non-linear effect. Sharma and Iselin (2006) find that, at very low or very high levels of cash compensation, independent directors do not reduce financial misstatements. Their results suggest that appropriate cash compensation is somewhere in the middle ground. If cash compensation is very low, and assuming firms use stock options to compensate directors, then low cash compensation suggests the possibility of greater stock option compensation. At the other extreme, high cash compensation, regardless of the form of compensation, may create economic bonding and cronyism in the boardroom. All three studies acknowledge that obtaining compensation data for directors has been a challenge due to poor disclosure. However, the SEC's new compensation disclosure rules effective for the fiscal years of 2006 onwards provides some hope that compensation data may now be available to conduct more reliable analyses. Future research can replicate the above three studies and also examine how the structure, amount, stock option vesting periods, the timing of the exercise of stock options, and spring-boarding or backdating of options, amongst other factors, affect financial reporting quality. In addition, a key question is whether independent directors should be given stock options at all. If so, then the recent stock option backdating scandals suggest that directors receiving stock options could be motivated to game the system and influence financial reporting to move stock prices in their favor. Rather, some commentators suggest that independent directors be given stock ownership in the firm and be barred from selling stock in the short term. In summary, the economic incentives facing independent directors provides a rich avenue for future research aimed at understanding threats to director independence.

7.4.2 *Interlocking Directorships*

Interlocking directorships at the board level has received considerable attention in the literature (e.g. Davis, 1996). However, we are not aware of any research that examines how director interlocks at the audit committee level affects the quality of financial reporting. The theoretical explanations of interlocking directorships at the board level would also apply at the audit committee level so the need to create a theory is not intense. Under the recent director independence rules, the NYSE and NASDAQ deem that a director is not independent if there is an interlocking directorship at the compensation committee level. What this means is that if an executive officer at Firm A serves on the board and also on the compensation committee of Firm B then an executive officer of Firm B who also serves as a director in Firm A, will not be considered an independent director on the board of Firm A. In this scenario, the director from Firm A on the board of Firm B will be considered independent because the executive officer from Firm B does not serve on the compensation committee of Firm A. If, however, both directors serve on each other's compensation committee, then both will be considered as not meeting the independence requirement. It is clear that the NYSE and NASDAQ believe that serving on the compensation committee is critical to ensuring independence because the underlying threat stems from economic incentives that could undermine a director's independence. Such a view strengthens our first potential research area on economic incentives.

While interlocking directorships at the audit committee level offers considerable scope for future research, its appeal may diminish because obtaining data on interlocking directorships is a challenge. With disclosures about directors improving and databases (e.g. Board Analyst, IRRC, etc.) providing more details about directors, the challenge is surmountable. The important question, though, relates to what nature of interlocking directorships is likely to threaten a director's independence? Is a simple audit committee interlock sufficient to create threats to independence or, as the NYSE and NASDAQ rules suggest, compensation committee interlocks ought to accompany audit committee interlocks before independence may be impaired? Shall the interlocks be confined to the compensation committee or shall nominating committee, governance committee and other sub-committee interlocks be deemed important? These are questions that could guide future empirical research to understand the group dynamics of the independent directors and help shape future corporate governance policies.

7.4.3 *Social Ties*

Almost every country's director independence rules include a criterion related to family membership where a family relationship will deem a director not independent. Interestingly, the Spanish rules extend family relationship to other affective relationships. As the audit committee should comprise 100 percent or majority independent directors, the idea of this criterion is to 'prohibit' a director on the audit committee from overseeing management who has a family relationship with the director because the family relationship may cause the director to not exercise independent judgment. It is understandable and clear that some form of nepotism could taint a director's exercise of objective judgment. However, it is not so clear whether other forms of non-business relationships affect a director's independence. A director's tenure on a firm's board is one of the factors proposed to influence a director's independence. Research, however, provides two alternative views on how tenure may affect a director's ability to monitor management.

Organizational behavior theory suggests that longer tenure increases an individual's commitment towards the firm (e.g. Buchanan, 1974; Salancik, 1977). Similarly, the expertise hypothesis suggests that directors with longer board tenure accumulate greater experience and knowledge about the firm and its business environment (Vafeas, 2003) and, therefore, such directors may be able to perform their monitoring responsibilities better.

There is, however, an alternative view which posits that director independence deteriorates with longer tenure. It is often argued that independent directors are less likely to discipline management when they develop friendship or social ties with management. Longer tenure develops a close social nexus and a strong affiliation between management and the independent directors. Independent directors with long tenure are, therefore, more likely to ratify management decisions that compromise the interests of shareholders (Kesner, 1988; Wade *et al.*, 1990; Boeker and Goodstein, 1993). Longer serving independent audit committee members may forge a stronger bond with management and consequently may not be willing to diverge on issues concerning the financial statements (Sharma and Iselin, 2006). The long tenure of independent directors at Enron supports this view (US Senate, 2002). Corporate governance activists such as the NACD are also concerned that directors who stay too long on corporate boards may be detrimental to the shareholders. The NACD (1996) argues that changing business conditions require changes in board composition and suggests a maximum of 10 to 15 years of board service in order to obtain fresh ideas and critical oversight which only new directors can bring to the board. If directors with long tenure indeed develop close ties with management, then it is likely that such directors could become complacent and compromise their objectivity (independence) and support management.

The only research to date that examines how the tenure of directors on the audit committee affects financial reporting quality is Sharma and Iselin

(2006). They posit that long-serving independent audit committee members accumulate firm-specific expertise which may enable them to more effectively oversee the financial reporting process. In contrast, long-serving independent directors may develop close social ties with management and hence they may not monitor management effectively. Sharma and Iselin (2006) find that the tenure of the independent directors on the audit committee is not related to financial misstatements. A plausible explanation for this finding is that long tenure is a double-edged sword which counter-balances empirical effects. A limiting factor in Sharma and Iselin (2006) is that tenure is based on the average tenure of the independent directors on the audit committee. As is widely acknowledged, an average measure has its limitations. An avenue for future research could be deriving alternative empirical indicators for tenure. Another research opportunity could examine how the tenure of the independent directors correlates with the tenure of the CEO, and whether a relationship of influence can be derived (e.g. CEO 'appoints' the director to the audit committee as distinct from appointing the director to the board) to examine how this affects the quality of financial reporting.

7.4.4 *Former CEO*

The listing rules in most countries bar a former CEO from qualifying as an independent director unless a period of three or five years has passed. The listing rules assume that once the three or five year cooling-off period expires, the former CEO becomes independent. Monks and Minow (2008) provide a 'catch-22' perspective on former CEOs as board members. The often stated benefit of appointing a former CEO of the firm as a board member is the CEO's unparalleled expertise and firm-specific knowledge. The disadvantage is that the former CEO may interfere with the management of the firm and dominate the board. This may be particularly so if the board and the new CEO want to make radical changes and move into a new direction. In relation to the audit committee, it is not clear how former CEOs of the firm affect the director's exercise of independent judgment and the audit committee's effectiveness. We are not aware of any research that examines how the presence of a former CEO on the audit committee is related to financial reporting quality. The focus has been on the current CEO's duality, stock ownership and compensation. Since the theory surrounding a former CEO suggests benefits and costs of appointing such a director on the board, the presence of a former CEO who meets or does not meet the relevant cooling-off period provides for an interesting research question in the context of the audit committee and financial reporting quality.

7.4.5 *Business Affiliations*

In the director independence rules detailed above, we have seen that all of the countries surveyed include a criterion that disqualifies a director as independent if the director has or has had, in the past three or five years, a material business relationship with the firm. The basis for this criterion is that economic incentives stemming from business transactions could impair the director's willingness to act in the most objective manner or create a perception that the director may not be independent. Such directors have typically been classified as gray directors and research provides little evidence on the effectiveness of gray directors on the audit committee and financial reporting quality. Related research finds evidence of gray directors adversely affecting the audit function (e.g. Raghunandan *et al.* 2001; Carcello and Neal, 2003). Under the new independent director rules, examining the presence of gray directors in the US and UK is virtually impossible because the audit committee in these two jurisdictions comprises independent directors. However, the scope to investigate the presence of gray directors provides opportunities in relatively smaller capital markets that do not require complete independence on the audit committee. Some of these markets include Australia, New Zealand, Singapore and many emerging economies.

The studies reported here do not distinguish between the types of business affiliation a director has. There is a body of research that examines how an *executive's* affiliation with the current or former audit firm is related to financial reporting quality. The evidence in this 'revolving-door' literature is mixed as some studies show affiliated executives do not undermine the quality of reporting (Geiger *et al.*, 2005; Geiger and North, 2006) whereas others show that it does (Menon and Williams, 2004; Dowdell and Krishnan, 2004; Lennox, 2005). To date, there is only one study that examines independent directors on the audit committee affiliated with a current or former audit firm and the quality of the financial reporting process. Naiker and Sharma (2009) show that former partners affiliated with the audit firm do not undermine the quality of financial reporting and the internal control system. Rather, their evidence suggests that affiliated partners bring considerable firm-specific expertise to the audit committee that leads to better monitoring of the financial reporting process. Naiker and Sharma (2009) are also the first to test whether the three-year cooling-off period applying to affiliated directors is necessary. Their results show that independent directors affiliated with the audit firm provide similar degrees of monitoring regardless of whether they meet the cooling-off period or not. This finding suggests that the cooling-off period may not be necessary.

Given the paucity of research on affiliated directors on the audit committee and financial reporting quality, there is ample scope to investigate how affiliation affects an independent director's effectiveness. Two issues worthy of future research is how different types of business affiliations affect a director's independence and whether variations in monetary thresholds of business transactions have a differential effect. Recognizing that it may be difficult to identify the value of monetary transactions from public sources and the fact that director independence rules appear to be converging, future research could perhaps employ experimental research methods to investigate such issues.

7.5 Concluding Comments

In this chapter, we provided an illustration of the most recent definitions of independent directors from around the world and reviewed selected literature on the association between independent directors on the audit committee and financial reporting quality. Our survey of the definitions suggests there are some common themes in the determination of director independence but considerable differences still remain. As each country has its own set of regulations, laws and corporate culture and extent of corporate scandals, variations are expected. Accordingly, we do not believe that there will be complete global convergence of the criteria defining director independence nor do we expect to see the establishment of a global corporate governance standard. However, what we can and do encourage is more cross-national studies on director independence. We have seen single country studies on director independence in the context of financial reporting quality but have yet to overcome the challenges of multi-country settings in a single study. We acknowledge that it is difficult to overcome institutional differences in a multi-country study but the evidence from such a comparative study has much to contribute to the development of the paradigm.

On the issue of factors affecting a director's independence, there is a broad array of opportunities that can shed further light on why some independent directors are vigilant and others not so when monitoring management. Such research is important because regulations governing director independence have been introduced hastily based on anecdotes rather than systematic scientific evidence. Future research can provide feedback on past policies and regulations and also shape the regulations to come. As data availability is often a limiting factor, we suggest the employment of a variety of research methods such as empirical archival, experimental, surveys and case studies to continue our pursuit of developing a rich and informative literature on director independence.

Chapter 8

CORPORATE GOVERNANCE AND THE SMALLER FIRM

CORAL INGLEY* AND LOTFI KAROUI[†]

Auckland University of Technology
[†]*Ecole supérieure de commerce de Troyes*

8.1 Introduction

The emphasis in corporate governance has been on large corporations and protecting investors' stakes (Roberts *et al.*, 2005) which, together, provide the basis for legislative frameworks and regulatory control of companies and for modelling principles and guidelines for board functioning and conduct. The dominant models, founded on agency theory, are based primarily on the role of boards of directors in publicly-listed firms that are subject to stock exchange listing rules and legal requirements for public reporting of their activities and performance to investors, shareholders and other interested stakeholders (Johnson *et al.*, 1996). The board in this context has traditionally functioned as a control mechanism, its role being mainly that of a watchdog, providing prudent oversight of the management's decisions and activities on behalf of the company's ownership (Carter *et al.*, 2003; Fama & Jensen, 1983; Voordeckers *et al.*, 2007). The theoretical basis for this view is that of the separation of ownership and management, requiring control through intermediation by boards of directors operating as agents for the owners. The main focus of governance in this setting is on compliance with legal requirements and safeguarding the shareholders' interests.

With the complexity of globalising markets and efforts to professionalize and improve the performance of boards, the traditional concept of the board's control role, based on the agency view, has expanded to include a service role where the board is expected also to be more active in setting the strategic direction and decision making of the firm in conjunction with management.

While the control role is aligned with the compliance dimension of governance, the service role is aligned with the performance dimension. With this extended board role, much debate has ensued regarding the theoretical adequacy of agency theory, on which current governance principles, laws and practices are based. From this debate, the board's service role concept seems to be better supported by other theories including stewardship, resource dependency and stakeholder theories (Voordeckers *et al.*, 2007).

We adopt the premise that smaller, private firms can benefit from the contribution that a board of directors can make to the development and success of the enterprise. This type of firm is beginning to receive academic attention with regard to governance due to the recognition of the sector's significance, depending on how such firms are defined, in representing the largest proportion of economic activity in most economies worldwide (Thomas & Coleman, 2005; Voordeckers *et al.*, 2007). Small and medium enterprises (SMEs), however, are not homogeneous (Corbetta & Salvato, 2004a). Various theoretical frameworks and prescriptions have been advanced with regard to the relevance of, and the appropriate role for, boards of such enterprises. Such approaches seem to assume that the dominant model of corporate governance developed for large corporations and publicly-listed companies can simply be adapted to fit the requirements of the smaller enterprise (Gabrielsson & Huse, 2002). Arguments supporting this governance architecture are based on a widely accepted set of general principles, together with an understanding of the role of the board of directors as being that of a combined control and service function. However, as yet, there is scant empirical information regarding the applicability of this approach in the context of the smaller firm, the main focus so far having been on aspects of the model such as board composition and independence (Voordeckers *et al.*, 2007).

In this chapter, we question the relevance of the dominant framework for SMEs and contend that, depending on both external (national culture, industry, technology, etc.) and internal contingencies (firm size, life cycle position, ownership structure, etc.), the purpose and function of a board in these firms may differ significantly from the board's role in large companies. We also challenge the appropriateness of the main underpinning theory for the SME context, on which the dominant model is predicated.

Agency theory is consistent with the notion of controlling managerial opportunism in the context of the separation of ownership and management in order to protect the interests of shareholders. This perspective assumes that the interests of management and owners are divergent and that management needs to be controlled in order to protect the investment and assets of the firm. Stewardship theory counters this perspective of management self-interest, arguing that managers are stewards of the resources entrusted to them and can be trusted to maximise profits for shareholders (Donaldson, 1990; Donaldson & Davis, 1991, 1994; Donaldson & Preston, 1995; Kiel & Nicholson, 2003). This means that demands for extensive monitoring and controls by external directors are not necessary because executives understand the business and external directors cannot match their level of firm-specific in-depth knowledge and expertise. Moreover, some proponents of stewardship theory contend that external directors do not have the skills, knowledge, time or resources to effectively monitor management, even if, given managers' basic trustworthiness, monitoring were necessary (Donaldson & Davis, 1994). Stewardship theory further holds that because executives have their reputations and future careers as well as their performance rewards at stake, principles of careful stewardship (i.e. protection and allocation) of the firm's assets and resources will guide their decisions and actions. Notable recent cases that tend to cast doubt on this view as representing a norm, however, include Enron and Tyco, where external directors have had their own agenda of opportunism, or of collusion, with internal directors in fraudulent behaviour, at the corporation's and shareholders' expense.

This debate between the role of internal and external directors is at the heart of both agency and stewardship theory. The Anglo, agency-based model of corporate governance focuses on the shareholder as the ultimate arbiter and promotes this influence via external (or non-executive) directors. However, with banks as major stock holders, the German–Japanese models of governance heavily favour internal (or executive) directors, as is more consistent with the stewardship perspective (Hackethal *et al.*, 2005). Thus, jurisdiction is also a relevant aspect in the debate with regard to the applicability of the dominant agency-based framework (Becht *et al.*, 2002).

Resource dependency theory and the resource-based view of the firm argue that the board is an essential link between the organisation and the key resources it needs to maximise its performance. From this perspective, the board is seen as an important resource for the business, particularly for the directors' external links which may include providing access to capital, customers, suppliers and other influential stakeholders. This is based on the directors' professional capabilities, commercial awareness and technical skills, as well as their own networks and linkages that represent a pool of social capital for the business (Ingley, 2004). Importantly, the directors provide access to their social networks which bring a reciprocal flow of information, services and cooperation. When considering the model for effective governance for small and young businesses it is apparent that using the board as a value-adding resource can be a key factor in helping the organisation to achieve its objectives (Ingley & McCaffrey, 2007) where the board fills a role more as a pilot than that of a watchdog in this setting. Empirical evidence in different SME contexts supports this view. Research on entrepreneurial SMEs (Daily *et al.*, 2002; Rosenbaum, 2005), venture-backed SMEs (Sapienza *et al.*, 1996, 2000; Fried *et al.*, 1998; Brunninge & Nordqvist, 2004) and family firms (Corbetta & Montemerlo, 1999; Corbetta & Salvatto, 2004b; Gallo, 2005) suggests that, irrespective of whether the board's involvement in the control role may help protect shareholders in certain situations, firms and their primary stakeholders usually use direct (shareholder–management) relations to deal with agency problems. These studies also suggest that board contributions are more effective in dealing with linking to resource providers, counselling management and helping with strategic decision making.

Beyond these main theoretical frameworks (agency, resource dependency and stewardship), various other theories have been used to address the role of boards of directors. Among other frequently-cited frameworks in this field of academic work are stakeholder theory, institutional theory and cognitive perspectives (Stiles and Taylor, 2001). These competing theoretical perspectives, as well as others such as managerial hegemony, the finance model (or shareholder theory) and so on, each provide partial support for explaining, understanding and prescribing the role of the board of directors in organisations. However, from all of these perspectives an integrated theory has failed to emerge that would indicate a single, unified model for corporate governance.

Conditioning further the theoretical arguments concerning the appropriate role of the board are contextual variables that militate against a single model for corporate governance. Some commentators contend that, while there is growing convergence globally in *principles* of corporate governance, the various *systems* of corporate governance will likely remain largely divergent and country-specific with regard to factors such as legal, regulatory and legislative frameworks and business practices (e.g. Bhasa, 2004; Davies & Schlitzer, 2008; Guillen, 2000; Jeffers, 2005; Ponssard *et al.*, 2005; West, 2009). In addition, the appropriate model of governance practice for a given company is also contextual and dependent on a range of firm-specific factors such as industry sector, market conditions, ownership structure, firm size, age, development phase, regulatory requirements and so on (Zahra & Pearce, 1989; Huse, 2005). Moreover, the concept of corporate governance is now widely applied, not just to large corporations and publicly-listed firms, as well as to small and medium-sized private companies, but also to non-profit organisations that likewise vary in type, scale and context. Thus, a contingency perspective is also applicable to corporate governance in relation to SMEs.

This chapter proceeds in the following way: the application of traditional approaches to the role of boards of directors is discussed in more depth, with elaboration of the control and service roles of the board. The theoretical rationale in respect of SMEs is considered in conjunction with this discussion, with regard especially to the value that a board might add to a smaller firm. Ownership and management expectations of performance are also discussed with regard to the role of the board in SMEs, along with the justification for having a board in relation to SME firm development, how such a board might be configured, and the level of engagement that might be relevant for such a board. This discussion leads to the consideration of several typologies of board involvement in SMEs where we argue that a continuum of engagement is a more appropriate conceptual framework for corporate governance in this context. We conclude the chapter with a proposition emerging from our discussion which calls for a new corporate governance architecture, not only for the governance of SMEs but also potentially for the governance of large corporations, as well as other types of organisations.

8.2 Traditional Approaches to the Board's Role in Corporate Governance

As indicated above, an assumption seems to prevail that the traditional overarching (Anglo) model of corporate governance applies to all types of organisation, with relatively minor modifications for context. Discussion and research has tended to focus on how the basic approach may be adapted by a shift in emphasis with regard to the particular attributes and role of boards in these organisations (Carver, 2000, 1997; Forbes & Milliken, 1999; Hermalin & Weisbach, 2003; Gabrielsson & Huse, 2005; Huse, 2000; Thomas & Coleman, 2005; Voordeckers *et al.*, 2007). However, concerning the fundamental purposes, drivers and expectations of governance, these can be seen to vary in important ways across these different types of organisations (van der Walt, Ingley & Diack, 2002).

To highlight ways in which the role of boards in SMEs, in particular, might differ from that prescribed by the dominant Anglo model, it is useful first to consider more closely the main theoretical streams and rationale on which the model is based.

8.2.1 *Board Role Perspectives*

We have highlighted the main theoretical contributions in corporate governance in relation to the role of the board as being those of agency theory, resource dependency theory and a stewardship theory. To these we also add and discuss below, the stakeholder perspective, which, together with the resource-based view, represent an external orientation by the board, while the agency and stewardship perspectives characterise an internal orientation by the board.

While many theoretical frameworks for the board's role in corporate governance have been derived from the economics, social, and organizational disciplines, two theories have dominated the field. These two main theoretical perspectives — agency theory and resource dependency theory — have resulted in a widely-held definition organized around two generic concepts covering the monitoring function and the collaborating activities of the board (Huse, 2007). Referred to earlier, these are respectively the control role and the service role. The control role relies mainly on the agency perspective which considers the board to reside at the apex of firms' internal control systems (Fama & Jensen, 1983). The service role is more collaborative and draws primarily upon resource dependency theory which considers the board to be at the frontier of the organization as its external interface.

8.2.2 *Control Role and Agency Theory*

Agency theory focuses on board accountability and the board's fiduciary responsibility to shareholders for financial performance, which is viewed as the primary measure of past and present value creation. This approach stresses the critical monitoring or control role of the board, because of its primary legal duty as the agent of shareholders, protecting their interests and maximising their wealth (Jensen and Meckling, 1976). While agency theory acknowledges a board's strategic contribution, especially its contribution to the organisation's mission and the development of strategy, under this perspective, the emphasis is more on decision control where the main contribution by board members is ratifying decisions. It is for this reason that critics claim poor director selection, and thus ineffective decision-making, are a handicap to this task (Zahra and Pearce, 1989). Agency theory, therefore, suggests that owners, as principals, should select board members who are able to monitor management effectively because of their primary duty as agents of principals/shareholders. However, this raises issues about shareholders' abilities to identify effective board members for their respective firms and their power to then orchestrate their admission to the board, as well as the organized departure of ineffective directors. Practice demonstrates that, in reality, shareholders have relatively little power in these situations to significantly influence the composition of a board (Ingley & McCaffrey, 2007; Fama & Jensen, 1983; Jensen & Meckling, 1976; Stiles, 2001; Voordeckers *et al.*, 2007, Zahra & Pearce, 1989).

Roberts *et al.* (2005) have argued that agency theory is inadequate as a rationale for the governance of the modern corporation, because it assumes the need to find ways to align only the interests of principals (owners) with those of their agents (the managers). Both principals and agents might seek to support other interests as well, such as employee or community well-being. Moreover, while recognising shareholder primacy, the modern corporation typically has multiple principals (e.g. institutional investors, individual shareholders) who hold some interests in common whilst also having individual interests that may conflict with those of other principals (Allcock & Filatotchev, 2009; Arthurs *et al.*, 2008; Child & Rodriques, 2003; Hoskisson *et al.*, 2002). The problem of addressing outsider interests is, therefore, compounded for non-executive directors.

In reality, non-executive oversight of the activities of the executive, and especially the chief executive, may not be as firm and critical as official institutional voices demand and the weight of prescription requires. This is due to the board decision-making culture, which weighs differentially insider and outsider interactions. Actual board practices appear to be more closely aligned to the needs and demands of internal actors who are generally considered to be the top management team (Huse, 2005). Having the same business background, non-executive directors usually subscribe to the same dominant business ideology as the executives. This means that they may intervene reactively rather than proactively in executive decisions and, therefore, be less effective as a check on management hegemony. However, Hill (1995) argued that while non-executive directors might be less effective in this regard than the expectations placed on them by regulators and investors, they are not without effect, although they may act more as a constraint in limiting the scope of managerial opportunism than in preventing such behaviour (Hill, 1995; Huse, 2005).

Given the recent strengthening of corporate governance codes and their emphasis on the importance of the board's control role, this constraint may be, to some extent, at the expense of both their external service role and their contribution to the decision making processes (Adams & Ferreira, 2007; Bezemer *et al.*, 2007; Hill, 1995). It is, therefore, useful to contemplate the extent to which, from an agency perspective, the much emphasised independence of outside directors (to minimise managerial opportunism and offset executive power) aligns with their role as mediators among different stakeholders and as advisors to managers (Aguilera, 2005).

From this discussion, the question arises, and will be addressed more fully later, as to the relevance for SMEs of the monitoring and control role of boards. Depending on the type of ownership structure and the distance in separation between ownership and management, the archetypal owner-managed small firm has little or no distance between ownership and management and so the agency-based view of the need for a monitoring and control mechanism as a constraint on managerial opportunism would render a board irrelevant in this context.

8.2.3 *Service Role — Resource-based, Stewardship and Stakeholder Theories*

According to resource dependence theory, the board is a provider or procurer of important resources rather than merely a controller and evaluator of management. In this service role, boards act as "boundary spanners" and networkers with external sectors or organisations such as financial institutions, or political bodies, finding ways to tap into these bases of power and influence for the benefit of the organisation (Parsons, 1960; Pfeffer, 1972 & 1973; Pfeffer & Salancik, 1978). This perspective arises from the idea of value creation and corporate citizenship and aims at facilitating and maximising value-enhancing behaviour. Its main emphasis is on the board as a strategic resource and as the primary source of leadership for the firm. In this role, the board provides strategic input (with strategy as the main driver of *future* value creation). Thus, director capability is a key requirement in board configuration (Corbetta & Salvato, 2004a & b; Freeman & Evans, 1990; Davis *et al.*, 1997; Donaldson, 1990; Freeman, 1984; Ingley, 2004; Pfeffer, 1972 & 1973; Pfeffer & Salancik, 1978; Voordeckers *et al.*, 2007).

Pfeffer (1972, 1973) found that by including non-executive members from diverse occupational and professional groups, a board could link an organisation to its external environment, thus helping to secure critical resources. Recent research confirms an interest in appointing directors with relevant practical work experience, "success stories" and global work history, rather than specific areas of contribution. This work thus supports the theories proposing that outside directors bring transferable skills and act as resources rather than auditors (Mueller *et al.*, 2008). While the main focus of the resource dependency perspective is on the service role, it recognizes that intermediating for resources implies aligning interests of the management and resource providers so that the control role is also supported by this framework.

According to these two dominating frameworks (agency theory and resource dependency theory), well-functioning boards should be involved in both of these generic (control and service) functions.

Stewardship theory counters agency theory by considering managers as loyal stewards. Without presenting a naïve vision of corporate leaders, stewardship theory posits that in many situations, the interests of the shareholders and those of the managers may converge. According to this view, in serving the interests of shareholders, the managers of a corporation may match their own interests, both directly (by means of financial incentives and bonuses), and indirectly (in desiring to protect their reputation and value on the labour market) with those of the owners.

Building on research findings from both psychology and sociology with regard to motivation at work, Donaldson and Davis (1991) consider that economic and financial benefits are far from being the only elements in managers' motivations. Donaldson and Davis also advance non-financial motivational factors, such as achievement and self-esteem needs, self-actualization needs, successful exercise of authority and power. From the stewardship perspective, one of the most important roles of the board of directors is to strengthen the power of the managers (Muth & Donaldson, 1998) so enabling a better use of their skills and capabilities in managing the firm. Donaldson and Davis (1991) have shown from their study of 337 American firms, and by controlling for industry effects, that where board structure strengthened the power of their managers, such firms presented a higher return on equity. In this respect, stewardship theory is complementary to the resource-based view of the board's service role which sees advising and counselling management as an important function for directors.

Stakeholder theory — a view that incorporates aspects of the theories outlined above (agency theory, resource dependency and the resource-based view of the firm, and stewardship theory) — is considered to be a more inclusive approach inasmuch as it takes into account the complex character of the corporate social context and the attendant obligation upon corporations to act as socially responsible citizens (Aguilera, 2005; Hillman & Hitt, 1999; Ingley & van der Walt, 2004a; Kiel & Nicholson, 2003; Maharaj, 2008). The stakeholder perspective begins with the premise that the creation of *shareholder* wealth is not the sole reason for companies to exist (Blair, 1995; Freeman, 1984). Stakeholder theory is based on the view that companies and society are interdependent and, therefore, the corporation and its board serve a broader social purpose than its responsibilities to shareholders, to whom it is primarily but not solely responsible (Donaldson and Preston, 1995; Kiel & Nicholson, 2003). Again, stakeholder theory complements the resource-based view of the board's role in emphasising the external interface as part of its service function.

Table 8.1 below summarises these theories according to key perspectives of board roles and tasks, as discussed above.

From a cognitive perspective, corporate governance researchers (e.g. Forbes & Milliken, 1999; Golden & Zajac, 2001; Rindova, 1999) have added arguments concerning individual directors as knowledge and expertise 'providers' and, in particular, as decision making experts (providing general

Table 8.1 Board Roles, Orientation and Task Expectations.

Board Role Theories	Generic Roles	Boards Central Mission	Board Task Expectations
Agency	Control, oversight, monitoring roles	Aligning shareholders and management interests	Compliance with legislative, statutory and regulatory requirements
			Company accounts relevance
			Financial performance
			Management decisions and actions
			Resource deployment
		(Primarily internal focus)	Appointing, evaluating, firing the CEO and succession (and senior management)
Resource dependency	Service, resource provision, networking, advisory roles	Linking/connecting the firm with key resource holders	Advising and counselling management
			Strategic network and access to key resources (boundary spanning)
			Managing corporate reputation
			Providing key expertise (decision support)
		(Primarily external focus)	Managing external dependencies
			Reducing environmental uncertainty
Stewardship	Service, facilitation, empowerment, service, advising, counselling, mentoring	Collaboration Strengthening managerial power	Advising, mentoring and counselling management
			Strategy formulation and implementation
		(Primarily internal focus)	Enabling better use of management's skills and capabilities
Stakeholder	Control, oversight, service, coordination	Balancing conflicting claims of multiple stakeholders	Coordinating stakeholder interests
			Risk management
			Strategic assessment of stakeholder influence
			Managing corporate reputation
		(Primarily external focus)	Corporate stakeholder engagement

management expertise). They have also strongly highlighted the collective dimension of boards. To this extent, boards can be seen as sharing a common interest with senior managers and supporting them in a service to management rather than having only a controlling and monitoring — and therefore adversarial or conflictual — relationship with them. Authors adhering to this perspective point out an additional service contribution of the board as a decision making group (e.g. Forbes & Milliken, 1999), placing emphasis on the group's strategising function in helping management deal with the complexity and uncertainty associated with strategic decisions (Rindova, 1999). This view of the board is consistent with strategic leadership arguments with regard to board members' directing role (e.g. Golden & Zajac, 2001; Davis & Thompson, 1994; Jensen & Zajac, 2004; Walsh & Seward, 1990). Finkelstein and Hambrick (1996, p. 277) see boards as "supra-top management teams" who are increasingly independent thinkers and who generally take an active role in influencing, sense-making and shaping the strategic direction of their organisation.

While some aspects of the service role are specified in corporate governance guidelines (such as the role of the board in strategy, see OECD Principles 2004, for example), unlike the control function, most service elements are not made explicit in legislative requirements but, rather, are advocated in prescriptions for best practice.

From the perspective of the SME, the service role of the board would seem to provide a more relevant theoretical basis as a rationale for boards in small firms, than theories emphasising the control role. This raises the question as to whether current governance frameworks are appropriate for closely held SMEs — one which is pursued later in the chapter.

8.2.4 *Expanding Role and Task Expectations*

The control and service roles of the board are consistent with the compliance and performance dimensions of corporate governance, respectively. While defined as separate board functions (see Table 8.1), in reality, the control and service roles represent dual aspects of the board's overall governing role (e.g. Carlsson, 2001; Carter & Lorsch, 2004; Garratt, 2003; Ingley, 2004). In modern corporations, expectations of the board's realm of responsibility have thus expanded beyond that of a control mechanism. As highlighted at the beginning of this chapter, the board is responsible for future performance and value creation as well as being accountable for past performance and asset protection. Given a global context of increased environmental and circumstantial complexity, it must, therefore, also play a greater role in determining the firm's strategic response to uncertainty. In this context, the firm is no longer regarded as an entity accountable only to shareholders, but as a corporate citizen responsible to a diversity of stakeholders and to society as a whole.

A difficulty arises, however, with regard to the seemingly dichotomous definitions of the role of the board in the context of the publicly-listed company. The specification of a control role and a service role implies that control is not a feature of the latter, yet both roles relate to oversight of management's decisions and actions by the board, which must involve monitoring and control. In this expanded view of the governance role, the board is ultimately responsible for the overall performance of the firm. Hilmer and Tricker (1994), for example, identified four board roles: strategy formulation, policy setting, executive management supervision, and accountability. Each dimension of governance (compliance and performance) requires the board to monitor and oversee the activities of the firm and the use of its assets and resources. The definition of control in relation to the publicly-listed company is, therefore, misleading. This is because "control", in terms of corporate governance, encompasses more than controlling for financial performance and managerial opportunism.

As shown in Table 8.2, the board's control tasks conceivably span both the control and service roles. Nevertheless, the terms "control" (as viewed by the agency perspective) and "service" (as identified in resource dependency theory) have passed into common usage as descriptors of the dual roles of the board (see e.g. Thomas & Coleman, 2005). Greater clarity may be gained from viewing the difference in orientation of the two roles in Table 8.2, where oversight in the control role (Louden, 1982) emphasises financial control and monitors past performance through financial accounting methods, while oversight in the service role (Hung, 1998) emphasises strategic control and supports future performance through the development of strategic capability.

Table 8.2 suggests that, in fact, there are not two but three *main* roles for boards: control, strategy and service (Zahra & Pearce, 1989), with multiple task expectations defining these main roles (Huse, 2007). For the private SME, control may feature as part of the board's role but, based on the control/service dichotomy and with a greater emphasis on the service dimension in the context of the smaller firm, control is more likely to be a component of the strategy dimension than the traditional agency-based internal control dimension.

8.2.5 *Board Roles and Value Creation*

From the preceding analysis of theoretical underpinnings for the board's role, the agency perspective considers the board as existing to protect anonymous and dispersed shareholders from managerial opportunism and value destruction. This perspective is primarily a framework for avoiding value destruction

Table 8.2   A Synthesis of Board Role Classifications.

Basic Framework Louden (1982)	Zahra & Pearce (1989)	Hung (1998)	Huse (2007) (Task Expectations)
Control Role	Control role	Control role	Output control
		Maintenance role	Internal control
	Strategy role	Coordinating role	Decision control
		Strategic role	Collaboration and mentoring
Service Role	Service role	Support role	Advising
		Linking role	Networking

Source: Adapted from Huse (2007).

and/or (unfair) value expropriation. Consistent with the neoclassical theory of the firm, the agency view assumes that the value creation process is a given so that boards will be mainly concerned with how this created value should be distributed.

These theoretical arguments can be also found in stakeholder theory where the focus is on protecting all the stakeholders from both managerial opportunism and shareholder primacy. Here, similarly, the board acts to safeguard the created value from expropriation and, therefore, its main role is concerned with balancing conflicting interests and guaranteeing that important demands are addressed. It is this view of the board's main role, as one of control in attempting to align competing and/or conflicting interests, which places the board in an adversarial relationship with management. Increasingly, however, as we have highlighted above, authors are questioning these underlying assumptions which focus on the board's role as mainly being that of value protection.

In contrast, stewardship, cognitive, resource and strategic leadership theories are more concerned with value creation processes. The service role, as derived from these theories, concentrates on how well-functioning boards can participate in value creation by collaborating with managers (Finkelstein *et al.*, 2009; Westphal, 1999). In all of these theories, the perspective shifts from a conflictual relationship between the board and management to more cooperative work between the two parties so that the firm can add more value (Adams & Ferreira, 2007; Huse, 1994).

A major point in common with these four theories concerns increased complexity. The two perspectives on board roles — the control role and the service role — have been considered by many authors as cumulative, resulting in the increasing demands and expectations of boards (e.g. Forbes & Milliken, 1999; Garratt, 2003; Huse, 2007). Both scholars and practitioners highlight the escalating levels of political, economic, technological and societal changes that have characterised the end of the last century and the beginning of the current one, and which have contributed to the increasing complexity and uncertainty faced by firms and managers. In this setting, some authors, as highlighted in the preceding discussion, have regarded the board as the central mechanism to help managers by counselling them — widening their perspectives, acting as sounding boards, involved in sense-making activities, and also in connecting with external actors, providing access to resources, and so on. All of these tasks may contribute toward helping managers to add value. These factors are all the more relevant as the psychological and social bases of these two roles are divergent and even contradictory. On one hand, the control role requires independence and social distancing and, on the other hand, the service role relies on collaboration, social closeness and some form of 'complicity' (see, for example, Finkelstein et al., 2009; Gulati & Westphal, 1999).

Building on these theoretical developments, we can consider that the central problem for corporate governance concerns creating and distributing value. The board as a key mechanism in the corporate governance framework needs to achieve a balance between two major and seemingly conflicting social demands relative to accountability on one side and enterprising on the other (see Short et al., 1999). However, to what extent might such a balance be required in the small private firm? Enterprising and value creation are clearly relevant issues but, unless the firm is publicly-listed, to what extent is public accountability an expectation of a board in this context? This leads to the question of what a board might contribute in an SME context.

8.3 Corporate Governance in SMEs

As we have highlighted above, the dominant overarching model of corporate governance, including the basic principles and guidelines that are essentially similar across jurisdictions, is assumed to apply to all organisations, with relatively minor adaptations for type and sector (e.g. private, public, non-profit, etc.). Consideration has also begun to emerge regarding the role of the board in small and medium businesses, of which family businesses are often included as a sub-set (Forbes & Milliken, 1999; Hermalin & Weisbach, 2003; Gabrielsson & Huse, 2005; Huse, 2000; Thomas & Coleman, 2005; Voordeckers et al., 2007). The common denominator is the assumption of closely-held private ownership. However, while family businesses are often also small businesses and, in fact, dominate the small business population (Voordeckers et al., 2007), many of the largest and longest surviving firms began and, for some, continue to exist as family businesses. Some also continue to be family-owned beyond the first generation or are publicly-listed with the family retaining a controlling share of the business (Corbetta & Salvato, 2004a). According to La Porta *et al.* (1999) this remains especially true for continental Europe where families continue to play an important ownership role and/or management function in many world class multinational firms. In countries such as France, Germany, and Italy, firms still under family influence include L'Oréal (Bettancourt family), Michelin (Michelin family), Porsche (Porsche and Piech families), Fiat (Agnelli family) and Benetton (Benetton family) (Kirchmaier & Grant, 2004). It is, therefore, inaccurate to regard family businesses as synonymous with SMEs. It is also inaccurate to equate SMEs solely with private ownership. Each of these factors represents a clouding of the discussion around the relevance to, and appropriate role for, boards in SMEs.

Definitions of SMEs vary internationally by measurement variable (Ayyagari *et al.*, 2007). Commonly used measurements of size are employment numbers and total annual revenues. Definitions based on qualitative measures have also been advanced. For example, Torres and Julien (2005) defined SMEs according to the concept of proximity (or closeness) to geographical markets, closeness of shareholding, organisational structure, and so on. In this chapter, we define SMEs as companies employing between 10 and 200 employees. While there is a large body of research on SMEs and considerable work exists regarding the need for effective boards in large publicly-listed companies, there are few studies on the need for boards in small non-listed companies (Teksten *et al.*, 2005).

8.3.1 *Rationale for Boards in SMEs*

SMEs contribute significantly to the total output of most developed economies and to the generation of jobs and wealth creation (Ayyagari *et al.*, 2007; OECD, 2008). The literature recognises the usefulness and relevance of well-functioning governance in SMEs as it leads to value addition to the firm, improved company structures as well as superior financial outcomes and firm continuity (Voordeckers *et al.*, 2007). Effective board contributions are also essential in the current global economic environment and can assist SMEs in their internationalization and in acquiring knowledge-based resources (Zahra *et al.*, 2007). Zahra *et al.* (2007) also highlight the positive link between good governance of SMEs and globalisation through acquisition, which is further enhanced and supported by the presence of outside and independent board directors.

The concept of corporate governance in smaller private firms gains its support from the idea that a board of directors can provide resources and strengthen such firms (e.g. Castaldi & Wortman, 1984; Forbes & Milliken, 1999; Johanisson

& Huse, 2000; Lorsch, 1995a, 1995b; Thomas & Coleman, 2005; Zahra & Pearce, 1989). This view is consistent with a generally accepted understanding of the purpose of a board being value creation, primarily as a financial return on investment for the ownership of the company. Based on this view, the type of role for the SME board, as we have indicated above, is more closely aligned with the service or performance role than with the compliance or control role of the board (Voordeckers *et al.*, 2007) and draws more readily from resource-based perspectives than from agency and other control-oriented theories. The control role of publicly-listed companies, in the sense of ensuring compliance with financial reporting requirements, is clearly not relevant in this smaller type of private firm. It is the service/strategy role of providing, or supporting and guiding, the strategic leadership of the firm that is perceived as the most relevant purpose and function for these boards (Borch & Huse, 1993; Gabrielsson & Winlund, 2000; George *et al.*, 2001; Voordeckers *et al.*, 2007).

When considering ownership type, however, such a clear-cut board role differentiation is problematic. As indicated above, an SME may be privately-owned or publicly-listed and while publicly-held companies have legal financial reporting requirements, privately-owned unlisted companies are not required by law to report publicly to shareholders on their financial performance. However, the compliance/control role of the board remains relevant for publicly-listed SMEs. Moreover, while Fama and Jensen (1983) argued that separation of ownership and control leads to agency issues and thus independent, outside directors are important in balancing boards of publicly-listed firms, with small private firms agency problems are not necessarily absent and can arise when owner-manager-directors of small firms perceive the addition of outside directors and professional managers with firm growth as a dilution of their control. While as indicated above, the control role is perceived as less important in small private companies, the possibility of opportunistic behaviour, especially in family firms, requires a focus on both roles by boards in these firms (Voordeckers *et al.*, 2007) as well as in large corporations. Accordingly, it is unhelpful to specify the role of boards in SMEs on the basis of closely- or widely-held public/private/family ownership alone as a defining characteristic (Huse, 1994).

8.3.2 *The Role of the Board in SMEs*

The debate on the role of the board in SMEs is not new and can be dated as early as 1948 when Mace outlined the advisory and counselling role of boards (Mace, 1948). Van den Heuvel, Van Gils & Voordeckers (2007) provide a useful review of the literature on the role of boards in SMEs and family businesses. Based on their survey of 286 firms in Belgium, they report that control and service are the two most acknowledged roles played by these boards. From their study, Zahra *et al.* (2007) observe that the strategy and enterprising role of the board comprising both outside as well as inside directors is very important as outside directors bring their unique experiences, skills and perspectives and complement the existing skill set of the board. The innovative process in strategy formulation has been emphasised in a number of studies where research has shown that the presence of outside directors on the board leads to 'positive tensions and instils new ideas and ways of doing business' (Zahra *et al.*, 2007). Outside directors are used by many SMEs to assist with strategy development. Thus, we reflect that more factors than that of serving as legal agents for shareholders identified in agency theory defines the role of directors on SME boards. It is the strategic/resource-based role which is more vital for SME boards where outside directors who are "not tied to the day-to-day operations of the firm, are likely to think more freely concerning the strategic alternatives open to the firm" (Brunninge *et al.*, 2007).

As outlined above, situations and reasons for developing effective board governance in SMEs include: management continuity and succession, acquisition of specialised expertise, innovation, crisis management and arbitration (Ford, 1992). Ford (1992) argued that a situational perspective is, therefore, a more useful basis for understanding the role of a board in a small company than that of ownership type. He contended that the board's role will vary with the life cycle of the firm, for which he identified six stages: embryonic/seed stage, start-up stage, early growth, rapid growth, maturity and instability. On this basis, the board's role will differ in the start-up stage from what it might be at the embryonic or seed stage and it will differ again during growth stages. During the start-up period, "an experienced team of board members could greatly assist in this organizational stage as the company acquires the initial resources of personnel and assets" (Teksten *et al.*, 2005, p. 54).

The role of a formal board in a small company is thus strategically important and dynamic since it evolves with the different stages from the company's early development through maturity. Accordingly, the company's objectives will also change as it moves through the various growth stages, so that the skill set and competencies of the board members should likewise evolve and be updated on a regular basis to help direct the company effectively through the challenges it will face through each stage.

8.3.3 *Configuring the SME Board*

Research indicates that SME boards often lack key skills expected from board members and that the majority of director positions are filled from a tight circle of insiders who comprise mostly existing board members and management. However, the transition from an owner-operated/controlled firm to power sharing with a board may not be a smooth one and can involve various issues including those of succession. In a study examining the issue of succession in the small firm context, Schnatterly and Johnson (2008) highlighted among inside directors and owners, a perception of a reduction in control through the dilution of authority as the possibility of the position of CEO being taken over by the outside directors. Coulson-Thomas (2007) found in his research, regarding the contribution of directors in SMEs, that non-executive directors were often perceived as "passengers who would get in the way or, worse, try to prevent the executives from doing what they thought was right for the growing company" (p. 4). In his UK study, Coulson-Thomas noted that founders of smaller companies like to take the key decisions themselves and, fearing a loss of control to "outside directors," seem reluctant to be "constrained" by a board. Greiner (1998) noted similar issues in the early phases of growth in young companies, which he termed as the crises of leadership, autonomy and control in his seminal (1972) "Phases of Growth Model", which, if not resolved at each stage, respectively, will prevent the firm from moving ahead in the development sequence.

Given this common fear of loss of control among SME owners (Daily & Dalton, 1992), the board is likely to function more effectively when the outside directors can, with their expertise, experience, and broad outlook, probe, challenge and offer recommendations in an atmosphere that is supportive rather than adversarial. According to Schnatterly and Johnson (2008), this balancing act necessitates maturity in outside directors and owner-manager/CEOs who are willing to be respectful and considerate, and who subordinate their sensitivities to the good of the company. This means that the CEO must terminate the aura of secrecy common to many privately-owned companies and be candid with the board. Metaphorically, most, if not all, of the skeletons must come out of the closet.[1]

Coulson-Thomas (2007) concluded from his research that many of the companies in his study would benefit from the addition of independent directors with experience and skills that complement the entrepreneurial and executive abilities of the founder directors and are related to their vision and aspirations for their businesses. Such benefits from adding one or two outside directors, who could act as a sounding board and balance the operational focus of the founder and managers, include open-mindedness, objectivity, fresh thinking, drive and purpose. Coulson-Thomas (2007) highlighted the

---

[1] http://pervinfamilybusiness.com/library/articles/creating-board-directors.asp.

need for controlling shareholders of SMEs to understand more fully the role and contribution of an appropriate board and the potential benefit of one or more non-executive directors. He points to the strategic value of such a board where independent directors can help executives to achieve a balance between different interests and contending factors, such as immediate issues and longer-term requirements. Where Greiner (1972, 1998) focuses on management capabilities as the key to resolving the developmental crises of a growing company, Coulson-Thomas (2007) argues that developing effective boards of competent directors can be a valuable way of encouraging and supporting the development of businesses beyond the limitations of the perspectives, ambitions and timescales of their founders.

Malizia (2008) suggests that in the search for board directors, small businesses should "look for leaders who can "roll up their sleeves to run [the] small company"; in other words, a hands-on approach that might be provided by high profile executives of large companies who have a good knowledge of processes. We contrast that prescription with the views of small business owners who want their boards to spend less time on operational (process) matters and more on strategic planning issues and guidance for management (see Mueller *et al.*, 2009).

If the idea of a formal board is threatening to SME owners, a stepwise approach may be a more appropriate way of addressing the issues of leadership and control in the context of firm development. Advisory boards could provide one such solution as a step towards the establishment of a formal board, where the SME can benefit from the contribution of expert external advisors who can guide and support the CEO without seeking control of decision making (Blumentritt, 2006; Ford, 1992). The advisory board may then evolve to a formal board at an appropriate stage of the firm's development as a planned step in the growth trajectory. According to Nadler (2004), what is essential in configuring the board for effective performance is the application of what he specifies as the seven Rs: the right mindset, the right role, the right work, the right people, the right agenda, the right information, and the right culture. This prescription is consistent with Ford's (1992) view of the board's role as varying with the life cycle stage of the firm.

8.4 Contingency Perspective and Board Engagement

Demb *et al.* (1989) examined the role of boards of directors in 70 large multinational corporations. Supporting the idea that boards have a more significant role than merely that of watchdogs, Demb *et al.* (1989) also highlighted the expanding nature of the board's role in today's firms: from the boards' mission statements they identified considerable variation in the intervention domain of the board of directors. According to these authors, "the board is one of many resources available to companies to use in pursuing their objectives. The board is a scarce and expensive resource and so should be used carefully for those activities where it can uniquely contribute" (p. 61).

With regard to increasing the proportion of non-executive directors for more effective monitoring and oversight, Demb and Neubauer (1992) contended that "no group of eight, twelve or twenty individuals can sensibly carry the full responsibility for assuring corporate accountability to the firm's stakeholders. Rather, boards are among a set of elements used by societies to make corporations responsive and accountable. Boards are designed to play an intervening role between the enterprise and society, and to help resolve competing claims on the corporation" (pp. 34–35). Boards, according to Demb and Neubauer (1992), function as an intermediary between the corporation and the other three governance elements or forces that shape the corporate life-space: regulations, ownership, and societal pressure.

Carter and Lorsch (2004) argued against the "...widely-held assumption that all boards do the same thing, and that each director, other than his or her committee responsibilities, has exactly the same job," with board responsibilities tending to be defined the same way across industries and geographies. Such a uniform grouping is problematic. However, because "...different boards face different circumstances, in terms of company complexity, company performance, the tenure of their CEO, as well as their own capabilities." Carter and Lorsch (2004) assert that "it makes no sense to assume that each board will undertake the same activities in the same "dosage" regardless of these differences, and indeed, despite the assumption that all boards do the same thing, our own observation confirms that individual boards do, in fact, play very different roles" (Carter & Lorsch, 2004, pp. 59–61).

While recognizing a variety of roles a given board may play, perspectives in empirical studies continue to consider board roles dichotomously, opposing active boards and passive ones at each extreme, where passive boards are considered to be weak monitors of management and often pawns under the domination of a strong CEO. This has resulted in an overemphasis on the composition variables of the board where non-executive directors, who are presumed to be independent *vis-à-vis* corporate directors (Fama, 1980), are associated with the board's control function. One of the most commonly prescribed measures for improving boards' governance effectiveness in reducing agency problems is to increase board independence from management through reinforcing the number or proportion of non-executive directors relative to executive directors on the board (Walsh & Seward, 1990) and duality in leadership structure (Finkelstein *et al.*, 2009; Huse, 2007), in conjunction with independent nominations committees.

8.4.1 *Contingency perspective*

Many authors have called for new theoretical perspectives addressing boards and management, especially in the SME context (see Gabrielsson & Huse, 2005; Huse, 1994). In line with this thinking, and based on the arguments we have presented in this chapter, we suggest working within an integrative strategic contingency perspective, taking into greater account both external and internal company contexts and considering board roles similarly as contextual in nature. Huse (1994, p. 60), for example, highlighted three sets of (internal and external) variables relating to the contingencies of independence versus interdependence and the degree of separation between management and ownership (different ownership structures and company size; different life cycle stages of the firm; and different types of organisation). Huse argued that interdependence and independence reflect two distinct dimensions, where the independence dimension considers mainly compositional aspects of boards while the interdependence dimension concerns process-related aspects of board management. He concluded from his research that a combination of both dimensions was likely to lead to the most effective monitoring in companies large and small, but that, at one end of the continuum, high independence was likely to be most characteristic of large companies while, at the other end, high interdependence was more characteristic of small firms.

Based on these two dimensions (independence and interdependence), Huse (1994, p. 65) developed a typology comprising four types of board-management relations: the "laissez-faire" board, the "independent" board, the "understanding" board and the "participative" board. From this typology, he suggested that small firms should especially aim to develop a participating board, where directors support management in decision-making and networking activities, monitor management on behalf of other stakeholders, take care of stakeholders' interests and, in the owner-manager context, where managers will listen to and will heed criticisms from the board because of their mutual trust.

Presenting a similar typology based on matching board configuration to the firm's circumstances, Nadler (2004) named five board roles, placing these on a continuum of engagement. These types of board role are: the passive board as the least engaged, the certifying board, the engaged board, the intervening board, and the operating board as the most engaged board. He emphasised the reality that boards move back and forth across the scale, their levels of engagement changing as issues and circumstances change, where, for example, a passive board may transform temporarily into an intervening board to remove a CEO and then into an operating board until a new leader is appointed.

If it is accepted that boards play different roles depending on the firm's circumstances, then, as argued from the life cycle perspective, the contingency approach would seem a more useful basis on which to develop regulatory frameworks for corporate governance that are applicable not only to large corporations but also to SMEs.

In terms of ownership characteristics, SMEs are present along a spectrum ranging from owner-managed firms to publicly-listed companies. We argue that because of variation in ownership structure it is difficult to conceptualise a single configuration of boards that, in terms of director independence based on the dominant agency paradigm, may capture this diversity. As stated by Huse (1994) governance and the role of directors in SMEs is more a matter of interdependence than independence because the issue is more about relational aspects of trust, solidarity and reciprocity than structural features. We also contend that in the SME context, the control role of the board needs to be adapted to the intensity of the conflicts of interest risks with regard to the distance between owners and managers and between shareholders/stakeholders and managers. Figure 8.1 below reflects this variability according to increasing distance or growing separation between

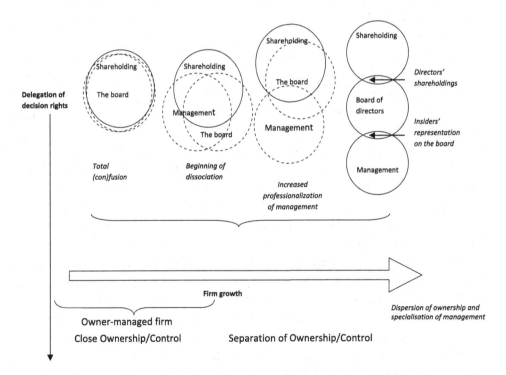

Figure 8.1   Firm Growth and Ownership Control.

ownership and management with regard to decision control, in relation to the growth and development of the firm.

8.4.2 *SME Diversity and Board Research Uniformity*

Research on SMEs has developed incrementally over the last century. Over this time, researchers have moved from an assumption of homogeneity among SMEs, to the recognition that the universe of small- and medium-sized firms is highly diverse in nature with regard to ownership and management structure, stage of development and other factors (Torres & Julien, 2005). This recognition has led to the development of a number of sub-fields within the SME research field. With regard to corporate governance in particular, around 50 academic studies have been published since the seminal work by Huse (2000) who set a research agenda for addressing board issues in SMEs, based on a contingency approach. Studies have since addressed corporate governance sub-fields with regard to ownership characteristics — family businesses, entrepreneurial firms, venture-backed start-ups, listed SMEs, and so on.

While recognizing, at least implicitly, the diversity in ownership settings with regard to boards, a majority of these studies have concentrated on board composition variables following the 'usual suspects' approach — the proportion of non-executive directors, director shareholdings, board size, and CEO duality — in relation to corporate performance (Finkelstein & Mooney, 2003). This has resulted in an over-emphasis on issues of board independence to enable greater control while accepting that the service role is a more accurate contribution in the context of smaller firms.

Aligned with Gabrielsson and Huse's (2005) argument concerning the problem with uncritical application of large company concepts in the small business and other contexts, we suggest that much recent research on boards in SMEs implies that, because of their smallness and presumed lesser complexity, the links between board composition variables and corporate performance may show a 'clearer' link, since leadership, rather than monitoring, may matter more in small firms. However, in agreement with authors such as Welsh and White (1981), we consider that SMEs are not 'little big businesses.' Thus, we contend that corporate governance scholars need to focus on arguments additional to smallness, and to address board characteristics and consequences in the SME context.

8.5 Toward a New Governance Architecture

In this chapter, we have highlighted the debate around the "one-size-fits-all" approach to corporate governance and questioned the relevance of the dominant agency-based framework for SMEs, which is predicated on the separation of management from ownership in the large publicly-listed corporation. In the absence of distance in separation between ownership and management in the context of the private SME or closely-held firm, there is no legal requirement for a formal board of directors. Boards are useful, but not essential to the effective management of small firms. Once we recognise current corporate governance reforms and guidelines as being ideology-based rather than representing empirically supported norms, we can then move away from the necessity of boards only as a controlling mechanism for managerial constraint to ensure compliance and protection of investor capital, to the strategic role of boards as facilitators of firm performance and economic and social value creation (Johanisson & Huse, 2000). Indeed, as we have discussed, evidence suggests that the very terms, "board" and "governance," are negative concepts for many small firms since they commonly imply a loss of control (Farrar, 2008).

We consider that if boards are needed for value creation, it will be for their ability to support executives in dealing with increased complexity. For us, the main change that has occurred in the business landscape over the last two decades, in particular, is increased interdependencies between societal components at the global level. This complexity introduces a major challenge for firms, large and small, and executive teams are, indeed, needing help from senior directors with interpretative capabilities. The board can represent a way of reinforcing these capabilities at the top (see Daft & Weick, 1984). This would suggest that in the SME context, boards may be more helpful in the sense-making process than in the accountability process.

Clarke (2006) suggests that a two-step legal governance framework, one for large firms and the other for SMEs, may be more appropriate than the prevailing single model. He further argues that this binary divide should provide opportunities for simple, principle-based governance for SMEs that can 'weave' its way up to large firms, rather than a continuation of the trickle down approach from large firms to SMEs. As Greiner (1972, 1998) identified in his "Phases of Growth" model, five key dimensions are essential for building a model of organization development: 1) age of the organization, 2) size of the organization, 3) stages of evolution, 4) stages of revolution, and 5) growth rate of the industry. Each dimension influences and interacts with the other dimensions over time. However, a dual model of corporation such as that suggested by Clarke (2006), would need to determine at what stage along the growth/development continuum an SME becomes a larger company, although public ownership would provide one legal determinant.

Farrar (2008) and Farrar and du Plessis (2009) present various governance frameworks adopted by different jurisdictions with regard to codes of self-regulation and private arrangements as well as legal vehicles to assist in the governance of SMEs. In particular, they highlight the South African model (the South African Close Corporations Act 69, 1984) for the smaller firm as an example worth consideration. With its two-tiered legal structure — one for large corporations and a separate one for small companies — this model is similar to the approach suggested by Clarke (2006). In the South African context, this framework has been highly successful in providing a more suitable legal setting for the formal governance of SMEs. After 25 years, however, this Act is undergoing change, which may not continue to benefit the SME sector to the extent that it has in the past. Nonetheless, the two-step model is advocated by Farrar and du Plessis (2009) for other jurisdictions in recognition of the inadequacy of the current single dominant model, and to encourage a formal approach to corporate governance in SMEs in the quest for better firm performance, given their economic and social importance.

McCahery and Vermeulen (2008) highlight four developments that they believe could indicate a new movement towards corporate governance initiatives focused on non-listed companies. The first development concerns the 'one-size-fits-all' and regulatory mentality of policy makers in attempting to mitigate governance failures and scandals of the last two decades. The tendency to overreact has arguably led to some undesired spill-over effects to non-listed companies. The second development relates to the rewards of joint venturing and the importance for business parties in both large and smaller enterprises to be made aware of the benefits of improved and stronger corporate governance structures for these joint operations. The third development concerns the widely-acknowledged economic significance of family-owned businesses and start-ups to national economies. With the typical life cycle of family-owned firms tending not to extend much beyond second or third generations, only companies with strong and professional governance structures are able to endure beyond these limits. Further is the expectation by funders that non-listed firms, which rely heavily on bank finance and venture capital, have a professional governance structure in place.

In view of the need for more professionally-managed non-listed businesses, McCahery and Vermeulen (2008) emphasise the importance of measures that are sufficiently attractive and coherent from a cost-benefit perspective to encourage non-listed companies to opt into a well-tailored framework of legal mechanisms and norms. They conclude that the realm of the non-listed company is a legitimate and important perspective for policy makers and lawmakers to consider when undertaking legislative reforms in corporate governance. This is because non-listed firms that operate under a well-designed and effective governance structure are likely to perform better and, in the case of joint ventures and cross-border ownership, will, therefore, be more attractive to external investors, especially in emerging market economies. McCahery and Vermeulen (2008) also highlight as important directions for considering the real amount of regulation needed for non-listed firms: the impact of the Basel II Accord on the availability of funds for SMEs, the development of an equity-oriented capital system with more closely-held and family-controlled firms expected to access these public capital markets for their financing needs, as well as the New Markets (second-tier listings exchanges) in Europe; the trend in de-listing by some public companies in the face of perceived exorbitant compliance costs with the rising regulatory burden and, conversely, the public listing of some large private equity firms in the US which have employed a limited partnership structure. Such companies choose to continue to operate as much as possible as a non-listed company to avoid excessive state and federal regulation that now threatens the public company. In owning units instead of conventional shares, investors in listed private equity firms employing this type of ownership structure are deprived of the normal complement of rights, such as fiduciary duties and voting powers associated with the corporate form. These developments may well lead to a different type of firm and new corporate governance structures.

8.6 Conclusion

We have presented in this chapter a series of typologies, settings, dimensions and frameworks leading to a contingency view of corporate governance and the role of a board in an SME context. In attempting to integrate these perspectives, we have also shown that a contingency approach moves beyond a "one-size-fits-all" single framework of governance developed for large publicly-listed corporations, to one which offers a basis for more general application to a wider range of organisational types and settings. Combining a contingency perspective with a staged/stepped approach to formal regulatory governance of companies large and small would seem an appropriate response to the complex environment with increased public concerns for corporate accountability and expectations of firm performance, resource use and wealth creation that characterise the emerging global marketplace.

Chapter 9

CORPORATE GOVERNANCE DEVELOPMENTS IN THE UK AND THE EVOLVING ROLE OF INSTITUTIONAL INVESTORS

CHRIS MALLIN

University of Birmingham

9.1 Introduction

Corporate governance has gained an increasingly high profile in the last decade or so. The interest in corporate governance spans countries and continents, and businesses both large and small; it is an area that has captured the interest of shareholders and wider stakeholder groups alike. Various corporate scandals and collapses over the years, and the recent financial crisis with the resulting collapse of long-established and well-known financial institutions, have increased interest in corporate governance even further. At the same time, questions have been asked as to whether more could have been done to prevent some of the problems that caused the financial crisis, including the apparent lack of appropriate risk management, and the excessive remuneration paid to executive directors who appear to have failed to protect the interest of shareholders in a number of ways.

It is pertinent to look at how corporate governance has developed in the UK, which has generally been seen as having a well-developed corporate governance system. However, before examining the development of corporate governance in the UK, let us consider some of the definitions of corporate governance. A widely recognised definition is one given by Sir Adrian Cadbury who chaired the UK's Committee on the Financial Aspects of Corporate Governance which reported in 1992. Sir Adrian Cadbury stated that corporate governance was 'the whole system of controls, both financial and otherwise, by which a company is directed and controlled.' This definition is succinct but clearly conveys the importance of controls in the company. A wider definition was given by the Organisation for Economic Co-operation and Development (OECD, 1999) which stated that corporate governance was 'a set of relationships between a company's board, its shareholders and other stakeholders. It also provides the structure through which the objectives of the company are set, and the means of attaining those objectives, and monitoring performance are determined.' As we can see, this definition views corporate governance from a much wider perspective and takes account of the various stakeholder groups, not just the shareholders. It also emphasizes the importance of corporate governance as an enabling device for setting, achieving and monitoring corporate objectives and performance.

Whilst these are just two of the many definitions of corporate governance, it is easy to appreciate from the above why corporate governance is so important to companies, investors, and stakeholders. Corporate governance is fundamental to well-run firms and helps ensure that the assets of the firm are secure and not subject to expropriation by individuals or groups within the firm who could wield excessive power. Corporate governance, therefore, helps a firm to be sustainable in the longer term.

This chapter discusses corporate governance developments in the UK and highlights recent changes that have implications for UK corporate governance, including the Companies Act 2006, Combined Code 2008, and other recent regulatory pronouncements. The chapter will also examine developments that impact institutional shareholders and how the role of the institutional investor is evolving. Finally, some recent examples of activism will be discussed which include executive directors' remuneration given this area's particularly high profile as a result of the recent financial crisis.

9.2 Corporate Governance in the UK

9.2.1 *Corporate Governance Codes and Guidelines*

In the early 1990s, there was a general lack of confidence in the financial reporting of many UK companies following various financial scandals and collapses (including Coloroll and Polly Peck). Therefore, the Committee on the Financial Aspects of Corporate Governance was established in the Spring of 1991. Subsequent scandals, including those at BCCI and Maxwell, occurred, leading to the Committee interpreting its remit more widely so that, rather than just looking at financial aspects, it broadened its view to look at corporate governance as a whole. The Committee reported in late 1992 and the report became widely known as 'the Cadbury Report,' as the Committee was chaired by Sir Adrian Cadbury.

The recommendations embodied in the Cadbury Report formed the foundation of the UK corporate governance system, and also came to be widely adopted in many countries around the world. The recommendations covered: the operation of the main board; the establishment, composition, and operation of key board committees; the importance of non-executive directors and the contribution that they can make; and the reporting and control mechanisms of a business. Arguably the most cited aspects of the Cadbury Report's recommendations are the recommendations that the roles of the Chair and CEO of the company be carried out by separate individuals; independent non-executive directors should be appointed via a transparent nominations procedure; executive directors' remuneration should be set by a remuneration committee comprised of wholly or mainly non-executive directors and there should be full disclosure including the various performance-related elements; an audit committee comprised of at least three non-executive directors should be established; and directors should report on the effectiveness of the company's system of internal control. The boards of all listed companies registered in the UK were to comply with the Code of Best Practice or explain why they did not. This 'comply or explain' approach has also been widely adopted around the world.

Following on from the Cadbury Report, there were a number of subsequent reports issued during the 1990s and 2000s which covered various aspects of corporate governance as shown in Table 9.1. Some were more specific in their remit. For example, the Greenbury Committee looked at executive remuneration disclosure, whilst others were focused on corporate governance more generally, like the Combined Code. The various codes and guidelines are summarized in Table 9.1 below together with the focus of each one. As can be seen, they cover a range of areas including executive remuneration, internal control, non-executive directors, and audit committees.

It should be mentioned that in the UK, the Financial Reporting Council (FRC) is responsible for promoting high standards of corporate governance. It publishes the Combined Code and instigates regular reviews of corporate governance. The Combined Code itself had a major revision in 2003 when many of the recommendations of the Higgs and Smith reports on non-executive directors and audit committees respectively were incorporated into the Combined Code. Since the last major revisions to the Combined Code in 2003, the FRC has reviewed the impact and implementation of the Combined Code every two years. The Code was last revised in 2008. A third review is now in process; as part of which there is a public consultation process. The FRC will report later in 2009 with any potential changes.

Table 9.1   Summary of UK Corporate Governance Codes and Guidelines.

Name	Year	Focus
Cadbury	1992	Established code of best practice for corporate governance in UK companies
Greenbury	1995	Directors' remuneration disclosure
Hampel	1998	Reviewed implementation of Cadbury and Greenbury
Combined Code	1998	Drew together findings of the above three reports
Turnbull	1999	Internal controls
Higgs	2003	Role and effectiveness of non-executive directors
Tyson	2003	Utilisation of wider pool for non-executive directorships to enhance board effectiveness
Smith	2003	Audit committees
Combined Code	2003	Incorporated many of the findings of Higgs and Smith committtees
Turnbull	2005	Updated previous guidelines on internal controls
Combined Code	2006	Updated previous Code including some provisions on voting
Combined Code	2008	Some minor changes to previous Code including that an individual can chair more than one FTSE100 company
Smith	2008	Revised guidance including appointment, re-appointment and removal of auditors

Having discussed the recommendations of the Cadbury Report and highlighted the various codes and guidelines that have been published since then, let us consider the latest UK corporate governance recommendations as embodied in the Combined Code 2008.

9.2.2 *Combined Code (2008)*

The Combined Code (2008) has two sections, one relating to companies and one to institutional investors. The section relating to companies is divided into four parts: Directors; Remuneration; Accountability and Audit; and Relations with Shareholders.

In relation to Directors, the Combined Code states that a company should be headed by an effective board which is responsible for the success of the company; the roles of chairman and chief executive officer should be separate (i.e. clear division of responsibilities); there should be a balanced board with an appropriate mix of executive and independent non-executive directors; there should be a formal, robust and transparent appointments process; directors should be provided with appropriate information in a timely fashion to enable them to carry out their duties effectively; there should be an induction for directors when they join the board and also training opportunities should be available to enable directors to keep their skills and knowledge up-to-date; there should be performance evaluation of the board as a whole, the board sub-committees and the individual directors; and directors should be re-elected at regular intervals.

In relation to Remuneration, the Combined Code states that remuneration should be set at such a level as to attract and retain the appropriate directors, but that directors should not receive more than is necessary. It is important to link a significant proportion of executive directors' remuneration to corporate and individual performance measures; directors should not be involved in setting their own remuneration and the procedure through which executive remuneration is set should be formal and transparent.

Regarding Accountability and Audit, the Combined Code states that the board should provide a balanced and comprehensible picture of the company's position and its future outlook; there should be a sound system of internal control which is able to safeguard shareholders' funds and the company's assets; there should be an audit committee which will be part of a formal and transparent arrangement for the application of appropriate financial reporting and internal control principles, and also for maintaining the relationship with the external auditors.

Finally in Section 1, regarding Relations with Shareholders, the Combined Code states that there should be a dialogue with shareholders 'based on the mutual understanding of objectives'; the company's Annual General Meeting (AGM) should be used to communicate with investors and also to encourage their participation.

Section 2 deals with Institutional Shareholders. The Combined Code mirrors the recommendation in the Relations with Shareholders part, as mentioned above, as it states that institutional shareholders should enter into a dialogue with companies based on the mutual understanding of objectives. In relation to this recommendation, the Combined Code also refers to the principles set out in the Institutional Shareholders' Committee's (ISC) guidance 'The Responsibilities of Institutional Shareholders and Agents — Statement of Principles' which is discussed further below. Section 2 also refers to institutional shareholders evaluating companies' governance arrangements, especially relating to board structure and composition, and giving due weight to relevant factors; and finally, it advocates that institutional shareholders have a responsibility to make considered use of their votes.

Before moving on to discuss the role of institutional investors in corporate governance, there are three other influential publications that should be discussed. The first of these is the Directors' Remuneration Report Regulations 2002, the second is the Companies Act 2006, and the third is the European Union directives.

9.2.3 UK Directors' Remuneration Report Regulations 2002

One of the notable developments in UK corporate governance in relation to directors' remuneration was the introduction of the UK Directors' Remuneration Report Regulations 2002. These state that quoted companies must publish a detailed report on directors' pay as part of their annual reporting cycle and that this report must be approved by the board of directors. A graph of the company's total shareholder returns over five years, against a comparator group, must be published in the remuneration committee report. The names of any consultants to the remuneration committee must be disclosed, including whether they were appointed independently, along with the cost of any other services provided to the company.

Companies must hold a shareholder vote on the directors' remuneration report at each general meeting. The vote is advisory in nature but, nonetheless, if shareholders vote against the directors' remuneration report then the board of directors would do well to heed the signal that the investors are unhappy with the directors' proposed remuneration. As can be seen in the section below on institutional investor activism, this advisory vote has been increasingly widely used to indicate institutional shareholders' disapproval of the executive remuneration packages recommended by various companies' remuneration committees.

9.2.4 Companies Act 2006

UK company law has been in need of an overhaul and modernisation for many years. Following a long consultation and review period, the Companies Act was published in 2006. Some of the main features are as follows: directors' duties are codified; companies can make greater use of electronic communications for communicating with shareholders; the requirement for an Operating and Financial Review (OFR) has not been reinstated, rather companies are encouraged to produce a high quality Business Review; enhanced proxy rights make it easier for shareholders to appoint others to attend and vote at general meetings; shareholders of quoted companies may have a shareholder proposal (resolution) circulated at the company's expense if received by the end of the financial year; whilst there has been significant encouragement over a number of years to encourage institutional investors to disclose how they use their votes, the Act provides a power which could be used to require institutional investors to disclose how they have voted.

The Companies Act (2006) has implications for directors and their relationship with stakeholders as more information has to be disclosed which is relevant to stakeholders (that is, the emphasis is not just on shareholders).

9.2.5 *European Influence*

The UK's system of corporate governance is comprehensive especially when compared to some of the fellow members of the European Union (EU). Therefore, when EU pronouncements are issued, the UK often already meets the corporate governance recommendations as they are already embodied in UK codes, guidelines or regulations. Nonetheless, it is important to discuss some of the recent EU pronouncements as they give a flavor of developments in the EU which, of course, impact on the UK.

In 2006, amendments to the EU 4th and 7th Company Law Directives were issued with the aim of enhancing confidence in financial statements and annual reports. The changes included the requirement that listed companies publish a separate corporate governance statement in the annual report, and that board members are to take collective responsibility for the annual report and accounts. The Directive on the statutory audit of annual and consolidated accounts clarifies the duties of auditors; a key provision being that listed companies should have audit committees with at least one member of the audit committee being independent and competent in accounting/auditing.

In 2007, the Directive on the exercise of shareholder rights was issued. It recommended that shareholders have timely access to information; and that there should be the facility to vote at a distance that does not require the need to be physically present at the meeting to vote. The practice of shareblocking, whereby if shareholders wished to vote their shares, they had to deposit them at a specified institution for a period of time around the company's AGM and so could not trade them during that time, was abolished.

After the onset of the global financial crisis, the High-Level Group on Financial Supervision in the EU, chaired by Jacques de Larosiere, published its report in February 2009. It highlighted failures in corporate governance as one of the most important aspects of the crisis, and made recommendations regarding compensation incentives and internal risk management.

9.3 Institutional Investors in the UK

9.3.1 *Growth of Institutional Investors*

In the US and UK, in particular, there has been a significant change in the pattern of share ownership in the last 40 years, with institutional shareholders (pension funds, insurance companies, mutual funds) becoming much more influential. For example, in the UK, according to the Office of National Statistics (2007) at the end of 2006, the largest owners of UK shares were the insurance companies with 14.7 percent (£272.8bn), the pension funds with 12.7 percent (£235.8bn) and the overseas investors with 40.0 percent (£742.4bn). This can be compared to 1963 when pension funds held 6.4 percent, insurance companies 10 percent, and overseas investors 7.0 percent (see Table 9.2).

The vast increase in overseas investors is of particular interest as many of these are US institutional investors who tend to be much more activist than their UK counterparts. They also regularly vote their shares — this stems from the fact that there is more of a culture of voting in the US with private pension schemes being mandated to vote by the Employee Retirement Income Security Act (ERISA) 1974. As private pension schemes vote, then the large public schemes such as the California Public Employees Retirement System (CalPERS) also tend to vote. When US investors own significant amounts of UK equity which they vote, this has tended to have the effect of also encouraging the UK institutional investors to vote.

Given the extent of share ownership by institutional shareholders, it is not surprising that they can wield substantial power and influence. This has been recognised by the UK corporate governance codes over the years. For example, Cadbury (1992) stated that we 'look to the institutions in particular...to

Table 9.2 Summary of Main Categories of Share Ownership in the UK 1963–2006.

Type of Investor	1963 Percent	2006 Percent
Individuals	54	13
Insurance companies	10	15
Pension funds	6	13
Unit trusts	1	2
Overseas	7	40

Source: Based on ONS Share Ownership 2007.
(Other categories owning shares include banks, investment trusts, public sector, and industrial and commercial companies).

use their influence as owners to ensure that companies in which they have invested comply with the Code'; and Greenbury (1995) stated that 'the investor institutions should use their power and influence to ensure the implementation of best practice as set out in the Code.'

Similarly, the Combined Code (2003, 2006, 2008) recommended that 'institutional shareholders should enter into a dialogue with companies based on the mutual understanding of objectives.'

There are various issues relating to corporate governance that are of particular interest to institutional investors. These include issues relating to the board such as splitting the roles of Chair and CEO, independent non-executive directors, and succession planning; issues relating to executive directors' remuneration; threats to shareholder rights, for example, company actions that result in dilution of shareholdings; and lack of appropriate disclosure on various matters.

Institutional investors are also increasingly aware of social, environmental and ethical issues that may impact the long-term sustainability of the business, and many screen companies to try to ensure that they have good corporate social responsibility and have taken account of the potential risks they may be exposed to, either through the nature of their business or the geographical locations in which they operate. The areas that institutional investors will generally try to avoid relate to child labour, slave labour, avoidance of certain types of industry, prohibition of testing on animals, etc., as well as environmental matters including harmful emissions to land, air, sea, including heavy metals, carbon emissions, oil, etc.

The Institutional Shareholders' Committee (ISC) is a forum which enables the UK's institutional shareholding community to exchange views and also to coordinate their activities in support of the interests of UK investors. Its constituent members are: the Association of British Insurers (ABI), the Association of Investment Companies (AIC), the Investment Management Association (IMA) and the National Association of Pension Funds (NAPF). These constituent members are professional organisations that act as representative bodies for their members, for example, the ABI represents the interests of companies in the insurance industry.

In 2002, the ISC issued the Statement of Principles on the Responsibilities of Institutional Shareholders and Agents. The statement issued was 'aimed at furthering the application of best practice to the relationship between institutional investors and the companies in which they invest, with the object of securing value for beneficiaries over the longer term.' The ISC states that the policies on activism that they describe are designed to deal with the under-performance of companies and, hence, ensure that shareholders derive value from their investments. They state that institutional shareholders should have a clear statement of their policy on activism and on how they will discharge their responsibilities; they should monitor performance, and intervene when necessary. Finally, they should evaluate and report on their activities. Overall, the statement aims to enhance 'how effectively institutional shareholders discharge their responsibilities in relation to the companies in which they invest.' In 2005, the ISC published its Review of the Statement of Principles and concluded that there had been a general increase in the level of engagement with investee companies. It made a few modifications to the original guidelines: 'activism' was replaced with 'engagement' to reflect the importance now attached by institutional investors to developing a high quality all-round relationship with the companies in which they invest; the guidelines now recommend that pension funds should incorporate the principles into their Statement of Investment Principles; and the corporate governance aspect should be more integrated with the investment process. The ISC (2007) again reviewed and updated the Statement of Principles on shareholder engagement. The only amendment relates to publishing a policy on voting disclosure.

9.3.2 *Tools of Governance*

It has become increasingly clear that institutional investors are expected to engage more fully with their investee companies, and, to act where there may be a lack of good corporate governance. Institutional investors have at their disposal a number of tools of governance, including dialogue/meetings, voting, shareholder proposals/resolutions and focus lists.

The Combined Code (2003), in the context of institutional investors, emphasised dialogue with companies, 'based on a mutual understanding of objectives.' Dialogue often takes the form of one-to-one meetings between the institutional investors and the company directors. Various issues are discussed at these meetings including strategy and corporate governance matters — executive directors' remuneration being a hot topic at the moment!

The various corporate governance codes have placed an emphasis on voting. The Cadbury Report (1992) stated that 'given the weight of their votes, the way in which institutional investors use their power...is of fundamental importance' and that 'institutional investors should make positive use of their voting rights and disclose their policies on voting.' Meanwhile, the Hampel Report (1998) stated that 'institutional shareholders have a responsibility to make considered use of their votes' which was reiterated in the Combined Code (2003, 2006, 2008) which stated that 'institutional shareholders have a responsibility to make considered use of their votes.'

Voting can be an effective means of exercising 'voice,' but there are significant barriers to both effective domestic and cross-border voting. In the UK, the Shareholder Voting Working Group, chaired by Paul Myners, has issued several reports with the fourth one being issued in July 2007. Voting levels have increased over time with voting levels have risen to over 60 percent up from 50 percent some three years ago. However, problems remain with the UK voting system. The report details the various impediments to voting, highlights the complexity of the voting system, and makes recommendations on a number of areas to help improve the situation and remedy the problem of 'lost' votes. The report recommended that the voting system should be more efficient and transparent, and specifically highlighted that institutional shareholders could be doing more to try to ensure that their votes were appropriately recorded. The report cited the Combined Code (2006) which states that 'institutional shareholders should take steps to ensure their voting instructions are translated into practice.'

Shareholder proposals or resolutions have traditionally been a little used tool in the UK (compared to the US where there can be 800 plus shareholder proposals each year). In the UK, a shareholder proposal can be put forward by either members having 5 percent of the voting power of the company; or 100 or more shareholders whose paid-up capital averages at least £100 each. The resolution may be circulated at the expense of the members making the request, unless the company resolves otherwise. Clearly the practical difficulties involved in putting forward a shareholder proposal mean that the number in the UK is small, of the order of 6–10 each year. However, there has been an increasing trend in the dissatisfaction of shareholders with various aspects of company performance in the financial crisis. Disagreement with executive remuneration packages seems to have already triggered an increased number of shareholder proposals.

Another tool of governance is the use of focus lists. Some institutional investors have established 'focus lists'; a good example of such an institutional investors is CalPERS. CalPERS targets underperforming companies and includes them on a list of companies that have underperformed a main index, such as Standard and Poor's or the Russell 1000 index. Underperforming the index would be the starting point for potentially being included on a focus list. However, this is usually combined with some weakness in the company's corporate governance structure, such as a lack of independent non-executive directors, and also a lack of responsiveness to the institutional investors' views.

9.3.3 *Institutional Investor Activism in Action*

In this section, some examples of institutional investor activism are discussed. Of course, constructive dialogue is often fruitful and, in those cases the general public are usually none the wiser as to issues being discussed as it takes place behind closed doors. Therefore, we concentrate on the more public effects of one of the other tools of governance: voting.

In terms of voting, at one time, it would have been rare for institutional investors not to have supported incumbent management and voted in favour of the resolutions they put forward. A signal of strong disapproval would have been for the institutional investor to abstain from voting, whereas now institutional investors will vote against. Most of the incidences of voting against tend to relate to executive remuneration. Whilst we might tend to think of the open disapproval of aspects of executive remuneration being a very recent phenomenon, the first example below highlights that this is not the case. It highlights how the shareholders of United Business Media voted against an ex gratia payment for the outgoing CEO following the successful handover of his CEO role to his successor. The second example reflects a more recent example in 2009 at Royal Dutch Shell when shareholders voted against the proposed payment of discretionary awards to executive directors as the company had failed to meet its targets.

United Business Media

In the UK, shareholders have a right to vote on the report of the Remuneration Committee which details the recommendations regarding the remuneration of the executive directors. The vote may be in favour of the report or against it. However, the vote is only advisory, although companies usually take note of it as it is a strong indicator of the way shareholders view the executive director remuneration policy in the company.

In 2005, when Lord Hollick, the Chief Executive of United Business Media (UBM) was about to retire, the Remuneration Committee agreed to pay him a special ex gratia bonus of £250,000 in recognition of a successful handover to his successor, David Levin. However, a number of institutional investors viewed this handover as part and parcel of Lord Hollick's role as Chief Executive and felt that a one-off payment of a quarter of a million pounds was inappropriate. Some 77 percent of shareholders, including many large institutional investors, voted against the Remuneration Committee Report, thus expressing their dissatisfaction with the proposed payment.

Following the vote, Lord Hollick decided not to accept the ex gratia payment based on the powerful message sent by the institutional investors and other shareholders. This was seen as a victory for the institutional investors who had proven that they could exert their power and influence via the advisory vote on the Remuneration Committee Report.

Royal Dutch Shell

In 2008 and 2009, there was intense public and investor disquiet with perceived excessive executive director remuneration in the UK corporate sector.
It seemed as though executive directors were being generously paid even
when the companies they looked after were experiencing falling share prices
and poor performance. Some directors who left their positions were being
paid 'golden goodbyes,' or receiving huge payments into their pension pots.

Against this backdrop, Shell's remuneration committee put forward a
remuneration report which recommended a discretionary award to executive
directors based on the 2006–8 performance even though the company failed
to meet its targets. The CEO received a bonus of £1.19 million. Not surprisingly, institutional investors from the UK and overseas all felt very strongly
about the discretionary awards and some 59 percent of Shell's shareholders
voted against the remuneration report.

Whilst the vote on the remuneration report is, as mentioned above, an
advisory vote, it would be a complacent board that ignored the very strong
signal being sent to them by their institutional investors. Shell has agreed to
consult its institutional shareholders more on the issue of executive director
remuneration.

The examples above also indicate the extensive technological advances
that we have witnessed in the last 50 years which have changed the way that
business, and investment, are undertaken. Information is much more widely
available, and it is available much more quickly. Institutional investors in different countries can communicate very easily to discuss issues which may be
of concern to them including corporate governance matters.

9.4 Concluding Comments

In this chapter, the development of corporate governance in the UK has been
examined and the evolving role of institutional investors discussed. We have
seen that financial scandals and collapses over the last decade or so, and the
more recent financial crisis, have had a significant impact on corporate
governance.

The evolving role of institutional investors has been examined. The
growth of institutional investors and the significant power and influence
which they can exert on their investee companies, means that there is a widely
held expectation that institutional investors will engage fully with their
investee companies and help ensure that best practice corporate governance
is followed.

Presently, the UK government, via the Financial Reporting Council, is reviewing the current corporate governance provisions in the UK; at the same time, institutional investors are being exhorted to engage more fully with the companies in which they invest, to act as owners and not as passive holders of shares. Certainly institutional investors now seem more activist and there are many more incidences of them being willing to vote against at companies' annual general meetings when constructive dialogue has failed. Corporate governance continues to develop and evolve in the UK, as in other countries, to try to meet the demands of a fast changing world where, increasingly, investors, government and other stakeholders demand that the nation's funds are appropriately invested in companies which competently manage the risks and opportunities presented to them, and where institutional investors engage fully with their investee companies to help ensure that companies have longer term sustainability.

Future research could examine to what extent institutional investors have become more active as a result of the global financial crisis, and the effectiveness of the different tools of governance could be examined in different scenarios to determine which tool might work better in a given type of situation. Finally, several international dimensions could be examined including a comparison of the market, political and other influences on institutional investors in different countries, the activism of institutional investors in different countries, and the variation in the adoption of different tools of governance in an international context.

Chapter 10

PENSION FUNDS AND SUSTAINABLE INVESTMENT: RETURN AND RISK?

ROB BAUER AND HARRY HUMMELS

Maastricht University, The Netherlands

10.1 Introduction

This chapter deals with the impact of sustainable investment strategies on risk and the return of funds with a special focus on pension fund investments. We define sustainable investment as follows:

Investment based on environmental (E), social (S) and governance (G) considerations and/or engagement of companies, governments and other relevant parties on the basis of such considerations. In the financial world, reference is often made to a pension fund's ESG policy.

In this chapter, we will discuss three forms of sustainable investment:

a) Negative screening by pension funds, i.e. exclusion of investments in companies that do not meet the ESG criteria defined by the pension fund's board.
b) The integration of extra-financial information in the investment decision making process, i.e. inclusion of ESG information when selecting investments, with a view to improving the investment portfolio's risk-return profile (RRP).
c) Exercising shareholder's rights, including voting rights and the right to engage a company's management.

We begin with a brief analysis of each form of sustainable investment and a discussion on the potential effects of an ESG policy on a pension fund's investment results. We review the integration of environmental (E) and social (S) as well as governance (G) characteristics into the ESG policy. We then extend the discussion to include other asset categories before summarising our findings and listing the implications for investors.

10.2 Return and Risk

10.2.1 *Negative Screening*

If a pension fund wants to avoid involvement with certain behaviour or activities of a company, governments, or other entities in which it may choose to invest, the fund can adopt an exclusion policy. Below, we limit discussion to the effects of such a policy on equity portfolios. In Section 3, we briefly discuss the effects of exclusion policies on other asset categories.

What influence does an exclusion policy based on ESG criteria have on the performance of the total portfolio of an investment fund? In the past few years, the academic world has put increasing effort into finding the answer to this question. It has to be said in advance that systematic exclusion of companies with a poor governance record is extremely rare. For this reason, our discussion will focus primarily on the exclusion of companies on the basis of social, ethical and environmental criteria.

In a recent study, Geczy *et al.* (2005) investigate the potential utility loss for investors resulting from the restriction of the investment universe through the application of socially responsible investment screens. Geczy *et al.* (2005) conclude that investors with a firm belief in the efficiency of markets probably have little to fear from limited restrictions imposed on the investment universe. These investors are convinced that the return and risk characteristics of excluded companies can be replicated fairly easily by adding other companies in the available universe. However, overly drastic and systematic exclusion based on an extensive set of very strict ethical standards, for example, excluding investments in the defence industry, aviation, oil and gas, transport and financials, can lead to inefficient portfolios. The situation is different for investors who are convinced in advance of their own stock-picking skills. They feel limited by the restriction of the investment universe, as this prevents them from making the most of their skills. If, for example, a portfolio manager who specialises in actively selecting defence stocks is no longer allowed to invest in the defence industry, the manager can no longer exhibit his full investment selection potential.

The study by Geczy *et al.* (2005) implies that the strategic view of a pension fund with regard to active investment is significant in determining the desirability of an exclusion or suspension policy. The study suggests that a pension fund, with a largely passive investment policy, need not expect negative effects from a limited exclusion policy on the risk-return profile of its portfolio. However, if a fund strongly believes in the added value of its (external) asset managers, then a strict exclusion policy may be counterproductive.

Other empirical studies indicate that sustainable investment funds, i.e. investment funds based on a form of ESG screening, have the same level of portfolio diversification as other investment funds and equivalent returns. An example is the study by Bauer *et al.* (2005), which demonstrates that SRI mutual funds do not perform better or worse than conventional investment funds that do not explicitly account for ESG factors. Bello (2005) demonstrates that sustainable investment funds and conventional funds have more or less the same level of diversification and equivalent long-term returns. Interestingly, both studies show that both sustainable and conventional investment funds underperform the broader market. A study by Schroeder (2007) examines the performance of sustainable indices such as the FTSE4Good. In most cases, these indices — which actively select stocks from the total available equity investment universe — do not produce lower returns than regular indices, for example, the Morgan Stanley Capital International index. However, some indices do entail a slightly higher risk. Some caution is in order when interpreting the studies of sustainable investment funds and indices mentioned here. Not all of the investment funds examined actually apply a strict exclusion policy. Others opt consciously for a "best-in-class" strategy or for positive screening. Consequently, it is difficult to draw strong conclusions on the basis of these studies about the influence of a certain form of exclusion policy.

Finally, a fact to remember about active investment policies is that every manager of an active portfolio actually applies an exclusion policy, albeit based on factors other than ESG considerations. After all, a large portion of the investment universe is excluded because the manager expects these companies to underperform the benchmark. Of course, a portfolio manager may later decide on financial grounds to include these companies again, but the fact remains that an active portfolio at any given moment excludes a subset of the index. The extent to which managers of active equity portfolios succeed in systematically outperforming the index by means of this "dynamic exclusion policy" has been discussed at length in the literature on fund management. Studies by Malkiel (1995) and Gruber (1996) provide conclusive evidence that managers of active investment funds generally are not capable of systematically outperforming the benchmark. Indeed, after deduction of costs, they turn out to significantly underperform the benchmark by about one percentage point a year. This raises the question of which exclusion policy has a greater impact on the investor — a limited exclusion policy applied to an otherwise passive investment strategy, or a systematically underperforming active portfolio?

In practice, pension funds seldom, if ever, exclude entire sectors of the economy from their investments. They do, however, sometimes actively terminate or suspend investments in individual companies, but this has far less drastic effects. In 2006, for example, the Norwegian Petroleum Fund, through its asset manager Norwegian Bank Investment Management, suspended investment in 19 companies until these companies met the fund's financial and ESG criteria.[1] The affected companies are primarily manufacturers of cluster bombs and land mines, although some multinationals corporations from other sectors were also excluded on ethical and environmental grounds. On the basis of the studies referred to above, the fund need not expect negative effects due to the exclusion policy on its risk-return profile. Another example is the exclusion in the seventies and eighties of companies with significant operations in South Africa (Munnell, 2007). Investment funds that excluded South African companies actually outperformed funds without exclusions. The reason, however, was that companies with links to South Africa were generally large corporations, so that portfolios with an exclusion policy were relatively overweight smallcap shares. During the period studied (1960–1983) smallcaps significantly outperformed largecaps (Grossman and Sharpe, 1986).

The above studies show that any exclusion policy, before being implemented, must be tested for its impact on the risk factors determining returns on listed shares. A priori exclusion of a large number of companies in a universe on account of their belonging to a particular industry, such as oil and gas, aviation, chemicals tobacco or alcohol can — if implemented rashly — lead to a drastic reduction in the number of companies in the investable universe. This means less choices for portfolio managers and can threaten the efficiency of their portfolios. By contrast, expectations are that a limited-scale exclusion policy, for example, excluding a small number of companies in a (global) equity index, need not have negative effects, as long as the risk factors are sufficiently taken into account during portfolio construction. The development of modern risk models and software has made this task steadily easier. Needless to say, the more companies that are excluded, the more difficult this task becomes. For active portfolio managers, for example, those using dynamic sector allocation, it becomes increasingly difficult to put all their skills into the selection of the portfolio. This can hurt performance, at least if they are indeed capable of systematically outperforming the benchmark.

---

[1] Council on Ethics for the Government Pension Fund — Global, *Annual Report 2006*, Oslo, p. 8.

10.2.2 *The Integration of Extra-Financial Information*

The integration of extra-financial information into the standard investment process is less controversial. Rather than a limitation, this presents an opportunity to use information from outside the realms of financial criteria as an input into the investment process. Relatively few portfolio managers explicitly integrate this information into their investment process as there is no consensus about the added value for investors. Opponents (including Friedman, 1970) point out that a company loses focus if it does not concentrate solely on making a profit and includes other goals, such as corporate social responsibility. In their view, investors in such companies will end up with lower returns due to the direct and indirect costs of pursuing objectives other than primary business ones. Supporters of the use of extra-financial information (including Porter and van der Linde, 1995), on the other hand, believe a high score on ESG factors enhances a company's image and competitive position. In their view, such companies are likely to be more innovative and to have better relationships with stakeholders. As a consequence, capital providers are likely to charge a lower risk premium, meaning that such companies enjoy lower financing costs. Investors ultimately benefit, as this information is probably not yet reflected in the stock market valuation of such companies. Unfortunately, these largely theoretical, and sometimes anecdotal, arguments have not yet been accompanied by fundamental and longitudinal empirical research, resulting in years of stalemate between the two camps. Research into sustainable investment has remained very much a niche activity.

Academic research into the impact of corporate governance (G)[2] has been continuing for some time. Most studies focus on the effect of corporate governance indicators on equity returns, equity market valuations of companies and earnings ratios. As long-term investors, pension funds are particularly interested in the impact of (G) on the long-term performance of companies. Unfortunately, only a few studies have the requisite long-term horizon. An exception is the research by Gompers *et al.* (2003), who had access to a sufficiently large sample (roughly 1,500 listed companies in the US) and time series data spanning 10 years. In this frequently cited paper, the authors analyse the impact of 24 governance mechanisms (based on takeover defences) on equity returns. After risk adjustment, they found that the portfolios of well-managed companies (defined here as those without takeover defence mechanisms) outperformed portfolios of badly managed companies

---

[2] For an extensive survey of studies into the impact of ESG-factors on investment portfolios, see, for example, Hummels and Bauer (2006) in chapter 5 and Bauer *et al.* (2004).

(with multiple barriers to takeovers) by as much as 8.5 percentage points between 1990 and 1999. Moreover, well-managed companies generally have higher stock market valuations, wider profit margins and higher return on equity (in accounting terms). Similar studies in Europe and Japan by Bauer *et al.* (2004) and Bauer *et al.* (2008) document comparable results.

According to a recent study by Core *et al.* (2006), however, information relating to corporate governance seems to be largely reflected in share prices. Moreover, they argue that the performance of the strategy based on Gompers *et al.* (2003) was, to a considerable extent, attributable to the internet hype. If they remove technology stocks from the data, the outperformance is much more modest and statistically insignificant. Cremers and Nair (2005) offer further rebuttal, demonstrating that the results are quite sensitive to the portfolio construction procedure.

These empirical studies show the need for additional data on corporate governance covering a longer time period and in more depth, rather than relying on takeover defences as a proxy for governance. Even where data is relatively abundant, caution is advisable. The large data supply coming from rating agencies needs to be concentrated and its quality further improved. In our view, the general conclusion that can be drawn from this type of research is that there is not a negative correlation between corporate governance characteristics and (long-term) equity returns. Although information on governance increasingly serves as direct or indirect input into the investment process, it does not seem likely that a simple strategy like investing solely in well-governed companies will work in the years ahead. It is far more likely that (unexpected) changes in the quality of corporate governance will impact investment risks and return.

There is considerably less empirical research into the impact of other ESG factors (E and S) on the financial performance of companies. Most studies present arguments from a management strategy perspective in favour of integrating sustainability into a company's business processes. The European Centre for Corporate Engagement (ECCE), a Netherlands-based international research network,[3] has published two studies based on "eco-efficiency data," an eco-management concept. Both studies combine insights from the theoretically oriented management literature with performance and risk measurement metrics from modern finance and investment literature. They demonstrate that portfolios of companies with high eco-efficiency scores outperform portfolios of companies with low scores. These results do not change after adjustment for market risk, investment styles and sector effects. Moreover, they show that

---

[3] Derwall *et al.* (2005) and Günster *et al.* (2006). For more information on ECCE, see: www.corporate-engagement.com.

companies with a low eco-efficiency score generally have low stock market valuations. The valuations of companies with high scores, however, are not higher or lower than average. Therefore, it seems that the stock markets tend to punish low scoring companies immediately, but take longer to price the good news. This may be due to bad news about a company attracting more press coverage (a case in point being the Exxon Valdez disaster and its very costly environmental consequences for Exxon). Apparently, investors respond immediately to unexpected bad news by adjusting their estimates of the company's future cash flows and risks. Positive news elicits a wait-and-see response, but eventually, the information finds its way into the price of the underlying shares.

The examples above suggest that equity investors can either earn higher returns or reduce their sensitivity to sudden bad news about a company if they integrate relevant elements of extra-financial information into the investment process. It is important to bear in mind, however, that this information is likely to explain only a limited portion of expected returns. Not all information in the spectrum of ESG factors is relevant. A company's share price is for the most part attributable to the company's profitability, which, in turn, is a function of the quality of its management, its innovativeness, its operational efficiency and the outlook for the sector in which it is active. Besides, a good score on ESG factors does not, by definition, imply that a company is a good investment, as the question must first be answered as to whether the relevant extra-financial information is already priced in. Although this is often unlikely to be the case, this type of information has only recently become available and has, to date, played only a very limited role in the investment processes of institutional investors and analysts.

An often-cited study by McKinsey (2002) confirms this: 80 percent of institutional investors indicate a willingness to pay a premium for shares of "well-governed" companies in developed markets. A recent study by Mercer Investment Consultants (2007) also demonstrates that US pension funds increasingly integrate ESG factors into their investment process and their range of financial products: a clear indication of a potential "early mover advantage." These findings are also consistent with recent ECCE surveys performed by Jaworski (2007) and Bauer *et al.* (2007) among European institutional investors, analysts (working for brokers) and European largecap companies. Analysts screen companies primarily for corporate governance and, to a lesser extent, for ethical, social and environmental aspects. Although institutional investors also rate corporate governance information as most important, they increasingly demand integration of relevant ethical, social and environmental information into the fundamental analysis of companies. The survey results clearly show that brokers are not responding to this need at present, despite initiatives like the Enhanced Analytics Initiative and the signing of the Principles for Responsible Investing by some of their corporate clients.[4]

Implicitly, the empirical studies referred to above test the null hypothesis that ESG factors do not play a role in stock market valuation. The crucial question is whether ESG information is relevant, and if so, whether it is reflected in the prices of securities. The alternative is that this information is not relevant to the investor because there is no relationship, or because the attending risks are not priced in. According to some studies, elements of extra-financial information do have an impact (certain governance characteristics and eco-efficiency, for example), while numerous studies claim to have found no relation with ESG factors.[5] It is the portfolio manager's responsibility to assess the merits of the ever-increasing flow of corporate information. A recent, contribution to the debate is an article by Hong and Kacperczyk (2009) titled: "The Price of Sin." The authors argue that investors in "sin stocks" (shares in companies that go against the social norm, for example, tobacco or alcoholic beverages producers) are only prepared to hold such shares if they receive higher returns. This premium for holding less marketable shares implies that these investors earn higher returns in the long run.

The current literature provides no unambiguous answer to the question of which factors are relevant and which are not. Supporters and opponents can always find a study to quote that confirms their ideas. For further reading, we suggest, to name a few, Hummels and Bauer (2006), Bauer et al. (2004) and Orlitzky et al. (2003).

10.2.3 *Exercising Shareholders' Rights*

Engagement and proxy voting are relatively new strategies used by investors to influence the management of a company. Unfortunately, this means that little research has yet been done into the effects of both strategies on companies' risks and returns, and on the risk-return profile of investments in such companies — let alone longitudinal research, which is simply not available.

Still, something can be said about the potential impact of engagement on the financial performance of companies. A case in point is the "CalPERS-effect." Years ago, state-run pension administrator CalPERS, in the US, began publishing a blacklist of companies with what it views to be poor corporate

---

[4] In 2008, the Enhanced Analytics Initiated ceased to exist as an independent organisation. The partners decided to continue their efforts to stimulate brokers to integrate ESG-information in their research as part of the UN PRI.

[5] See Hummels and Bauer (2006, chapter 5).

governance records: its "focus list of corporate laggards." For the years before these companies were placed on the list, they significantly lagged the index. In the years after the public announcement that these companies had been black-listed by CalPERS, they significantly outperformed the index. This improvement may be attributed to the negative press of being blacklisted or to the assistance from CalPERS to the firm's management to assist it to improve. Apparently, this kind of engagement produces positive results.

To an increasing extent, influence is being wielded with regards to not only corporate governance, but also on social, ethical and environmental policy. What distinguishes an ESG strategy is that it imposes no restrictions on portfolio managers in the composition of their portfolios. On the contrary, one needs to be invested in the companies to exercise shareholders' rights. It should be remembered, however, that there are costs involved in exercising voting rights and entering into a dialogue with companies. These costs do not automatically produce financial benefits, although the CalPERS example shows that the costs of engagement are certainly not a poor investment.

10.3 Extension to Other Asset Categories

A second element in the debate is the reach of ESG factors in the investment spectrum. In both practise and academia, attention has focused mostly on shares, a fact that was confirmed by the ECCE study by Hummels (2007). For the sake of consistency, the same debate could — and indeed should — also be held with regards to investments in fixed-income securities, for instance, or in real estate. Unfortunately, there is little empirical research concerning these asset categories linked to extra-financial information. There are a few exceptions, including a recent study by Cremers *et al.* (2007) which focuses on the relationship between governance characteristics (mainly takeover defence mechanisms) and corporate bonds, and a recent study by Bauer *et al.* (2009) on the relationship between employee relations and bonds spreads and credit ratings. The conclusion is that providers of loan capital accept lower spreads (that is, lower risk premiums) from companies with takeover defence mechanisms, while shareholders see such mechanisms as negative (Gompers *et al.*, 2003). Good scores on employee satisfaction lower bond spreads as well. Interestingly, pension funds often own both shares and bonds issued by the same company, and they should bear this in mind when executing their corporate governance and engagement policies. Despite these examples, research into the relation between corporate bond spreads and ESG factors is still in its infancy.

Similarly, there is little empirical research into the impact of extra-financial information on real estate investments, apart from two ECCE studies on the governance structure of REITS and the impact of green buildings on the (effective) rents and transaction prices of office buildings. We will not discuss this further here, but refer the reader to Bauer, Eichholtz and Kok (2010) and Eichholtz *et al.* (2008).[6] In the case of REITs (real estate investment trusts, which are listed property companies), the management must distribute practically all the free cash flow to the shareholders. This implies that managers of REITs have relatively little scope to redirect shareholder value for other purposes. A study comparing ISS[7] governance ratings of 220 US REITs shows that the valuation and the profitability of REITs are not correlated to their ISS governance ratings. A similar analysis of listed large cap companies confirms the findings of Gompers *et al.* (2003) with regard to shares. Among regular (non-REIT) companies, the authors find a positive relationship between profitability and valuation on the one hand and the governance score on the other. In the market, moreover, there are numerous initiatives to incorporate (E) and (S) into property investment products, but the scientific basis is largely absent.

We also see the integration of ESG factors in so-called targeted or impact investments. Unlike equity or fixed-income investments, targeted investments involve investing directly in areas like forestry, climate change and clean tech projects or microfinance institutions. Pension funds are front runners in this field, with substantial sums invested in projects of this kind. Because the investments are made in non-transparent markets, projects and companies, investors who possess the right information at the right time can earn handsome returns on their investments. The aim of these investments is not only to help increase the diversification of the total investment portfolio and earn strong absolute returns, but also to do this in a way that advances social goals. Academic research into the risks and returns of this new asset category is not yet available. The history is simply too short. An asset category such as microfinance — if indeed it can be called an asset category — is, by nature, very much mandate-driven. As for funds that offer access to targeted investments, there are only a handful that meet the demands and needs of institutional investors. The situation is similar for investments in forestry, alternative energy and clean technology, although the range of available funds is slightly wider.

---

[6] The paper of Bauer *et al.* (2009) contains references to a limited number of other studies of the governance structure of REITs.

[7] Institutional Shareholder Services (ISS): a provider of information on various governance characteristics of individual companies.

10.4 Implications for the Investor

In our view, implementing a sustainable investment policy does not necessarily conflict with the fiduciary duty of the pension fund board. Suspending investment in companies that do not meet ESG criteria, if done sensibly, need have no negative impact on the risk-return profile. In other words, as long as a pension fund does not, as a matter of principle, exclude entire sectors of the economy from its investments and does not formulate its criteria so strictly as to exclude a significant portion of the investment universe, the effect on the risk-return profile will, as a rule, be acceptable.

As a qualification of the above, we wish to point out that active asset management is in itself a form of dynamic exclusion. On average, active mandates significantly underperform the benchmark. Pension funds should give the decision to actively manage their assets just as much consideration as the decision whether to apply exclusions on the basis of ESG considerations. This is all the more important because many sustainable portfolios are a combination of some form of exclusion and a form of active management. Most pension funds appear, however, not to give much conscious thought to their strategic decision to invest actively. Pension funds that decide to take a limited set of exclusion criteria on board in their investment policy would do well to look at passive as well as active strategies.

In the case of positive as opposed to negative screening, some elements of extra-financial information seem to be positively correlated with the returns and valuations of companies (G: absence of takeover defence mechanisms and E: eco-efficiency). Others, again, seem less relevant or even negatively correlated. Generally, it can be said that information about the quality of corporate governance (G) seems particularly relevant. Research into (E)- and (S)-related information has produced ambigious results. Portfolio managers have a duty to take all the relevant and available information (and data) into account in their investment decisions. With the increasing amount of extra-financial information now at their disposal, it is up to them whether to attach importance to that information. In either case, they need additional sources of information, knowledge, scientific research and tools to process this information efficiently. The most important assessment they need to make, however, is whether or not ESG factors are already reflected in the prices of the securities. Especially in the case of (G), it appears to be already too late to benefit from the insights of scientific research. Be this as it may, good governance does form a prerequisite for investors to engage companies on (E) and (S) issues.

The way a pension fund uses its voting rights as a shareholder cannot be viewed in isolation from its position as an investor in other asset categories, such as corporate bonds. Sometimes, for example, the pension fund's interests as a shareholder can conflict with its interests as a provider of loan capital. Pension funds would do well to bear this in mind in the execution of their engagement policies.

Finally, investors need to realise that engagement involves costs. A direct relationship with investment results is often absent. Indirectly, engagement can produce financial benefits, if it prompts companies to improve their business practice, thus saving them money or reducing their extra-financial risks, including reputation risk. Such benefits are hard to quantify, however. Research on the efficiency of engagement strategies is necessary for the next evolution of shareholder engagement.

Chapter 11

SUSTAINABILITY REPORTING AND THE IMPORTANCE OF STAKEHOLDER ENGAGEMENT

CORAL INGLEY

Auckland University of Technology

11.1 Introduction

Corporations today can rarely afford to adopt the view articulated by Milton Friedman (1970, pp. 32–33) that "the social responsibility of business is to increase its profits..." and that "the responsibility of the corporate executive is to conduct business in accordance with the desires of the owners of the business, which generally will be to make as much money as possible while conforming to the basic rules of the society, both those embodied in law and those embodied in ethical custom." Friedman's (1970) views on the social responsibility of business may well have seemed tenable 40 years ago. According to Friedman (1970), not only was the idea of Coporate Social Responsibility (CSR) a passing fad that should not be taken seriously, but it was also "a fundamentally subversive doctrine" with heavy overtones of socialism. He argued that the responsibility for imposing taxes and the expenditure of tax proceeds is a governmental function and that when corporate executives effectively levy taxes by making expenditures to foster social objectives they are acting as civil servants and are part of a political process. The doctrine of "social responsibility" is thus inappropriate because it implies that political mechanisms are more appropriate than market mechanisms in determining the allocation of scarce resources. Friedman argued that "there is only one social responsibility of business — to use its resources and engage in activities designed to increase its profits so long as it stays within the rules of the game, which is to say, engages in open and free competition without deception or fraud."

Four decades later, companies are expected by the public to demonstrate good corporate citizenship, being accountable not only to shareholders, but also to other stakeholders and to the wider community within which they exist (Clarke, 2005, 2007; Huse, 2005; Maharaj, 2008). While Friedman (1970) did not argue against being socially responsible, viewing this as a prerogative of individuals rather than a corporate obligation, the requirement of companies in the contemporary environment is for wider accountability for their use of scarce resources and for the associated impact of their activities. They are accountable to a greater number of stakeholders and to society itself. This requirement has come into sharper focus with growing acceptance of and concerns about the inescapable realities of climate change, carbon footprints, environmental and business sustainability and the moral imperative of avoiding doing harm. In fact, we are now confronted almost daily in the media with sustainability issues and concerns.

In practical terms, all companies have to secure a franchise from society. The franchise comes partly from consumers and other pressure groups in the private sector (Clarke, 2005, 2007). Large corporations, especially those that are global in their reach, are among the heaviest consumers of resources and leave the largest footprints in the environment (McDermott, 2009). With increasing urgency around issues like resource depletion and environmental degradation, society has a keen interest in holding companies accountable for their actions when their impact reaches far beyond their physical presence and immediate activities (Valor, 2005).

But responsible business is not just about large companies — small businesses also can make a significant contribution to their own and their community's economic health and well-being by adopting sustainable operational practices and by engaging in meaningful ways with their communities. In Europe, for example, increasingly SMEs and those in sectors that are low in environmental impact (e.g. banking, securities) are now energetic reporters on their social responsibility and sustainability performance. For example, see Fortis Group, a Belgian-Dutch Group and international provider of banking and insurance services and recent acquirer of ABN-AMRO. Since 2004, Fortis has used the Global Reporting Initiative (GRI) reporting guideline criteria in developing their CSR reports (see http://www.fortis.com/sustainability/gri.asp). Such programmes range from individual corporate giving to working jointly with local government and community groups on projects that contribute to greater social and economic wealth creation.

Not only is CSR becoming established as a critical element of strategic direction and one of the main drivers of business development as well as an essential component of risk management; a greater recognition of a direct and inescapable relationship between corporate governance, corporate responsibility, and sustainable development is also emerging. Mainstream international investors are showing increased interest in socially responsible business. For instance, Goldman Sachs finds that oil and gas companies with the best track records on CSR now dominate their market. The global investment banking and securities firm has stated that these companies' attention to CSR issues will have a direct and growing impact on their long-term performance and valuation (The Global Compact, 2004).

According to Massie (2003) sustainable governance is not an option.

"It is a fundamental expectation … from governments, markets and every part of civil society. To restore [public] confidence, to build… trust, companies must commit themselves to openness, transparency and fairness. They must do this through innovations in listings exchanges, governance reform and disclosure through [organisations such as] the Global Reporting Initiative."

(Keynote Address: "Global Agenda," World Economic Forum, Annual Meeting, Davos, Switzerland). Dr Robert K. Massie, is former Executive Director, Board member and Senior Fellow of the Coalition for Environmentally Responsible Economies (Ceres), Board member and co-founder Chair (1998) of the Global Reporting Initiative. The Global Reporting Initiative is a long-term, multi-stakeholder, international process to develop and disseminate globally applicable Sustainability Reporting Guidelines. Initially published in 1982 and updated in 2006, these guidelines include reporting principles, recommended report content and a series of Triple Bottom Line (TBL) performance indicators for key sustainability issues on a sector basis. According to the Environmental Agency, UK (2004) report "There is a 'clear' link between sound environmental governance policies and practices and financial performance…evidence of higher returns, business opportunity and competitive advantage and…a marked difference between [the financial] performance of environmental leaders and laggards."

Various other international environmental and investment agencies are increasingly reporting a clear link between sound social investment and environmental governance policies and practices. Examples include the Dow Jones Sustainability Index, FTSE4Good, Corporate Responsibility Index (UK, Australia, New Zealand), and Reputex (Asia, Australia, China) who make use of reports as an indicator of a company's willingness to publicly disclose information on their social and environmental performance and to assess an organisation's publicly reported Triple Bottom line (TBL) performance. Citigroup (2006) notes from a recent report on investment in the mining industry, that "We see …a strong correlation between companies that don't report [at all] and companies that score poorly in our index." Clearly, businesses can no longer afford to ignore their corporate social responsibilities without also increasing their risk profile in areas such as reputation and market performance.

11.2 Value of CSR

The past few years have seen a rapidly increasing interest from the financial community in the broad area of sustainability and ethical investments, with growth rates in Europe and North America of up to 70 percent per year in these funds. The more professional investors enter this market, the larger is the need for active screening of portfolios and for consistent rating and benchmarking to assess the triple bottom line of companies and the implications for value creation for investors. This need prompted the launch in 1999 of the Dow Jones Sustainability Group Index (DJSGI) as the first global sustainability equity index. In its first year of operation, the concept led to a favourable risk/return profile for investors and shows better than average returns on equity, on investments and on assets for the sustainability companies assessed in the DJSGI, than in its benchmark, the Dow Jones Global Index (DJGI) (Consolandi *et al.*, 2009, Knoepfel, 2001; McPeak & Tooley, 2008).

In the UK, the July 2000 amendment to the Pensions and Investments Act has supported this trend. The Act calls for pension fund trustees to disclose in their annual statements the extent to which social, environmental or ethical considerations are taken into account in the selection, retention and realisation of investments. Estimates for the value of ethical funds in the UK range from around 54 billion pounds sterling for core funds to almost 710 billion pounds in broad funds as at end 2007 (UK Social Investment Forum, 2008). The total value of European socially responsible investments was estimated to have grown from 1 trillion Euros in 2005 to 1.6 trillion Euros in 2007 (Celent, 2007). In the US, socially screened funds were estimated at around US$2.7 trillion dollars in 2007 (Powley, 2009; Manoje, n.d.) while predictions are that such investments will reach US$3 trillion by 2011 (Celent, 2007). Consultancy firm Booz Allen has recently predicted that the Responsible Investing (RI) market will reach US$26.5 trillion worldwide in 2015 or 15–20 percent of total global assets under management. As a percentage of total assets under management, the UK is reported as having the highest proportion of RI funds invested at 20 percent while the US has just 10 percent (Powley, 2009). A large portion of these assets is screened according to simple negatives such as avoidance of companies with sales in tobacco and alcohol (Knoepfel, 2001; Michelson *et al.*, 2004) and many SRI funds have been criticised as simply matching the investment mainstream (Schwartz, cited in Powley, 2009).

The fact that mainstream investors are showing increased interest in socially responsible business and that many of the globe's largest companies are making room at board level for CSR issues is an indication that there is perceived value in doing so. Today this requires new structures for considering social and environmental questions that some boards may be ill-prepared to oversee and traditionally have not been theirs to answer. As public attention to social and environmental issues grows, boards are finding that these issues do have a material impact on performance. They affect reputation and other intangible assets and have direct bearing on financial performance.

The business case for CSR concerns not just the notion of whether or not CSR is "good," but rather, the extent to which there is a payoff from investing in socially responsible and environmental issues. In other words, it is a matter of whether it is not only in society's interest but also in the company's interest and that of shareholders to do a better job at socially responsible decision-making in CSR issues (Stenzel & Stenzel, 2005).

According to *The Economist* there are two main reasons why acting responsibly is in the company's and shareholders' interests. The first reason is that it builds trust and trust gives companies the benefit of the doubt when dealing with key stakeholders such as customers, workers and regulators, allowing them greater leeway when difficulties arise. The second reason is the edge it gives in attracting and retaining good employees and in building superior customer loyalty (*The Economist 12/14/2002*).

In the long term, companies with a sustainability focus deliver more predictable results and fewer negative surprises. Investors seek out these companies for reliable above-average growth rather than more temporary outsized performance. Increasingly, investors use corporate sustainability as a proxy for enlightened and disciplined management. The five most important factors they use when buying a stock include investment in innovation, setting high standards of corporate governance, meeting shareholders' expectations for returns, long-term growth and productivity increases, competitiveness and contributions to intellectual capital, providing industry leadership by setting standards for best practice in sustainability and maintaining superior performance, and encouraging long lasting social well-being in local and global communities, thereby securing from stakeholders a "license to operate" (Knoepfel, 2001).

11.3 CSR and Sustainability

The rapidly developing interest in CSR has led to a variety of terms and a multiplicity of definitions in the literature. The terms used, sometimes interchangeably, to describe CSR include business ethics, corporate citizenship, corporate accountability, and sustainability. Definitions and interpretations of these concepts range from a basic level of engagement to the most demanding degree of system-wide commitment (Clarke, 2007; Russell, Haigh & Griffiths, 2007; Schacter, 2005).

In defining social and environmental sustainability, Clarke (2007) notes the confusion around the various acronyms commonly associated with the idea of CSR. He observes that in some definitions, CSR is subsumed under sustainability, while in others, sustainability is included within CSR. For this reason, Kidd (1992) emphasises the importance of analysts describing clearly what is meant by "sustainability," given the existence of multiple meanings for the term based on differing but equally valid concepts.

According to Clarke (2007), part of the confusion exists around different levels of analysis where, at the highest levels, global sustainability is at issue while at lower levels, the term is used to refer to economies, societies, industries and organisations. Definitions also vary with level of commitment, ranging from basic engagement in selected activities to demonstrate "doing sustainability," to wider general commitment with a comprehensive, integrated, entity-based approach to CSR. Clarke observes that at the global level of commitment a wider definition than CSR is required, but emphasises that corporations have a role to play, beginning with the recognition of the need to sustain a balanced ecosystem.

Business for Social Responsibility defines CSR as "achieving commercial success in ways that honour ethical values and respect people, communities and the natural environment" (Schacter, 2005, p. 12). According to Schacter (2005), CSR is the notion that corporations must address social, environmental and economic demands from stakeholders, as well as financial demands from shareholders. For companies, wherever they are operating, this means attending to the legal, ethical, commercial and other expectations society has for business and making decisions that fairly address the interests and claims of all key stakeholders (Cramer & Hirschland, 2006; Schacter, 2005).

The Global Reporting Initiative's (GRI) *Sustainability Reporting Guidelines* (2002, pp. 44–45, 48) state that:

— Environmental impact refers to an organisation's impact on living and non-living natural systems, including eco-systems, land, air and water. Examples include energy use and greenhouse gas emissions.

— Economic impact means an organisation's impact both direct and indirect on the economic resources of its stakeholders and on economic systems at the local, national and global levels.
— Social impact relates to an organisation's impact on the social system within which it operates. This includes labour practices, human rights and other social issues.

These guidelines indicate the extent of sustainability reporting that is expected in triple bottom line reporting. Companies vary, however, in the degree of substance and the level of integration between financial and non-financial components of such reporting, according to their understanding of and commitment to corporate sustainability.

Russell, Haigh and Griffiths (2007, p. 42) identified four distinct categories of understanding with regard to corporate sustainability, noting that these understandings vary by organisation type according to differences in the arrangement of their governance structures:

1.   A corporation working towards long-term economic performance;
2.   A corporation working towards positive outcomes for the natural environment;
3.   A corporation that supports people and social outcomes;
4.   A corporation with a holistic, integrated approach.

11.4 CSR and Stakeholder Engagement

According to the MORI Reputation Centre (Pendleton, 2004), seven in ten British adults think industry and commerce do not pay enough attention to their social responsibilities; approximately one in five has chosen a product because of a company's ethical reputation; and conversely a similar proportion has boycotted a company's product on ethical grounds. Ipsos MORI, part of the Ipsos Group, is a leading UK research company with global reach. In a 2005 survey by Community Service Volunteers, 92 percent of employees said that they would prefer to work for a company that has an employee volunteering project than with one that does not (Business in the Community & Accenture, 2007).

It would be rare today to hear companies saying they do not care about stakeholders and expecting to get away with such disregard. Businesses recognize that they live in an increasingly interconnected, globalised world where the Internet facilitates vast global communication so that corporate interactions are constantly under close and immediate scrutiny. This has caused companies to pay closer attention to all of their stakeholders and become more sensitive to their employees, customers, suppliers, community groups, corporate governance, and shareholders.

The interrelatedness of these factors means that creating shareholder wealth requires thinking about how a company impacts society and how society's various stakeholders might react to that company's decisions. Employees can either decide to work for a given company or go elsewhere. Customers can decide to buy the company's products or the products of their competition. Regulators can decide to impose greater or lesser levels of regulation. All of these possible responses mean that improving shareholder wealth requires thinking broadly about future impacts of today's business activities and products.

It also means that in an interconnected, globalized world, a well-run company that will be a good investment for the short and the long run, will engage, disclose and act. But while some forms of engagement are superior to others, a company that does not know how to integrate issues of sustainability into its long-term strategy is increasingly likely to be considered by investors as a poorly run company that is incurring large and potentially unacceptable risks for its shareholders.

In addition, a concurrent set of forces in the form of changing stakeholder expectations can lead to trigger events or incidents ranging from boycott campaigns to investors voting on CSR-related issues at corporate annual general meetings. The interaction between a company and its stakeholders is now so critical to a business being able to fulfill its purpose and achieve its corporate goals that the consideration of potential triggers caused by changes in the external environment, specifically from the perspective of stakeholder expectations, is a crucial additional filter for business (Grayson & Hodges, 2004).

Decisions taken in response to triggers can be tactical and short-term or they can lay the foundations for forward-thinking systemic change in operational behaviour or corporate strategy. A positive approach in assessing the impact of triggers is necessary if a company wishes to turn the burden and obligation of managing corporate responsibilities into the benefits that typify the management of corporate social opportunities.

11.5 Sustainability Reporting

Reporting on sustainability activities provides a potentially important tool for companies to present the outcomes they have achieved. The preparation of the reports raises issues of importance for organisations which may not previously have been considered by their management teams and boards. The frameworks (e.g. GRI Guidelines) provide a context for dealing with non-financial performance and managing emerging issues. Reporting provides a tool for discussing sustainability issues with stakeholders and also for gaining confidence with investors, insurers and financial institutions. The report can also be a way of demonstrating a commitment to core values and providing leadership in CSR as well as a tool for identifying risk and opportunity.

Less than a decade and a half ago, business resistance to the concepts of environmental responsibility, transparency and sustainability was deep and strong. According to Massie (2002) and others (such as the SustainAbility Group) the picture is now different. SustainAbility's report "Tomorrow's Value: The Global Reporters 2006 Survey of Corporate Sustainability Reporting," asks the question: How far has the value light bulb switched on in corporate brains and boardrooms? On current evidence [from the report], the links between the evolving sustainability agenda and wider market opportunities are now better understood — with a small number of companies reporting the relationship with value in increasingly interesting ways. Partly, as a result, some parts of the financial community are gearing up their use of non-financial, extra-financial and/or sustainability disclosures to better understand emerging environmental, social and governance risks. Many of the world's corporations are now exploring, in great depth and at their own expense, their effects on biodiversity, water and energy use, and climate. In the face of this progress, however, Massie (2002) sees the danger that business, by seeming to embrace the idea of sustainability, may co-opt it and strip it of any real challenge. He argues that some corporations pursue genuine and substantive actions, while others simply re-label their existing practices as sustainable. The challenge for the environmental and investor community is to retain the right and responsibility to determine and set the standards of behaviour in CSR and sustainability.

Massie (2002) acknowledges that individual firms have gone a long way toward engaging with stakeholders, disclosing their performance through environmental and other reports and taking specific actions on matters ranging from greenhouse gas emissions to labour practices and supply chain management. Yet he notes that while they are asked to engage, disclose and act, too often companies are selective among the options. Massie (2002) points out that some engage but do not disclose. Some disclose but do not act. Some act but never engage. This means that a distinction must be made between high quality and low quality in each of these areas, since some forms of engagement and reporting are superior to others and companies need to disclose their impacts in a candid, comparable manner that is useful to investors. In some countries, such as France, England, South Africa and Australia, governments, stock exchanges and large pension funds are pressing for increased disclosure through the GRI (Massie 2002). Leading corporate sustainability reporters are recognising that the focus needs to shift beyond disclosure and reporting, to communication with key stakeholders such as financial analysts and financial institutions, and the wider innovation agenda.

Key challenges in sustainability reporting are related to core principles of balance, materiality and transparency. The role of the accounting professional is, thus, in keeping abreast of developments in reporting, as well as fuller participation in benchmarking against leading practice. At the same time, it is important to recognise the limits of entity-based reporting with regard to addressing the full extent of sustainability issues at a national and global level. It is also important that the process of reporting is not equated with "doing sustainability" and become merely a box-ticking exercise. Triple bottom line reporting does not stand alone but, rather, is a valuable tool for businesses to engage in the meaning of sustainability for them and for the world in which they operate.

11.6 Non-financial Reporting

Non-financial reporting (NFR) practices have become an integral part of the business operations of most large international corporations. Companies most directly identify CSR with a notion of corporate citizenship, tied in with stakeholder relations (especially focusing on human resources and customers), and meeting the concerns of environmental interest groups and the communities in which they operate. The overall goal is to address important and shared social and environmental issues. Companies tend to select specific CSR issues that they consider strategic — for instance, those related to health, safety and environment (e.g. carbon emissions and aiming for carbon neutrality). Companies focus on these to differentiate themselves from other socially responsible competitors in order to increase the sustainability of acquired advantages (Perrini, 2006).

Non-financial reporting can be defined as the attempt to open corporate borders to stakeholder management. NFR represents the result of companies' thoughts about what constitutes CSR and sustainability, about its importance and how it can be shared with stakeholders. These reports are a good window on companies' attitudes and priorities. For example, non-financial information on the quality of risk management, corporate governance, strategic direction, quality of management, and social and environmental performance can provide investors and other stakeholders with indications about the future potential of a company and help stakeholders better understand a company's overall performance, business strategy and growth perspective.

The GRI Guidelines 4.14 to 4.17 provide a basis for identification and selection of stakeholders with whom to engage, for the organisation's process for defining its stakeholder groups and for determining the groups with which to engage and not to engage. The Guidelines outline the specification of approaches to stakeholder engagement, including the frequency of engagement by type and group and include, but are not limited to, disclosure about engagement implemented for the purposes of preparing a sustainability report. These approaches could include surveys, focus groups, community panels, corporate advisory panels, written communication, management/union structures and other vehicles. The Guidelines urge organisations to indicate whether any of the engagement is or has been undertaken specifically as part of the report preparation process. Disclosure items also include key topics and concerns that have been raised through stakeholder engagement and how the organisation has responded to those key topics and concerns, including through its reporting.

11.6.1 *Non-Financial Reporting Methods and Measures*

According to recent studies of the nature and content of non-financial components of CSR reports, reporting practices are no longer restricted to traditional CSR-related issues, such as the description of environmental protection and employment relations, although these topics remain the most covered. For example, Perrini (2006) examined 90 companies from 150 included in the Ethical Index Euro; Makower (2006) reported the findings of a study of corporate citizenship and sustainability issues among 198 global companies; Cramer & Hirschland (2006) reported the results of a study by the UK-based SustainAbility Consultancy on triple bottom line reporting. Knoepfel (2001) outlined reporting methods of the Dow Jones Sustainability Index (DJSGI) which covers the economic, social and environmental dimensions of corporate sustainability (the triple bottom line), and identifies and ranks companies according to their corporate sustainability performance. In a yearly review, 10 percent of leading companies in each of 64 industry groups are selected for inclusion in the index. They are monitored continuously throughout the year and, if necessary, down-rated or excluded from the index. Among the sources used for the assessment and for cross-checking information are company questionnaires, company documents, publicly available information, stakeholder relations, media screening and company interviews. The selection process is externally verified and the methodology is reviewed yearly to capture the increasing knowledge and standardisation of sustainability issues and aligned with ongoing initiatives such as the GRI. The methodology is further developed on an ongoing basis to reflect increasing knowledge about the linkages between corporate sustainability performance and long-term shareholder value creation. Increasing numbers of themes and topics have been added so that non-financial reporting now often provides a complete synopsis of corporate behaviour. Reporting can be considered the most external and direct expression of managerial CSR concern, providing transparency indicators (transparency in disclosure) and merit indicators (substance in CSR and stakeholder engagement) (Perrini, 2006).

Transparency indicators include staffing, capital stock composition, salary schemes, taxes and duties, etc. By providing such information, companies aim to provide stakeholders with a clear representation of the company's situation and how it fits into their local context, as well as allowing them to recognise the company's evolutionary path. Transparency indicators are often associated with merit indicators. Merit indicators focus most directly on making it possible to express judgment on the level of CSR attained by the company, for example, descriptions of health benefits that allow assessment of the level of corporate concern about the well-being of its human resources (Perrini, 2006).

Specific stakeholder categories in CSR reports include shareholders, reporting on corporate governance, investor relations, shareholders returns, capital stock composition, rating, stock price, benefits and services for shareholders. Also reported on in stakeholder categories are the prevention of corruption and unethical behaviour and community engagement with citizens, non-government organisations and the media. In this type of reporting, community engagement and stakeholder engagement are often considered as being synonymous in that all categories of stakeholders are part of the community and can be regarded as citizens (Perrini, 2006).

Three subject areas tend to be included in the community relationship section of non-financial reports: local-global community, the media, and the virtual community. Reporting on local-global community involvement is of two kinds: active commitment in community causes and corporate giving. The areas of direct involvement that are mentioned in such reports, are numerous and varied, ranging from training and education to sports, culture and research. These social and ethical activities further indicate a company's desire to contribute proactively to its community at large. With corporate giving, firms contribute to social causes with both monetary and non-monetary resources (Perrini, 2006).

The DJSGI framework for sustainability monitoring covers illegal commercial practices (e.g. tax fraud, money laundering, antitrust, balance sheet fraud, corruption cases), human rights issues (e.g. cases involving discrimination, child labour), workforce conflicts (e.g. extensive layoffs and strikes) and large disasters or accidents (e.g. fatalities, workplace safety, technical failures, ecological disasters, product recall) (Knoepfel, 2001). Where virtual communities are included in CSR reporting, this comprises data on, and analysis of, contacts and their characteristics, and also addresses the security systems and policies created to manage the relationship with all stakeholders via the internet. The relationship with the media analyses the degree of attention received from the media concerning the company's CSR activities and initiatives, as well as the attention paid by the company to media queries (Perrini, 2006; Knoepfel, 2001). Monitoring media and stakeholder information assesses a company's ongoing involvement in critical social, economic and environmental issues and its management of these situations.

Corporate sustainability monitoring in the DJSGI also assesses the quality of management. According to Cramer and Hirschland (2006), companies' ability to manage the ever complex, ever-changing kaleidoscope of CSR issues provides an increasingly robust proxy for their management quality. As mainstream financial analysts from New York to Tokyo confirm, management quality is viewed as the single most important determinant of companies' ultimate competitiveness and financial performance (Knoepfel, 2001).

11.6.2 *Extent of Reporting*

CSR reports are usually produced as a direct result of an accountability process, representing the progression in becoming an open and responsive organisation that is able to balance the interests of various stakeholders. A company may begin to adopt a CSR approach with selected sustainability elements such as environmental reporting (e.g. on carbon emissions) and expand their commitment to CSR with more substantial reporting on a wider range of subjects and in greater depth. To the extent that these reports are part of an accountability process, they are, therefore, expressly outside-oriented, aimed at sharing information systematically about the exchange relationships between companies and their stakeholders.

Results of recent studies of CSR reports indicate as a shift from what has been identified as a "trust me" culture, in which stakeholders had implicit and explicit faith that corporations would act in their best interests, to an "involve me" culture in which companies ask their stakeholders to help them understand the right way to be effectively responsible. Although in these studies there is evidence in companies' documentation of how stakeholder concerns have been fed into corporate decision-making processes, concrete examples of when and where outcomes have been directly influenced are still scarce (Perrini, 2006).

In one such study comprising of 90 companies out of 150 included in the Ethical Index Euro, Perrini (2006) found that only 31 percent of non-financial reports were expressly stakeholder-oriented, these being organised into sections addressed to specific categories of stakeholders. Rather than by stakeholder category, the majority of reports instead present data according to triple bottom line reporting criteria (social, economic, environmental activity). Shareholders represent the missing element in non-financial reporting, with issues directly relating to shareholders the least covered in these documents.

Criticisms of the degree of substance in these reports highlight a lack of detailed description of policies for shareholder relations, with the reports less well-developed than, for example, information on employee relationships. With regard to shareholder concerns, most often reports focus on corporate governance and the existence of independent directors on the board as well as descriptions of corporate compliance with self-regulatory measures. In Perrini's (2006) study, the topics most reported on were corporate governance (45–67% of sample) and investor relations (17–45%), while the least reported on were stock price fluctuations and shareholder benefits and services (negligible — between 0–11%). Around one third of reports described the routine communication of information to shareholders — from road shows to one-on-one meetings and open-house days. Rarely are such aspects as shareholders' return, capital stock composition, rating, stock price fluctuation or benefits described in depth.

Perrini (2006) believes that the reason lies in the fragmentation that characterises reporting. Descriptions of the relationship between a company and its financial community are usually contained in other documents expressly focused on corporate governance issues. This fragmentation points to the greatest weakness of the overall reporting practice — the lack of integration between the non-financial topics and financial performance within the reports. In general, companies are perceived as failing to explain the implications of the sustainability agenda for their business prospects and in convincing shareholders of their capability to integrate social and environmental needs into day-to-day operations.

In a 2004 study by the UK-based SustainAbility consultancy, most companies were found to be failing to identify the material strategic and financial risks and opportunities that arise from the triple bottom line agenda. In turn, corporate boards are not disclosing to financial investors how environmental and social issues can provide both risks and opportunities for the companies in which they are invested. These data are not being reported despite legal requirements in many jurisdictions, suggesting that numerous companies remain unaware of the full array of risks and opportunities they face (Cramer & Hirschland, 2006).

Similarly, Perrini's (2006) study showed that there is little reporting and disclosure on the attitude of financial partners. Including banks, insurance companies and other financial partners in the reports as relevant stakeholders in the accountability and reporting process can have an impact on a company's risk profile. Account needs to be taken of the existence of a positive correlation between the quantity and quality of disclosed information about the net financial position and the cost of having access to credit. Investments in CSR activities and the ability to manage stakeholders have a direct impact on lenders and potential investors' perceptions of company risk. This can increase a firm's access to capital and disclosure can play a fundamental role in the process. The ability of a company to manage multiple stakeholder relationships decreases risk. With the visibility gained through disclosure, shareholders and financial partners can use CSR activities as a signal of a firm's successful attempts at satisfying stakeholder groups (Perrini, 2006).

In a study of 198 global companies (Makower, 2006), almost two thirds (62%) had formal programmes to manage their corporate citizenship and sustainability (CC&S) practice, while almost all the remainder (35%) conducted regular reviews of these activities, and most companies (71%) reported publicly on CC&S performance. Corporate citizenship and sustainability issues were found to be of growing importance for the majority of respondents and while large companies perceived a greater potential risk from these issues, they are struggling to find concrete ways to capitalise on their programmes in the marketplace. Despite their CC&S practice and performance, a large majority of companies (59%) in Makower's (2006) survey lacked an active strategy for developing new business opportunities arising from meeting these needs. While progress is slow, given the scope and urgency of some of the planet's social and environmental problems, four decades on from Friedman's article, there is clear support for the idea that companies can operate in ways that strengthen their various stakeholders while providing solid, sustainable returns for their shareholders (Makower, 2006). As stakeholders become more active and are able to make a greater contribution to the development and evaluation of company policy, their needs must be given priority.

To report in greater depth on these activities, a non-financial report that is a systematic and coherent forum can contribute to building a new corporate identity as an open and transparent organisation based on reciprocal listening and wide-ranging involvement. These areas are also of crucial importance to stakeholders trying to fully understand a company's state of health and its ability to create and share value and wealth. Including this information, especially in the context of multi-year trends, could allow for further opportunity to demonstrate the relationship between CSR and financial performance (Perrini, 2006).

11.7 Creating Value

While for corporations the prospect of meeting the demands put forward by organisations such as the GRI is challenging, indications are that they are taking their social and environmental responsibilities seriously and that these issues are gaining greater prominence in the business agenda. As the *Economist Intelligence Unit* states, until recently, board members often regarded corporate responsibility as a piece of rhetoric intended to placate environmentalists and human rights campaigners. But now, companies are beginning to regard corporate social responsibility as a normal facet of business and are thinking about ways to develop internal structures and processes that will emphasise it more heavily. In the not too distant future, companies that are not focusing on corporate responsibility may come to be seen as outliers (*The Economist 12/14/2002*). Without a careful process for identifying evolving social effects of tomorrow, such firms may risk their very survival.

Companies that understand environmental, social and governance issues as being central to their success and manage them effectively, create value. Rather than seeing CSR as yet another demand for compliance, companies are beginning to recognise the concept as presenting a new business model and an opportunity for building innovative forms of competitive advantage. Boards are instrumental in shaping and overseeing such strategies and active engagement around what it means to be a responsible and responsive enterprise which can strengthen the board's potential as a strategic influence on long-term value. The boards of many corporations have yet to recognise CSR as a corporate social opportunity for value creation.

Chapter 12

PUBLIC–PRIVATE PARTNERSHIP ARRANGEMENTS: PROBLEMS AND PROSPECTS

CHANDRASEKHAR KRISHNAMURTI

University of Southern Queensland

ALIREZA TOURANI-RAD

Auckland University of Technology

12.1 Introduction

What should be private and what should be public has been an exigent question facing societies for centuries. In recent years, a new organizational arrangement with a mixed mode of ownership between public and private sectors has become popular: Public-Private Partnerships (PPPs). Contracting between government and the private sector is currently regarded as a common form of public service delivery (Brown and Pitoski, 2003). While PPP arrangements, depending on their scope, are diverse and used differently throughout the world, a general definition could be the following: "the government has a business relationship, it is long-term with risks and returns being shared and that private business becomes involved in financing, designing, constructing, owning or operating public facilities or services" (Hodge, 2000). PPPs offer government new means to finance projects, build infrastructure, deliver services and improve the efficiency of public sector organizations leading to substantial economic gains. It is estimated that even a relatively small improvement in operational efficiency of about 5 percent could free up 1 percent to 5 percent of the GDP of a developing country's resources.

The main difference between PPPs and traditional procurement is that with PPPs the private sector returns are related to service outcomes and performance of the assets over the life of the contract. The private sector is responsible not only for asset delivery, but also for overall project administration and implementation, and successful operations (Davis and Eustice, 2005). De Palma *et al.* (2009) argue that there is a strong economic justification for close cooperation between the public and the private sectors, especially when: (a) PPPs offer governments new means to finance projects, build infrastructure and deliver services as the public sector could leverage its limited resources; (b) the public sector wants to benefit from the knowledge and expertise of the private sector, which could provide better management in some cases; and (c) the private and the public sectors would try to limit their exposure to the risks involved in large-scale projects by allocating these risks among themselves or transferring them to a third party.

As for the popularity of PPP arrangements, a recent study reports that in Europe, over a thousand PPP contracts were entered into during the 1990–2005 period, accounting for the investment of over 200 billion Euros.[1] PPP arrangements have been utilised for building schools, hospitals, roads, sanitation facilities and sports stadia, to name a few. PPPs are prevalent in both developed and developing countries. According to the World Bank, the private sector financed 20 percent of infrastructure investments in developing countries during the 1990s, amounting to US$850 billion in monetary terms. In the US, PPP agreements have been employed in the context of the privatization of utility companies in the eighties and toll roads in the nineties. However, the employment of PPPs has accelerated in recent years, especially from 2005 onwards (de Palma *et al.*, 2009).

Despite the growth and attractiveness of privately financed infrastructure projects, there have been several high profile cases where such arrangements have collapsed. More recently, as a result of the financial crisis, many PPP projects have been negatively impacted. We, therefore, consider it important and relevant to understand global PPP experiences and draw some useful lessons from the past. We believe that the successful implementation of a PPP project involving the use of highly complex financial arrangements is predicated on understanding some of the key risk and governance issues.

The remainder of this chapter proceeds as follows. In Section 2, we discuss contract types prevalent under PPP arrangements. This is followed by a discussion of the determinants of PPP arrangements in Section 3. Section 4 summarises country level experience under PPP frameworks and covers the working of PPP arrangements in different sectors. Section 5 investigates the

---

[1] Delivering the PPP Promise: A Review of PPP Issues and Activity. *A Price Waterhouse Coopers Report.*

impact of the recent financial crisis on PPPs. Section 6 analyses the problems and risks of PPP engagements. The final section contains our conclusions and a discussion on the future prospects for PPPs.

12.2 Contractual Types in Public-Private Partnerships

In order to reduce the gap between the huge costs involved in public infrastructure projects and the available financial resources, PPP arrangements are increasingly being employed to deliver new funding for infrastructure projects. The overriding argument, of course, should be that where PPPs are the most suitable arrangement, they should deliver better value for money than alternative arrangements. Contractual arrangements are an important component of a successfully implemented PPP project. There are several variations of PPP arrangements which include combinations of design, ownership, operation, and asset transfer, and they do not conform to one organisational type (Pollitt, 2003). European public authorities, for instance, use the concession system by which it grants specific rights to an organisation to construct, refurbish, maintain and operate an infrastructure project for a given period. It is called a concession when the payment received by a company is in the form of a fee paid mainly by users; and it is called a public/private partnership contract when payment is made mainly by a public authority. The concession arrangement is tantamount to a contract under which a public authority entrusts a company with making the required investments to generate and operate the services at its own cost and risk. There are two salient features associated with the concession system: *transfer of risk* and the notion of *contract globality*. The concession arrangement involves the *transfer of risk* from the concession authority to the concession company. The notion of *contract globality* relates to a number of functions (construction, financing, exploitation, maintenance, etc.) over a long period (averaging from 10 to 75 years). In this respect, the concession arrangement is different from a contract for infrastructure construction which is concerned only with the task of construction and not the subsequent operation. A concession contract typically involves, in addition to the construction work, a long-term service agreement to operate the infrastructure.

Based on the Canadian Council for Public-Private Partnership definitions, we describe commonly prevalent arrangements:

Design-Build (DB): The private sector is charged with designing and building the infrastructure in accordance with performance specifications of the public sector, generally at a fixed price, the risk of cost overruns being transferred to the private sector.

Design-Build-Finance-Operate (DBFO): The private sector is entrusted with the designing, financing, and constructing of a new facility under a long-term lease. The private partner operates the facility and transfers it to the public sector at the end of the lease term.

Build-Own-Operate (BOO): The private sector finances, builds, owns and operates a service in perpetuity. The constraints are specified in an agreement entered into by the private sector entity with the regulatory authority.

Build-Own-Operate-Transfer (BOOT): The private entity is granted a franchise to finance, design, build, and operate a facility (and to charge a user fee) for a specified period after which ownership is transferred to the public sector.

Build-Transfer-Operate (BTO): The private entity funds and constructs the infrastructure, but transfers ownership to the public authority immediately after the completion of construction. The private entity is then allowed to operate the infrastructure for a limited period after which all rights are transferred to the public sector.

Lease Contract: The public authority grants a private entity a lease to operate the service for a given period. Typically, the lessee makes payments to the public authority but is allowed to charge a fee to the users.

Based on a report by the IMF (Hammami *et al.*, 2006), the most popular contract used is the Build-Own-Operate (BOO) model, representing close to 40 percent of total contracts, and the Build-Own-Transfer (BOT) being the next most popular contract. Figure 12.1 shows a graphic representation of the number of projects by types of contracts.

12.3 Determinants of PPPs

What determines the extent of private sector participation in ventures with the public sector? Hammami, Ruhashyankiko and Yehoue (2006) (hereafter HRY) examine this issue in a cross-country context with a special focus on developing countries. HRY identify five channels that affect the prevalence of PPP arrangements in infrastructure taking into account different incentives and constraints faced by the public sector and the private sector. These are *government constraints, market conditions and macroeconomic policies, political environment, institutional quality and legal system,* and *prior experience.* Using the World Bank's private participation in infrastructure (PPI) database covering the 1990–2003 period, HRY study the relative importance of the different channels in four sectors — Energy, Telecommunication, Transportation and Water.

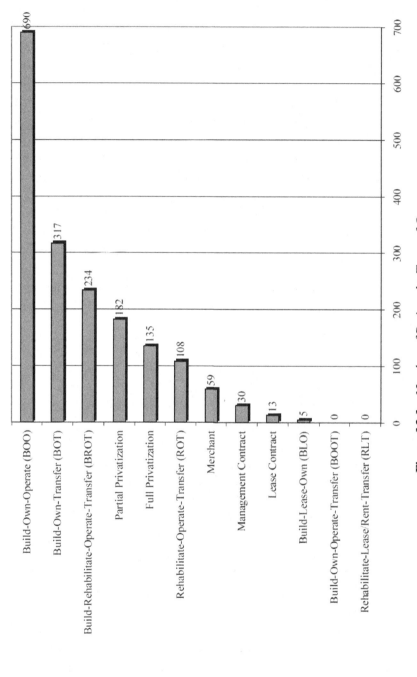

Figure 12.1   Number of Projects by Types of Contract.

Government Constraints

PPP arrangements permit the public sector to consider projects that are otherwise unaffordable. PPPs can facilitate the closing of the infrastructure gap between what the government can fund and what people require by allowing the public sector to leverage its financial resources using the private sector as an intermediary. Employing PPPs also enable the public sector to allocate scarce public funds to worthy causes that are commercially unviable. Empirically, HRY show that both the number of PPP investments and the investment in PPP as a percentage of GDP increase directly with total debt as a percentage of exports.

Countries which lack external sources of revenue such as oil, other natural resources, or aid, tend periodically to experience severe financial crises. Therefore, they tend to be more responsive to alternate means of financing infrastructure investments. They are thus more willing to engage in PPP arrangements. HRY show that the number of PPP investments is decreasing in fuel exports (as a percentage of merchandise exports). This relationship is particularly strong for PPP projects in transportation and energy infrastructure. Apparently, this is because fuel producers and exporters may already have built their infrastructure before 1990. Alternately, governments without access to external resources tend to resort to PPPs in order to erect their energy related infrastructure.

Market Conditions and Macroeconomic Policies

A prerequisite for the successful execution of PPP arrangements is the existence of incentives for the private sector to engage in PPP contracts. As a result, market conditions and stable macroeconomic policies are expected to play a vital role. The existence of a large market with sufficient purchasing power is likely to be a precondition for successful implementation of PPP engagements. Thus, we expect PPPs to be much more common in large markets where demand and purchasing power are greater. Another requirement for attracting private investors is the presence of stable macroeconomic conditions, adequate tariff regimes, reasonable economic policies, and a track record for honouring commitments. Thus, PPPs are expected to be more prevalent in countries with stable macroeconomic policies, ceteris paribus.

As expected, empirical results show that market size plays a significant role in explaining the popularity of PPP programmes in telecommunications, transportation and water sectors. In addition to market size, market demand as proxied by population and real GDP per capita also play a critical role in determining the number of PPP programmes in the transportation sector.

Political Environment

Other things being equal, ethnically divided countries require a larger number of infrastructure projects for public goods and services. These needs arise due to the differing individual preferences of people belonging to different ethnic groups. As the number of projects increase, there is increasing financial pressure on the public sector for resources. This necessitates private sector participation. Thus, PPP arrangements would be more common in countries with ethnic fractionalization. It is also to be expected that governments that are more willing to adapt to market-oriented policies are more likely to engage in PPPs. Finally, we expect widespread use of PPPs in politically stable countries with accountable governments.

The empirical work of HRY demonstrates the importance of the political environment in PPP arrangements. They show that centre-right governments tend to engage more in PPPs in the energy sector. Also, market-friendly governments are more likely to employ PPP arrangements in the telecommunication sector. Interestingly, HRY find that ethnically fractionalized societies with centre-left governments are more apt to PPPs in the transportation sector.

Institutional Quality and Legal System

Since PPP arrangements are contractual agreements, their sustainability is contingent on the regulatory environment. Therefore, strong institutions and effective rule of law will be associated with higher occurrences of PPP arrangements. Empirical evidence on the impact of the legal channel is weaker than that of other channels. The rule of law is significant only for transportation PPPs.

Prior Experience

The final channel that affects the utilization of PPP arrangements is a government's reputation and private sector experience. Prior experience in executing PPP projects should critically impact successful future arrangements. Thus, we expect PPP arrangements to be higher in countries with prior PPP experience. This belief is supported empirically (Hammami *et al.*, 2006).

12.4 PPP Contracts by Country and Sectors

The most active PPP markets in the world are Australia, Canada, Japan, UK and USA. Figure 12.2 shows the sectoral activity in some of the major countries where PPP arrangements are prevalent.

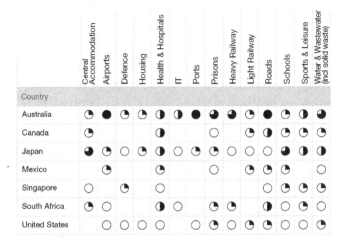

Figure 12.2   Selected PPP Activity by Country and Sector.
Source: Pricewaterhouse Coopers, October 2005.

We highlight some of major arrangements in countries using PPP below.

12.4.1 *Australia*

PPPs are in widespread use in Australia for delivering economic and social infrastructure. In the transportation sector, toll roads such as the A$2.5 billion Eastlink in Melbourne, the A$1.5 billion Western Sydney Orbital, and Brisbane Airtrain are prominent examples. The flagship social infrastructure schemes utilising PPP are the A$250 million Brisbane Education and Training Precinct and the A$350 million Royal Women's Hospital. Victoria and New South Wales are at the forefront of PPP use, followed by Queensland, Western Australia and the Northern Territories. In general, the State's Treasury manages the PPP policy and guides and oversees the projects. Australia is the originator of the ABN model, where investment bank-led consortia win most deals, take on most of the equity and specify the terms under which subcontractors participate and underwrite the bonds for financing the project.

12.4.2 *Canada*

PPP arrangements have gathered significant momentum in the provinces of Alberta, Ontario, and British Columbia. In the transportation sector, the Confederation Bridge and the Kicking Horse/Trans Canada Highway are the most well-known examples utilising PPP arrangements. Dartmouth Water and Wind Power are eminent examples of PPP in the utility sector. UNBC Northern Sports Centre, Nova Scotia Schools, and Paramedic HQ are the prominent instances of social infrastructure PPPs delivered in Canada. The Canadian Council for Public-Private Partnerships provides institutional support for interested counterparties. The demand for PPP arrangements is likely to be strong in the future given estimates of a current infrastructure backlog of US$45 billion which is projected to increase to over US$100 billion by 2027.

12.4.3 *United States*

Political support for PPPs remains strong in the US due to tight state budgets and public opposition to tax increases. Road and rail infrastructure have dominated the executed projects. Notable projects include the sale of Chicago Skyway to a consortium led by Macquarie, the Comprehensive Development Agreement for the Trans-Texas Corridor and the sale of Dulles Greenway to Macquarie. Oregon, Georgia, New Jersey, New York, and Virginia are some of the states engaged in launching new projects under the PPP framework. More recently, an important initiative under consideration is the use of PPPs in the financial sector. The US Department of Treasury is contemplating the application of the Public-Private Investment Program (PPIP) to tackle the challenge of legacy assets and improve balance sheets of financial institutions. It is hoped that this application of the PPP concept will ensure that credit is available to households and businesses. The scheme is expected to utilize US$75 to US$100 billion in capital from different sources to generate up to US$1 trillion over time for the purchase of legacy assets (De Palma *et al.*, 2009).

12.4.4 *Europe*

PPP arrangements are also widely prevalent in EU countries as summarised pictorially in Figure 12.3. The UK is the forerunner of PPP arrangements in several sectors. According to the UK Treasury, over 450 deals with a cumulative value of more than £35 billion were signed between 1999 and 2004, while 118 deals were closed between 2004 and 2005. The Midland Expressway and the Ministry of Defence Military Accommodation are significant instances of projects executed within the PPP framework.

PPP arrangements are popular across a range of sectors such as social infrastructure, transportation and utilities. PPP in social infrastructure comprises projects in accommodation, defence, education, health, leisure, justice, and social housing. The typical PPP projects in the transportation sector include

Figure 12.3 shows PPP arrangements by country and sector across the following sectors: Central Accommodation, Airports, Defence, Housing, Health & Hospitals, IT, Ports, Prisons, Heavy Railway, Light Railway, Roads, Schools, Sports & Leisure, Water & Wastewater (incl solid waste).

Legend

- ○ Discussions ongoing
- ◔ Projects in procurement
- ◑ Many procured projects, some projects closed
- ◕ Substantial number of closed projects
- ● Substantial number of closed projects, majority of them in operation

† Procurement activity in these sectors relates to traditional style concession contracts

Member States

Country	Central Accommodation	Airports	Defence	Housing	Health & Hospitals	IT	Ports	Prisons	Heavy Railway	Light Railway	Roads	Schools	Sports & Leisure	Water & Wastewater (incl solid waste)
Austria	○	○			◔	○		○	◔		◔	○		○
Belgium		◔		◔				◔	○		◔	○		◔
Denmark	◔							○		○	○	◔	○	
Finland			○		○			○	○		◔	◔		○
France	◔	○	○		◑		○	◔	◑	◑†	●†		◕	●†
Germany	◑	○	◑		◔	◔		◑	○	○	◑	◕	◔	◑
Greece	◔	●			○					◕	○	◑		
Ireland	○			◑	◔			○		◔	◕	◑		◕
Italy	◑	◔		◔	◕		◔	○		◑	◕		◕	◕
Luxembourg		○			◔									
Netherlands	◔		◔	○	○		○	◔	◑		◑	◑		◕
Norway (not EU)	○		○		◔			○			◑	◔	○	
Portugal	○	○		◔	◔	◔	◑		◑		●	●		●
Spain	◔	◔			◑		●	◔	○	◕	●	○	○	◕
Sweden		○		○				○	◑	○				
UK	●	●	●	●	●	●	●		●		●	●	●	●

New Member States

Country	Central Accommodation	Airports	Defence	Housing	Health & Hospitals	IT	Ports	Prisons	Heavy Railway	Light Railway	Roads	Schools	Sports & Leisure	Water & Wastewater (incl solid waste)
Cyprus		◔					◔				◔			◕
Czech Republic	○	◔	○	○				○	○	○	◔	○	○	◕
Estonia			○	◔	○	○				○	○	◔		
Hungary	○	○		◑	◔	◔		◔		○	◑	◑	◔	
Latvia	○			○	○			○			○	○		○
Lithuania					○				○	○		○	◔	
Malta				○	◔	◔	○				◔	○	◔	
Poland	○	○		○		◔			○	○	◑		○	◑
Slovakia	○										○			○
Slovenia														◑

Acceding and Candidate Countries

Country	Central Accommodation	Airports	Defence	Housing	Health & Hospitals	IT	Ports	Prisons	Heavy Railway	Light Railway	Roads	Schools	Sports & Leisure	Water & Wastewater (incl solid waste)
Bulgaria		◔†				◔†			◔					◕
Romania	○		◔	◔							◑		◔	◕
Turkey	◑		○	○					○	○	○			◑

Figure 12.3 PPP Arrangements by Country and Sector in Europe.

Source: Pricewaterhouse Coopers, October 2005.

airports, bridges and tunnels, rail/light rail, ports and roads. PPP projects in utilities encompass the energy, water, wastewater and waste management sub-sectors. Figure 12.3 summarises the PPP opportunities in the various sectors.

We expand on the opportunities and challenges in each of these sectors below.

12.4.5 *Transport*

Internationally, the transportation sector has been the largest recipient of investment under PPP arrangements. PPPs are common in delivering infrastructure services associated with roads, bridges, tunnels, airports, railways and ports. PPP arrangements in the road and airport sector are elaborated below:

Roads

Australia's road sector was one of the first to use PPPs to deliver highway infrastructure. Sydney now has the world's largest network of urban toll roads. Spain and Italy have developed considerable experience in using PPPs in the road sector. In the US, over US$21 billion is devoted to highway projects under PPP arrangements, with California, Florida and Virginia accounting for 50 percent of the total invested funds.

Airports

Airports are complex enterprises which provide highly technical aeronautical and commercial services. Some of the services are natural monopolies while others permit vigorous competition. Traditionally, airports have been owned and operated by federal or local governments since airport infrastructure is generally believed to be a public utility. However, as governments have faced resource constraints, the practice of engaging private sector participation has grown in recent years. Furthermore, efficiency considerations have also accelerated the tendency to incorporate a role for the private sector in airport services.

The UK is the forerunner of privatization in the airport sector. The privatization of BAA (British Airports Authority) in 1987 started this trend, which has since grown rapidly in several parts of the world. The private sector plays a major role in the provision of airport infrastructure in Australia, Austria (Vienna), Denmark (Copenhagen), Germany (Frankfurt, Hamburg), India (Bangalore, Hyderabad), Italy (Naples, Rome), and New Zealand. In 2008, the United States joined these countries with the announcement by mayor Richard Daley of Chicago of a landmark deal to privatize the Midway Airport in Chicago for a sum of US$2.52 billion.

Privatization of airports is in progress in several Latin American countries such as Argentina, Chile, Costa Rica and Dominican Republic. During the 1990–2005 period, 38 low and middle income countries entered into more than 100 contracts ranging from short-term management contracts to long-term BOT (build-operate-transfer) arrangements, divestitures and concessions.

Concessions, accounting for more than 40 percent of airport contracts and 60 percent of the value of investment commitments have remained the most prevalent form of private participation in airport infrastructure in developing countries. Initially employed in Latin America and Sub-Saharan Africa during the 1990s, the concession model has now spread to Eastern Europe, Central and South Asia. Greenfield projects have been the second most frequent contract type accounting for 28 percent of the contracts and 20 percent of investment commitments and are especially popular in East Asia, Eastern Europe and Central Asia. Management and lease contracts have increased in popularity, growing from about 7 percent of transactions in late nineties to 20 percent during the 2002–2005 period. Several countries including Bangladesh, China, Djibouti, and Egypt have used management contracts since 2002. Divestitures have become less popular and declined from 17 percent of transactions in the nineties to less than 10 percent during the period of 2002–2005.

12.4.6 *Utilities*

Most of the PPP arrangements have taken place in the sub-sectors of Water and Sanitation and Power. According to World Bank estimates, the power sector accounts for a total private investment of US$213 billion during the 1990–2001 period. The bulk of these projects were executed in Latin America an East Asia.

Water and Sanitation management is one of the fast growing areas for PPPs. PPP projects in the Australian states of Victoria and New South Wales account for about US$132 million. In Canada, several municipalities engaged PPPs in this sub-sector. In Europe, the largest water PPP is in the Netherlands with a 1.58 billion Euro contract awarded by the Water Board of Delft.

12.4.7 *Social Infrastructure*

PPP arrangements are prevalent in Education, Hospitals, Public Housing, Defense and Prisons. We describe the intricacies of the working of PPPs in each of the sub-sectors below.

Education

Typically, the private sector finances, designs, constructs and operates a public school facility under a contract with the government for a given period such as 20 years. At the end of the concession period, the ownership of the facility is transferred to the government. A common alternative PPP arrangement in education to that detailed above entails private sector investment in school infrastructure and delivers related non-core services such as cleaning, food services, and transport. The government takes care of the core service of teaching. The UK is the forerunner of PPPs in schools. A total of nearly 100 deals in education worth £3.5 billion have been signed. During the next decade, a total investment of £37 billion is envisaged to refurbish and construct new buildings. Australia has followed the UK lead in PPP school projects in New South Wales. Encouraged by its positive experience, new projects worth A$3.7 billion are being executed.

Hospitals

The growing demand for health care infrastructure has necessitated private participation. In general, a private consortium designs, builds, owns and operates a hospital for a fixed period of time and leases it back to the government. The UK National Health Service has extensively used PPPs since 1987 with 130 privately funded projects as compared to 12 publicly funded ones. The public service provides clinical services and some of the cleaning services while the private sector constructs and operates the facilities. Portugal has also engaged PPPs in its hospitals. Ireland is another entrant in this area.

Public Housing

With over two years experience, the Netherlands is the pioneer of PPP in public housing. Joint ventures are commonly used. Typically, the ownership is transferred after a period of 5 to 10 years. Australia and Ireland have conducted pilot projects utilising PPP arrangements for public housing.

Defence

Equipment maintenance and installation, supply chain integration, operational support, specialised training, and real estate management are some of the common projects under the purview of PPP arrangements. The UK Ministry of Defense has utilised PPP arrangements in over 56 projects involving £4.65 billion. Germany and the US are other countries with PPPs in place for managing some of their defense projects.

Prisons

Australia, the US and the UK use PPP arrangements to house their inmates. The private sector builds and operates these facilities and leases them back to the government for a fixed period of time. The benefits are shorter construction times and lower running costs.

12.5 Recent Financial Crisis and Its Impact on PPPs

A recent report by the World Bank Public-Private Infrastructure Advisory Facility (PPIAF) clearly indicates that the financial crisis has affected new PPP projects, especially in emerging markets. More than 30 percent of 316 projects monitored between July 2008 and February 2009 reported delays due to the financial crisis, mainly in larger projects in excess of US$250 million, with the majority of delays experienced in the energy and transport sectors. A recent survey carried out by Pricewaterhouse Coopers of banks which are active in PPP transactions, showed that unless there were strong client relationship and refinancing opportunities, there is a significant shift in the preference of financial institutions from long-term maturity bonds to short-term ones. Moreover, due to capital constraints, banks increasingly are unable and/or unwilling to enter into long-term contacts (Davies, 2009).

A major financial and economic crisis could potentially affect all the parties involved in a PPP project, including the relevant government agency and the private sector partner responsible for an asset's construction, operation, financing and service delivery, as well as direct beneficiaries of the services (tax payers and users). Burger *et al.* (2009) contend that the recent financial crisis impacted PPPs both in financial and real terms. According to Burger *et al.* (2009) the likely effects on PPPs among others which could be transmitted through multiple channels are the availability and cost of credit and lower economic growth, First, while currently the level of interest rates is historically at low levels in developed countries, sovereign and corporate bond rates have been on the rise. Moreover, in both developed and emerging markets spreads between corporate and sovereign rates have increased since mid 2008. The resulting increase in the cost of credit has an effect on projects in the pipeline phase as well as on existing projects with refinancing needs (most likely those in the construction phase) and/or variable interest payments.

Second, in most countries, the financial institutions have been severely impacted resulting in a reduction in the availability of credit. "Banks are wary of extending loans and the downgrading of monocline insurance companies (who guaranteed the repayment of infrastructure bonds at a fee) has shrunk the bond market for infrastructure projects" (Burger *et al.*, 2009). The most affected PPPs are those in the pipeline phase. Those projects in progress, both in the construction and operational phases, will already have obtained for a large part the credit needed through agreements with financial institutions. Third, the impact of lower demand for services on the revenue/cash flows will have severe consequences for the debt servicing capacity and ultimate success of PPP projects. This endangers not only those projects in the pipeline phase but also those in operational phase. The latter PPPs, especially those that are dependent on direct user charges, will experience a reduction in cash flows. As for the former PPPs, the recession could affect their future cash flow estimates and their viability as a whole.

Burger *et al.* (2009) provide a list of intervention measures by governments to attenuate the impact of this crisis or to improve the attractiveness of PPPs for private investors. These include concession extension, tax breaks, subsidies and grants, minimum revenue guarantees, repayment of all or part of the debt, extra standing loan facilities, and ultimately step-in rights where, in the case of private sector failure, a government could step in and re-tender the PPP contract or could take over the entire operation.

12.6 Risk, Financing and Governance in PPPs

Despite the widespread acceptance of the PPP model for executing projects which have traditionally been under the purview of the public sector, we cannot conclude that all is well. Frequently, in the past decade or so, there has been an increasing number of renegotiated contracts. Andres *et al.* (2008) points to the fact that about 56 percent of the PPP contracts in the transportation sector and 81 percent in the water sector in Latin America were renegotiated in the period of 1990–2004. What are the lessons we can draw from the last decade of experience? We first highlight a few major cases of failure to depict the critical factors that are quintessential for the successful execution of projects under PPPs and then provide a broad set of issues faced by both public and private partners in PPP arrangements.

The first case deals with the privatization of water services in Cochabamba, the third largest city of Bolivia. This resulted in substantial increases in the price of water and led to massive protests between January and April 2000 that led to civil unrest and a state of emergency. The concession agreement was thereafter terminated. Going into the reasons behind the failure of the PPP in this case, it appears that a lack of transparency was the major issue.

The second case relates to the power crisis in California stemming from failed privatisation. High energy prices resulting from the strategic behaviour of participants exploiting their market position was the major contributing factor behind the problem. This case highlights the role of market and regulatory design.

The third case pertains to the Brisbane Airtrain in Australia. The PPP project involved setting up a new rail line to link Brisbane airport, the city and to the Gold Coast. Although the construction and operation costs were within budget, the project was plagued by significantly low ridership levels. This resulted in revenue shortfalls forcing a restructuring of the debt and equity. Clearly, private investors overestimated the demand. It was a public gain but a private loss. This case emphasises the role of risk. As long as risk is shared in an efficient manner and the outcome is transparent to all parties, PPP arrangements can still work.

The last case involves a PPP in the school sector in Nova Scotia, Canada. In this case, the problems were driven by cost overruns as a result of 'gold plating' compounded by a weak government and problems with the contract terms. Once again, the role of regulatory supervision and clear specification of contracts is underscored.

Based on a recent study by the IMF (Andres *et al.*, 2008), we can generalize the following limitations in PPP arrangements. There has been only partial interest by the private sector, concentrated in geographical regions and specific sectors, most notably energy, telecommunication and transport. There has been limited sustainability of some contractual arrangements for private participation. Private investment in infrastructure projects has led to unexpected fiscal costs due to the provision of poorly conceived guarantees and risk assignments in the concession contracts. Governments have had to provide the private sector with generous assurance schemes to attract them into the new investment environment or to compensate them for various types of project risk. From the private sector's point of view, participation in PPP projects has not always been as profitable as originally hoped for (Andres *et al.*, 2008).

Hodge (2004) indicates that the return on investment in public or private sectors alike should be a function of the inherent risk and that this should be incorporated in the design of the contract. Hodge argues that this issue is currently not being fully addressed. Risk transfer from one party to another or risk sharing over the life of a project under a PPP contract is different from the risk of traditional public infrastructure projects where the government takes over all the risk apart from the risk of construction borne by the contractors. In PPPs, risk transferred to private parties is paid for by the government. Alternatively, if risks are borne by the government, this should result in a cheaper up-front project price.

Harris (2003) contends that well-designed private participation plans could produce real improvements in the quality and quantity of infrastructure services, as well as major benefits for the efficiency of provisions. However, "private infrastructure schemes that fail to see commercial risk shifted to the private sector will bring fewer benefits, if any. Risks have to be shifted to the private sector, either through competition for consumers, or through effective regulatory frameworks" (Harris, 2003, p. 27). Indeed, a major benefit of PPP arrangements is the transfer of risk from the public sector to the private sector. According to a UK study, risk transfer accounts for 60 percent of the total cost savings attributed to PPPs. (Anderson and LSE Enterprise, 2000, cited in Hodge, 2004).

Another important factor is the financing aspect of PPP companies and the related agency costs. Especially significant are the exclusive governance issues in debt and equity financing in regulated PPP organisations. In the standard agent-principal finance literature, there exists a conflict of interest between the lenders and the shareholders. The company is viewed as the agent in the use of the funds raised by the loan from the principal, i.e. the lender. The company is required to use the funds prudently and pay back its loan. However, as discussed by Scheinkestel (1997), due to various layers of debt financing and the involvement of various financial institutions, the distinction between debt and equity in PPP organisations can become blurred. This would lead to higher agency costs for debt. In addition, in PPP organisations, the agency costs of equity could be higher. This is mainly due to managerial incentives that could lead to expropriation of shareholders' wealth. Alexander and Mayer (1997), for example, investigate the influence the market for corporate control could exert over the incentive for management to achieve efficiency in PPPs. They find the traditional channels, such as threat of bankruptcy or hostile takeovers or direct shareholder actions, are somehow weakened by the existence of institutional barriers and regulatory approaches. This is largely due to the fact that the public sectors are required to ensure security of supply of goods and services. This makes it difficult to allow any interruption resulting from these traditional incentives for efficiency.

Using a survey on debt and equity arrangements in regulated PPP organisations across different infrastructure sectors and developing markets, Devapriya (2006) conducts empirical tests and finds that debt has not been an effective apparatus for controlling managers' behaviour. He argues that managerial decisions on debt and equity arrangements in the capital structure are impacted by not only regulatory risks but also institutional risks to which PPP organisations comprising private ownership and private operations are exposed. In regulated PPP organisations, debt is often shared by banks as subordinate financiers. Thus, his findings suggest that tying the performance of managers to the financial structure of regulated PPP organisation could be undermined, particularly in developing and emerging economies. He contends that these governance issues need to be considered in developing alternative benchmarks to weigh up the efficiency of PPPs under different regulatory regimes to ensure better investment performance in developing country environments.

12.7 Prospects for PPPs

Besides enhancing efficiencies and utilising the expertise of private enterprise, PPPs serve to release financial capital for funding other core economic and social programs. Research by McKinsey and Company (Cheatham and Oblin, 2007) indicates that PPPs in transportation infrastructure alone (including airports, roads, rail and seaports) are likely to be worth US$330 billion from 2005 to 2010. The rail subsector dominates the projections (44%) followed by the roads subsector (44%). Although opportunities for PPPs exist in continental Europe, the biggest investment opportunities are in the US, the UK, China and South Korea. The most stable and attractive opportunities are present in markets that have a large number of feasible investments in the pipeline and possess features termed by McKinsey as "PPP readiness." A country's readiness for PPP is characterized by the extent of a government's commitment to public-private arrangements. This includes clarity of vision, transparency, legal and institutional frameworks, clear parameters and stakeholders' perceptions. Countries with a successful track record of execution score higher in the PPP Readiness Index. The best locations according to Cheatham and Oblin (2007) are Australia, South Korea, UK, and US, China and Germany. India represents emerging opportunities that are, however, riddled with substantial risks. Russia, Thailand, and Brazil are grouped into the "Proceed with Caution" category with respect to PPP Readiness.

The first key lesson learnt from past PPP experiences, according to Harris (2003) is that governments must address the key issue of the pricing of infrastructure services. Second, governments must allow sufficient flexibility in service options to increase coverage of services to the poor. Third, competition should be allowed to play a role where possible to help reduce prices and improve access. Fourth, the quality of regulation is critical. Fifth, financing issues must be addressed. Finally, politics is important. It is vital to build consensus and ensure trust and support between the partners for key PPP projects.

Chapter 13

STRENGTHENING DEMOCRACY THROUGH GOVERNANCE IN AFRICA — THE ROLE OF THE UN GLOBAL COMPACT

DANIEL MALAN

University of Stellenbosch

13.1 Introduction

The African continent does not have a good track record in either democracy or governance. Global rankings usually put Africa at the bottom of the scale on both accounts, and these shortcomings are often used to explain Africa's lack of development, extreme poverty and inability to attract foreign investment. Discussions about democracy usually focus almost exclusively on the role of governments, while governance is interpreted more broadly to include both the private and public sector. The link between democracy and governance has been explored in detail before. As early as 1991, a conference on this topic was held in Ota, Nigeria, and more recently, the Ibrahim Index of African Governance has focused extensively on governance issues that are very closely related to the concept of democracy.

In his opening remarks at the Nigerian conference in 1991, then-President Olusegun Obasanjo stated: 'Africans are now clamouring for greater responsiveness of their political leaderships, respect for human rights, accountability and a two-way channel of information between the people and their leadership. These related issues of governance can only be guaranteed under a pluralistic political framework' (Obasanjo, 1991, p. 22). Almost 20 years later, the 2008 Ibrahim Index of African Governance (Mo Ibrahim Foundation, 2008) addresses many of the same ideals in its ranking of African states:

> "All citizens of all countries desire to be governed well. That is what citizens want from the nation-states in which they live. Thus, nation-states in the modern world are responsible for the delivery of essential political goods to their inhabitants. That is their purpose, and has been their central legitimate justification since at least the seventeenth century. The essential political goods can be summarized and gathered under five categories: Safety and Security; Rule of Law, Transparency, and Corruption; Participation and Human Rights; Sustainable Economic Opportunity; and Human Development. Together, these five categories of political goods epitomize the performance of any government, at any level" (Mo Ibrahim Foundation, 2008, p. 1).

The purpose of this chapter is not to investigate the state of democracy on the African continent. The desirability of a democratic system is taken as a given without delving into the complexities of different definitions, democratic models, etc. The primary objective is to investigate ways in which private corporations can make a contribution to strengthen democracy. More specifically, the focus is on how the United Nations Global Compact can be used as a framework for private corporations to improve their corporate responsibility and corporate governance and, thereby, make a contribution to the strengthening of democracy.

Following a few introductory remarks about the concepts of democracy, a number of direct as well as indirect links between the two concepts will be explored. Thereafter, the United Nations Global Compact and its uptake on the African continent will be introduced. The King Reports on Corporate Governance (South Africa) and the Global Reporting Initiative will also be discussed briefly. Finally, a basic model will be described that attempts to explain the various links between the concepts and sectors. It is hoped that this model could assist corporations in their strategic thinking about the value of corporate social responsibility and corporate governance.

13.2 Conceptual Clarification

13.2.1 *Democracy*

Democracy is an elusive and often abused concept. Historically, democracy was defined in contrast to other forms of government such as a monarchy, aristocracy and oligarchy, but nowadays it is often compared with the more familiar examples of authoritarian regimes or theocracies (government by religious leaders). Abraham Lincoln defined democracy as a government of the people, by the people, for the people. One modern definition of democracy is that it is a 'form of government, where a constitution guarantees basic personal and political rights, fair and free elections, and independent courts of law.'[1] The following key elements of democracy are described on the web site, www.democracy-building.info:

- A guarantee of basic human rights;
- Separation of powers between government (executive power), parliament (legislative power) and courts of law (judicial power);
- Freedom of opinion;
- Religious liberty;
- Equal right to vote (one person, one vote);
- Good governance (a focus on public interest and absence of corruption).

It is interesting to see how these key elements are also reflected in the definition of corporate governance, discussed below.

13.2.2 *Corporate Governance*

As is the case with democracy, there are many different definitions of corporate governance. One of the most useful and succinct definitions of corporate governance has been provided by the OECD: corporate governance is the way in which organizations are directed and controlled. Garratt (2007) provides an extensive discussion of the history of the term "governance," tracing it back to its Greek root of *kubernetes*, and describes how it has found expression in modern English through the concepts of governance, government and cybernetics.

A big problem with governance standards is that there is often an overemphasis on the control aspects; in other words, corporations go into compliance mode and simply look for boxes to tick in order to fulfill the letter, but not the spirit, of a particular governance standard. Once the performance aspect of governance is understood, compliance does not necessarily take a back seat, but takes up its rightful place as one — and not the only element — of a governance system. The focus on performance enables a more strategic understanding of governance, which then makes it far easier for the board to become supportive — or even excited — about its governance function.

---

[1] http://www.democracy-building.info/definition-democracy.html, accessed 1 July 2009.

Hilb (2008) describes the difference between the shareholder-focused (Anglo-American) model of governance and the relationship-based model (e.g. Germany and Japan) which emphasizes stakeholder interests. Hilb (2008) proposes a third "new corporate governance" that integrates the strengths of both models. Any model of corporate governance that acknowledges the importance of ethical principles and responsibilities to stakeholders other than shareholders would support the idea of the three fundamental corporate governance values of honesty or openness, transparency and accountability (Garratt, 2003).

It is interesting to note that these values are also in line with the basic definition of democracy that has been discussed earlier. Openness is important in terms of freedom of opinion, the protection of human rights and religious liberty; transparency can be linked to the public interest and absence of corruption; whilst accountability relates to the separation of powers as well as the electoral system of one person, one vote.

It is, therefore, not unreasonable to conclude that — as a minimum — the concepts of democracy and governance are interrelated and that — possibly — one could view them as mutually reinforcing.

13.3 The Direct Link

The obvious link between democracy and governance can be stated as follows: in a democracy, there should be high levels of public sector governance, and this commitment to good governance should also filter through to the private sector, through regulation but also in the interaction between the public and private sectors. One of the most notable results should be low levels of corruption.

It is to be expected that government regulation will have a direct impact on corporate behavior. If the legal and regulatory framework of a country supports international conventions on, for example, human rights and anti-corruption standards, there will automatically be higher corporate performance levels in these areas in such countries. By implication, it also becomes much easier for corporations in such countries to support voluntary codes such as the UN Global Compact (discussed later), because compliance with many of the principles will be obligatory in any case.

Table 13.1 compares the results of selected African countries in terms of their performance in the 2008 Ibrahim Index of African Governance (Mo Ibrahim Foundation, 2008), which will be discussed later, and Transparency International's 2009 Global Corruption Barometer (Transparency International, 2009). Although not conclusive, there seems to be some correlation between the

Table 13.1 Comparison between Transparency International Index and 2008 Ibrahim Index of African Governance.

Country	Country governance	Business corruption	Parliamentary corruption
Ghana	1	4	2
Senegal	2	3	4
Kenya	3	6	7
Uganda	4	1	3
Zambia	5	2	1
Sierra Leone	6	8	6
Liberia	7	7	8
Nigeria	8	5	5

countries' governance ranking and perceived corruption in the business and parliamentary domains.

It could, therefore, be argued that if corporations improve their governance, it will result in lower levels of business corruption in a particular country. Since corruption in the private sector is very often connected to public sector corruption (e.g. through the payment of bribes by the private sector to public sector procurement officials), an improvement on the private sector side will inevitably filter through to the public sector. This will improve perceptions about public sector corruption, lead to improved governance ratings and ultimately impact positively on perceptions about democracy through an emphasis on fairness and the public interest.

13.4 The Indirect Links

There are two indirect ways in which good governance will improve democratic processes. These relate firstly to an internal perspective which results in the encouragement of the principles of democracy within corporations, and secondly, an external perspective where the activities of corporations themselves can have a direct impact on democratic processes in a particular country.

13.4.1 *The Internal Perspective*

Through their internal policies and activities, corporations can demonstrate a commitment to governance and democracy. At a very basic level, voters can be compared with shareholders and the principle of "one share, one vote" will give an indication of the commitment to internal democracy. Do shareholders have the ability to participate fully in decision making processes, or are these processes steamrolled by unresponsive boards of directors or powerful and non-communicating chief executive officers, or both? If minority share-holders are sidelined and voting processes undermined through the introduction of different classes of shares that create the impression of shareholder rights only, the corporation fails the test of fair treatment and its responsibility to act in the interest of all its shareholders. If senior manage-ment acts in an autocratic manner, the basic rights of shareholders and other stakeholders are undermined.

Another analogy in terms of the democratic model is that one would like to see a clear separation of powers between the board and management. The private sector hierarchy of shareholders, board of directors and executive management is mirrored to some extent by the public sector system of voters, parliament and cabinet. One of the problems of democracy is short-termism — the inclination of elected officials to disregard the bigger picture in favour of the next election date. This problem also finds its way into the corporation, where executive managers and directors often focus only on the short term, predominantly because their remuneration is linked to the quarterly or annual results of the corporation.

The issue of how the corporation treats its workforce is also relevant here. Do workers have the right to organize, to elect representatives and to engage with management about issues that are important to them? Transparent and fair processes will demonstrate a commitment to democracy, and they have to take place within the context of recognition of all stakeholder interests and rights, including those of shareholders. The corporation cannot simply acknowledge any group as legitimate and with an equal right to be engaged — there has to be a clear process of stakeholder analysis and stakeholder engagement. This process can be compared to the democratic processes of determining legitimate and reasonable requirements for being placed on the voters' roll (e.g. age and citizenship).

13.4.2 *The External Perspective*

Secondly, the more sensitive question should be asked: does the corporation have a moral responsibility to intervene in political processes to further democracy, or should it remove itself as far as possible from the political process? Corporations respond in different ways to this question, mostly by making a bland statement that they do not get involved in the political process, but merely monitor and engage on certain issues (e.g. regulation and taxation) where they feel that there is a direct impact on the ability of the corporation to operate in a particular environment. However, it is very clear that many corporations — especially large multinational corporations operating in developing countries — often go very far beyond this restrained method of engagement. In some cases, corporations assume governmental functions, e.g. through the provision of basic infrastructure, medical and educational services, and sometimes they even have to make use of military assistance from governments to be able to operate.

Elsewhere (Malan, 2005), I have proposed the following basic model (see Figure 13.1) to explain decisions corporations need to make about their social and political involvement. Corporations have choices with regards to the levels of social and political involvement at home but, more specifically, in host countries. Depending on the combination of the two elements, they can be classified as either corporate citizens, colonialists, tourists, or activists.

Corporate citizens can be described as responsible corporations with a desire to make a real contribution to the countries and communities within which they operate. Corporate colonialists are corporations that pursue policies of economic colonialism — exploiting the resources and cheap labour of host countries without making any real contribution to the economic wellbeing of their hosts. The early charter companies from the British Empire and the Netherlands provide good examples of corporate colonialists. One of the best examples is the British South Africa Company of Cecil John Rhodes, which was formed in the second half of the 19th century with the blessing of the British government. This company had its own army and police force — even its own flag and logo with the motto 'Justice, Commerce, Freedom.' Litvin provides a fascinating account of the activities of Rhodes' company, and quotes him after one of the military battles between the company and the Matabele tribe in what was later to become Rhodesia: "'You should kill all you can; it serves as a lesson

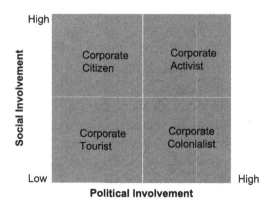

Figure 13.1   Understanding the Interaction between Social and Political Involvement.

to them when they talk things over at night. They count up the killed, ... and they begin to fear you," Rhodes explained to an officer after one battle' (Litvin, 2004, p. 65). Corporate tourists can be described as corporations that are "only visiting," i.e. scouting for opportunities and making modest investments without real commitment. When things go wrong, they can easily leave and find other opportunities elsewhere. Corporate activists combine social and political involvement, with the understanding that political involvement will be in support of democracy, human rights or other plausible ideals and not to look after narrow commercial interests. There are not many examples of corporate activists, with the early period of The Body Shop International and the aggressive campaigns in support of human rights and against animal testing being, perhaps, the best example of a true corporate activist. Because the line between the corporation's own commercial interests and broader political ideals is often not very clear, it makes this position even more difficult to define.[2]

The way in which corporations make decisions about such involvement depends on their approach to the very evasive term of corporate social responsibility (CSR). Jonker laments the lack of a theoretical basis underpinning the CSR movement, and suggests that this is why the debate about CSR lacks realism and is often "evangelical" (Jonker, 2003, p. 427). Jonker concludes that the social responsibility of corporations should become a business strategy: "a way of determining direction and creating and maintaining relationships and structures that enhance performance" (Jonker, 2003, p. 437). This strategic role is also emphasized by Porter and Kramer:

> "Boosting social and economic conditions in developing countries can create more productive locations for a company's operations as well as new markets for its products. Indeed, we are learning that the most effective method of addressing many of the world's pressing problems is often to mobilize the corporate sector in ways that benefit both societies and companies" (Porter & Kramer, 2003, p. 33).

However, there are certain constraints on what corporations can and cannot do. Millstein and Katsh argue that the large size of many corporations "brings with it discretionary powers which can be — and are being — undemocratically used in disregard of societal objectives and the public interest" (Millstein and Katsh, 2003, p. 16). They list various legal (corporate, state and administrative), tax and economic constraints, and then proceed to discuss the constraints of social forces on corporate conduct. The most important social

---

[2] For a more detailed discussion of these four roles, see the original article (Malan, 2005).

forces discussed by Millstein and Katsh include public opinion, news and broadcast media, industry associations, employees, shareholders and institutional investors, the intellectual community and public interest groups (Millstein & Katsh, 2003, pp. 231–251). These social constraints, as described by Millstein & Katsh, can also be viewed as a list of key stakeholders, and corporations that engage in effective stakeholder engagement will realize that they should not merely be viewed as constraints, but could be regarded as opportunities for corporations to improve their reputation and performance.

Dealing with these constraints is not easy, especially since many corporations struggle to understand the business case, and in almost all cases, they lack the ability or the inclination to understand the theory, as pointed out by Jonker (2003). The easiest way forward is to look for a standard or a code that a corporation can subscribe to. This provides an immediate framework, and enables a corporation to leapfrog much of the conceptual and theoretical processes that early pioneers had to go through. Sethi discusses the benefits of such codes:

"From the [multi-national corporation's] viewpoint, codes provide the corporation with a voluntary and more flexible approach to addressing some of society's concerns. They create mechanisms through which a corporation can fashion solutions that are focused, cognizant of the corporation's special needs and public concerns, and economically efficient. They also have the benefit of anticipating societal concerns in general and those of important stakeholders in particular. They engender public trust through the reputation effect, while avoiding being tainted by the actions of other companies" (Sethi, 2003, p. 81).

He describes three such initiatives in detail: the Sullivan Principles in South Africa, the code of the Fair Labor Association and the United Nations Global Compact. It is to this last initiative that we turn in the next section.

13.5 The UN Global Compact

In 1999, Kofi Annan, then secretary general of the United Nations, introduced the concept of a Global Compact to multinational corporations gathered at the World Economic Forum in Davos, Switzerland. On the 31st of January 1999, Annan stated the following:

"Globalization is a fact of life. But I believe we have underestimated its fragility. The problem is this. The spread of markets outpaces the ability of societies and their political systems to adjust to them, let alone to guide the course they take. History teaches us that such an imbalance between the

economic, social and political realms can never be sustained for very long ...
I call on you — individually through your firms, and collectively through your
business associations — to embrace, support and enact a set of core values in
the areas of human rights, labour standards, and environmental practices."[3]

Although this call was not meant to result in a formal structure, the response
from the business sector was so encouraging that the concept was formalized
soon afterwards. Today, the Global Compact is the world's largest voluntary
corporate citizenship initiative (Hall, 2007, p. 30) and describes itself as "a
framework for businesses that are committed to aligning their operations and
strategies with 10 universally accepted principles in the areas of human rights,
labour, the environment and anti-corruption"[4] (www.unglobalcompact.org).
The 10 Global Compact principles are:

- Human Rights

  o Principle 1: Businesses should support and respect the protection of
    internationally proclaimed human rights; and
  o Principle 2: make sure that they are not complicit in human rights abuses.

- Labour Standards

  o Principle 3: Businesses should uphold the freedom of association and
    the effective recognition of the right to collective bargaining;
  o Principle 4: the elimination of all forms of forced and compulsory
    labour;
  o Principle 5: the effective abolition of child labour; and
  o Principle 6: the elimination of discrimination in respect of employment
    and occupation.

- Environment

  o Principle 7: Businesses should support a precautionary approach to
    environmental challenges;
  o Principle 8: undertake initiatives to promote greater environmental
    responsibility; and
  o Principle 9: encourage the development and diffusion of environmen-
    tally friendly technologies.

---

[3] http://www.un.org/News/ossg/sg/stories/statments_search_full.asp?statID=22, accessed
25 September 2007.
[4] The Global Compact initially comprised a set of 9 principles (environmental, human rights
and social), with the 10th principle added a few years later as a result of consistent lobbying by
anti-corruption agencies and initiatives.

- Anti-Corruption
  - o Principle 10: Businesses should work against corruption in all its forms, including extortion and bribery.

According to Williams (Williams, 2007, p. 619), the

"Global Compact offers a forum under the umbrella of the United Nations with its visibility, global reach and convening power where some of the best members of civil society — non-government organizations, academic and public policy institutions, individual companies, business associations and labor representatives — can come together to discuss the changing role of business and its moral purpose."

13.5.1 *African participation in the Global Compact*

Since its launch on 26 July 2000, more than 8,000 participants from 130 countries (including more than 8,000 businesses) have signed up to the Global Compact.[5] African participation in the Global Compact got off to a slow start with one solitary participant signing up in 2000. The South African electricity utility corporation, Eskom, became the first African corporation to sign up on day one: 26 July 2000. More than a year elapsed before the second African signatory joined in August 2001 — once again it was a South African corporation (Sasol). Again, there was a waiting period of more than a year before the third participant, the Coca-Cola Bottling Company of Ghana, joined on 31 August 2002. There were three new joiners in 2003, five in 2004 and only two in 2005, before a sudden surge of 32 corporations in 2006 and 26 new joiners in 2007. On 11 April 2008, 17 South African corporations signed up simultaneously at an event in Johannesburg, coordinated by the National Business Initiative, the South African focal point of the Global Compact. At the end of June 2009, the total number of African company participants stood at 104. At this time, there were also 153 African SME participants (according to the Global Compact, companies are classified as entities with 250 employees or more, while entities with less than 250 employees are classified as Small and Medium Enterprises, or SMEs.

---

[5]http://www.unglobalcompact.org/ParticipantsAndStakeholders/index.html, accessed 8 June 2010. On this date, there were 8,291 participants, including 6,015 businesses of which 2,058 were listed as companies (i.e. more than 250 employees).

Table 13.2 African UNGC signatories per country.

Country	Number joined
South Africa	23
Kenya	12
Nigeria	11
Mauritius	10
Ghana	8
Zambia	6
Namibia	5
Malawi	4
Mozambique	4
Sudan	4
Côte d'Ivoire	3
Cameroon	2
Congo, The Democratic Republic of	2
Gabon	2
Madagascar	2
Senegal	2
Uganda	2
Cape Verde	1
Lesotho	1
Total	104

In terms of country participation, South Africa is currently the leader with 22 percent of all participants. As can be seen in Table 13.2, South Africa, Kenya, Nigeria and Mauritius jointly provide more than 50 percent of all African participants.

13.5.2 *Communicating on Progress*

Once a corporation has signed up as a member of the Global Compact, certain conditions must be met, including the need to publish in its annual report or similar public corporate report (e.g. sustainability report) a description of the ways in which it is supporting the Global Compact and its principles — this document is referred to as a Communication on Progress (CoP). The CoP is the most important indicator (at least to external stakeholders) of how successful members of the Global Compact have been in supporting its principles. It remains a subjective account, even if verified externally, but does provide useful insight into the activities of Global Compact signatories, and is probably the most important way in which stakeholders can assess the performance of a participating corporation.

The Global Compact rule in terms of an initial CoP reads as follows:

"Company participants are required to submit a first CoP within two years from the date of joining the Global Compact. Should a company fail to meet this initial submission deadline, they will be marked as non-communicating in the participant database of the Global Compact website. Furthermore, should a company also miss the second CoP deadline after an additional year, the company will be removed from the Global Compact database of active participants and listed as inactive on the Global Compact website."[6]

The way in which the CoP system is administered has created the impression amongst some stakeholders that the Global Compact is a compliance-based system. Although the CoP system is there to provide some consistency and accountability, it should not be viewed as a compliance-based initiative. In the words of Georg Kell, CEO of the Global Compact:

"the Compact never pretended to [be compliance-based], nor was it designed as one. The fact that some observers continue to criticize the Compact for something it never pretended to be is remarkable. Ever since the inaugural launch on 26 July 2000, we have been very clear that the Compact is about learning, dialogue and partnerships. The UN does not endorse companies or their performance. Rather, it seeks to promote collaborative efforts, transparency and public accountability."[7]

Of some concern is the fact that 27 percent of all African signatories have been listed as non-communicating by the Global Compact Office. Approximately 50 percent of corporations (those that joined after June 2007) must publish a CoP before 31 December 2009. This means that relatively few corporations are communicating regularly, and unfortunately, the quality of a large number of CoPs is also questionable.

The non-communicating companies are listed in Table 13.3.

It should be acknowledged that CoPs by themselves cannot provide a comprehensive indication of the quality of participation in the Global Compact. Even though it is relatively easy to highlight examples of bad practice, comparisons can be dangerous. By way of example, both FirstRand's action of merely copying the Global Compact principles in the inside back cover of its sustainability report and presenting that as its CoP, and Sun and

---

[6] http://www.unglobalcompact.org/COP/FAQ.html#7, accessed 29 February 2008.

[7] http://www.ethicalcorp.com/content.asp?ContentID=5898&newsletter=24, accessed 13 May 2008.

Table 13.3   Non-communicating African companies (1 July 2009).

Communicating company	Country
African Petroleum PLC	Nigeria
Celtel Zambia	Zambia
Chemical and Allied Products Plc — CAP Plc	Nigeria
Coca-Cola Bottling Company of Ghana Ltd	Ghana
Cybersonic Constructions Lda.	Mozambique
Dunlop Nigeria PLC	Nigeria
Floribis S.A.R.L.	Madagascar
Ghana Bauxite Company Ltd.	Ghana
Golden Gate Group of Companies	Nigeria
Haco Industries — K — LTD	Kenya
Lafarge Zambia — Chilanga Cement Plc	Zambia
Limbe Leaf Tobacco Company Limited	Malawi
Magadi Soda Company	Kenya
MTN Cameroon	Cameroon
National Airports Corporation Limited	Zambia
Nestle Cote d'Ivoire	Côte d'Ivoire
Nestle Ghana Limited	Ghana
Nestle Nigeria Plc	Nigeria
Nitrogen Chemicals of Zambia Limited	Zambia
Pharmakina s.c.a.r.l.	Congo, The Democratic Republic of
Safetech Services Inter Ltd.	Malawi
Satemwa Tea Estates	Malawi
UAC of Nigeria Plc	Nigeria
UNAD — United D'appi Pour Le Developpement Integral	Congo, The Democratic Republic of
Unilever Ghana Limited	Ghana
Zambia National Building Society	Zambia
Zesco Limited	Zambia

Sand's submission of a photocopied newspaper article are problematic. However, FirstRand's report and the newspaper article contain important information on relevant practices, which could be linked to Global Compact principles, even though not explicitly stated. It could even be argued that Rand Water's "CoP" that does not contain a single reference to the Compact contains relevant information in terms of the environmental principle.

A key challenge in moving forward is to focus on "localization" practices, e.g. to identify the extent to which corporations allow relevant interpretations of the principles to fit local conditions and different standards that might be regarded as acceptable at the local level. A theoretical framework that could assist in this regard is Integrative Social Contracts Theory (ISCT). ISCT was developed by Tom Donaldson and Thomas Dunfee from Wharton University to provide guidance on ethical issues in international business (including social and political involvement of corporations), and in essence, suggests that there is an absolute moral threshold (so-called hyper norms) that would apply anywhere in the world, that large corporations should have respect for local customs and traditions and can, therefore, negotiate micro contracts without transgressing this moral threshold, and finally, that context matters when deciding between right and wrong.[8]

In terms of ISCT, the ten principles of the Global Compact can be regarded as hyper norms — they are based on widely accepted international norms and enjoy a very high level of support in terms of country legislation and international conventions. In addition, the application of the ten principles should be seen within the context of micro contracts — the activities that corporations report on are always context specific. In the case of large multinational corporations, one would expect to see differences in global and local reporting practices, hopefully, with a consistency between local applications and the ten principles. In the case of local corporations (i.e. corporations without a global presence and/or SMEs), one would expect to see local interpretations of the ten principles. By way of example, it would be largely ineffectual for any corporation to simply re-affirm a commitment to human rights or fair labour conditions, without answering the question: What does this principle mean for our corporation in our current location within the current timeframe? For Tata Zambia to merely state that they have a disciplinary code, therefore, does not add any real value to the discussion about their contribution to the anti-corruption principle. Compare this approach to that of Coca-Cola in Ghana, which provides detailed information on the code in an earlier CoP, as well as local audit findings and reports on business fraud. This local information is also demonstrated clearly by Coca-Cola in terms of the environmental responsibility principle — this is information with which stakeholders can identify:

"[The Coca-Cola Bottling Company of Ghana] has invested about $2 million in waste water treatment in two plant operations in Ghana. We are the only bottling plant in Ghana with a functioning wastewater treatment system ... We provide financial support for the protection of Sakumono Ramsar Site into which our discharge flows. We have adopted the La Pleasure Beach, a large span of beach in Accra, as a Coca-Cola "Clean Zone." The project is a campaign to

---

[8] For a more detailed discussion of ISCT, see *Ties that Bind: A Social Contracts Approach to Business Ethics* (Donaldson & Dunfee, 1999).

keep the beach as a model of environmental cleanliness to serve as a model for all other beaches in Ghana. We participated in ECOFEST 2004 — an ecological preservation festival. We used the platform to create awareness on need to treat waste water before disposal into natural water bodies. The effluent discharged from our facilities support aquatic life. EPA monthly monitors all discharges from the facilities and reports on findings. Summonses are issued if violations or non-compliances are noted. There have been no summonses since the installation of the Waste Water Treatment plants."

It should be noted that it is potentially dangerous for corporations to merely submit their annual report (or even an annual sustainability report) as a CoP. Although there are excellent tools and templates available on the Global Compact web site (www.unglobalcompact.org), even advice on how to link with the Global Reporting Initiative's G3 Reporting Guidelines, there is no substitute for a detailed, internal process to critically think through the requirements and implications of the principles for individual firms. Just as with sustainability reporting in general, the danger is that corporations will spend more time on trying to find things to report on, than spending time to do meaningful things that could be reported on.

The jury is still out on the success of the Global Compact in terms of providing the framework that corporations require to fully understand and fulfill their CSR responsibilities. There is the danger that signatories will use the Global Compact merely as a public relations exercise. Sethi describes the early trend where corporations with reputational problems supported the initiative and "were only too eager to gain respect by hanging onto Kofi Annan's coattails" (Sethi, 2003, p. 125). At this stage, the advantages of support for the Global Compact seem to outweigh the disadvantages by far. Although there are many non-communicating and, no doubt, some non-supportive participants in the initiative, the majority of participants have found a comprehensive and structured framework to improve their corporate social responsibility activities. This will have a positive impact on governance practices and, ultimately, also on many of the elements which support democracy, wherever these corporations operate.

13.6 Other Relevant Standards

13.6.1 *The Ibrahim Index*

The ability of corporations to adhere to their own corporate values, and to any voluntary codes they might have subscribed to, will be influenced by the countries within which they operate. As was mentioned in the introduction, the African continent does not have a good track record in terms of democracy or governance. Someone that is single-handedly trying to make a difference is Mo Ibrahim, entrepreneur and self-made billionaire, who is making a huge contribution through his somewhat controversial leadership prize worth millions of dollars which is awarded to retired African politicians who demonstrate support for sound governance, as well as his Ibrahim Index on African governance. This index ranks 48 African countries in terms of the quality of their governance. The criteria that are used to develop the rankings focus on the following main categories: Safety and Security; Rule of Law, Transparency, and Corruption; Participation and Human Rights; Sustainable Economic Opportunity; and Human Development.

The aggregated results of the 2009 Index are displayed in Table 13.4.

Table 13.4 2009 Ibrahim Index on African Governance.

Rank	Country	Score
1	Mauritius	82.83
2	Cape Verde	78.01
3	Seychelles	77.13
4	Botswana	73.59
5	South Africa	69.44
6	Namibia	68.81
7	Ghana	65.96
8	Tunisia	65.81
9	Lesotho	61.18
10	Sao Tome and Principe	60.23
11	Egypt	60.09
12	Tanzania	59.24
13	Madagascar	58.37
14	Algeria	58.36
15	Benin	58.20
16	Morrocco	57.83
17	Senegal	55.98
18	Zambia	55.30
19	Gambia	55.13
20	Mali	54.55
21	Gabon	53.92
22	Kenya	53.74
23	Libya	53.69
24	Uganda	53.57
25	Malawi	53.03

(Continued)

Table 13.4   (*Continued*).

Rank	Country	Score
26	Mozambique	52.38
27	Burkina Faso	51.58
28	Mauritania	50.57
29	Swaziland	49.43
30	Sierra Leone	48.91
31	Comoros	48.58
32	Rwanda	48.53
33	Cameroon	47
34	Niger	46.59
35	Nigeria	46.46
36	Djibouti	46.04
37	Ethiopia	45.59
38	Burundi	45.27
39	Liberia	44.92
40	Guinea-Bissau	43.50
41	Congo	42.79
42	Angola	41.02
43	Togo	40.83
44	Guinea	40.41
45	Equatorial Guinea	39.39
46	Eritrea	36.96
47	Cote d'Ivoire	36.61
48	Central African Republic	35

13.6.2 *The King Reports on Corporate Governance*

The King Reports on Corporate Governance contain non-legislated codes developed by the King Committee on Corporate Governance, a committee that was established by the Institute of Directors of Southern Africa. Named after the chairperson of the committee, Judge Mervyn King, the so-called King I (1994), King II (2004) and King III (2009) reports have received international recognition for being forward-thinking and innovative (du Plessis *et al.*, 2005), especially in terms of recognizing sustainability and corporate citizenship as key requirements for good corporate governance. There was also substantial progress from King I to King III in terms of how ethics was handled. Whereas King I merely required a code of ethics, King II emphasized the need to demonstrate a commitment to organizational integrity and King III focused on the need for ethics practices to be integrated within the corporation.

King III was launched on 1 September 2009 and has been adopted as a listing requirement by the Johannesburg Stock Exchange, as was the case with King II. Corporations that comply with King III will, therefore, be obliged to demonstrate ethical behavior and corporate responsibility, and the positive effects of such compliance will be felt in South Africa as well as in all countries where South African corporations operate.

13.6.3 *The Global Reporting Initiative*

Measurement and reporting remain critical from a compliance as well as stakeholder engagement point of view. Just as the Global Compact requires Communications on Progress, stakeholders legitimately expect corporations to report on their social, economic and environmental performance against the so-called triple bottom line. The term that is used most often for this activity is sustainability reporting, and has clear implications for how corporations report on their governance processes.

The Global Reporting Initiative (GRI) is currently leading the field in terms of reporting guidelines for sustainability reporting. The mission of the GRI is to develop and globally disseminate applicable sustainability reporting guidelines for voluntary use by organisations reporting on the economic, environmental, and social dimensions of their activities, products and services (GRI website: http://www.globalreporting.org). This standard is important within the context of governance, since the elements of corporate social responsibility and sustainability are regarded as integral to sound corporate governance. The need to accurately measure and report on any activity is a key requirement for transparency, hence, the importance of this standard. The GRI embraces the principles of transparency, inclusiveness, auditability, completeness, relevance, sustainability context, accuracy, neutrality, comparability, clarity and timeliness. In 2006, the GRI published its G3 Reporting Guidelines, comprising of reporting principles, reporting guidance, a set of standard disclosures on strategy, company profile and management approach, as well as specific economic, social and environmental performance indicators. According to the GRI, these elements are all considered to be equally important.

13.7 A Proposed Conceptual Model

In a world that increasingly focuses on a broader range of stakeholders instead of only shareholders, a more democratic approach to the corporation will be advantageous — not only to the corporation itself — but also to the broader society. Internally, a democratic approach will lead to satisfied and more loyal

Table 13.5 Governance Values, Elements of Democracy, UN Global Campact Framework, Global Reporting Initiative Framework.

Openness/honesty	Freedom of opinion Religious liberty Basic human rights	Focus on all aspects of corporate citizenship, including human rights, environment and labour	Honest assessment and reporting of performance
Transparency	Serving the public interest Absence of corruption	Regular communications on progress Focus on anti-corruption	Making available relevant information, including positive and negative data
Accountability	Acknowledgement of stakeholders (voters, shareholders) Fair treatment (one person, one vote; one share, one vote)	CEO has to publicly commit support for the Global Compact	Reporting on relevant governance structures, policies and procedures

employees, shareholders and other stakeholders, and externally, this will make a contribution to more democratic societies by minimizing corruption in the public sector and putting pressure on governments to treat its citizens with respect and fairness. To make sense of all of this, corporations need to understand how the concepts and the values that underpin them support each other. The model displayed below might be useful (Table 13.5).

13.8 Conclusion

Just as citizens desire to be governed well (Mo Ibrahim Foundation, 2008, p. 1), corporations desire to operate in well-governed countries. With the exception of those unscrupulous corporations that benefit from corruption, bribery, fraud and other forms of misconduct, the majority of corporations benefit from democracy where fairness, transparency and basic rights are respected. By demonstrating support for good governance, corporations can make both direct and indirect contributions to democracy, and once involved in such a virtuous cycle, can once again benefit from the positive climate they co-create with governments and other stakeholders. The UN Global Compact has its limitations, but provides both a framework and range of role models to assist committed corporations to make such contributions.

Chapter 14

PERFORMANCE GOVERNANCE: STRATEGY, STRUCTURE AND SYSTEMS — THE THREE DIMENSIONS OF BOARD PERFORMANCE

RAM RAMAKRISHNAN

Organisation Development Pte Ltd

14.1 Performing Boards Understand Expectations

Boards are formed to oversee performance; to ensure that stakeholder expectations are met or exceeded while complying with the legal, statutory and regulatory norms within the society in which they operate. A company is incorporated to deliver sustained returns to the shareholders and other stakeholders. Social equity requires that this performance is achieved within the regulatory statutes. However, compliance is a social necessity and not the sole reason for boards to exist. Regulation and laws are essential to ensure that the people who 'steer' the business do so within socially accepted norms. Essentially, the performance-compliance nexus is the basis of civilized society where the common good is placed above individual greed, by law or by convention. Thus, both compliance and performance are necessary.

In the context of this chapter, performance is defined as the ability of an organization to deliver results at or beyond stakeholder expectations. Thus, boards need to understand that stakeholder expectations go beyond compliance, requiring a return on investment or creation of value, which means that boards must ensure the firm is not only legally compliant, but also delivers on performance. As part of effective strategic management and planning for performance, there is an active and ongoing need to understand the market, customers, employees, suppliers, environmental and societal expectations — both current expectations and also as these are likely to evolve in the near to medium term. The time frame for strategy formulation depends on the nature and situational dynamics of the business and should be such that it is sufficient for the directors to plan, initiate and ensure that the required resources to implement the strategy are available at or slightly ahead of the need. This chapter suggests that there is a need for boards to switch from a focus on mere oversight for compliance to active involvement in delivering firm performance and outlines a structured approach to developing high performance in the boardroom.

Performance governance is about setting the direction for the firm based on meeting an array of expectations. This requires alignment of the firm's competencies to deliver according to market expectations, linking the actual results to the desired outcomes based on feedback, in real time. Having worked at understanding factors such as market trends, technology development and customer expectations, strategy can then be developed and translated into a set of policies or guidelines that can help to establish the intended performance trajectory for the organization and align the key objectives.

14.1.1 *The Rule of Three*

Effective governance, in practice, can be encapsulated in three interconnected sets of three dimensions: the first set comprising the performance dimension, the conformance dimension, the compliance dimension and within which sits the second set of dimensions of strategy, structure and systems, supported by the third set of dimensions: policy, people, and processes. The first set of dimensions: performance, conformance and, compliance, are the three dimensions of governance. They represent the thinking for execution dimension. The second set of dimensions: strategy, structure and systems, are the three dimensions of board performance. These three dimensions encapsulate the three main duties of the board and reflect the planning for execution element of the board's working. The third set of dimensions: people, policy and processes, are the three dimensions that facilitate board performance through implementing strategy and constitute the three main tasks which the directors have to execute, on an ongoing basis, to ensure quality performance, conformance and compliance.

Directing the development of strategy, developing appropriate structures, and laying out working systems are the three dimensions on which boards work to deliver sustained performance. When combined and integrated in an ethical manner, the three S dimensions may deliver sustained value to the firm's stakeholders. The 3Ss — strategy, structure, and systems — derive from and impact the functioning of the board and what the directors perceive and do as their job.

For coherent development and cogent deployment of strategy, a board must approve a suitable structure for decision-making that will provide the links through which the strategy will be deployed. But practical execution of strategy also requires a system comprising a collection of relevant procedures to power the linkages. Systems ensure the communication of the necessary information to make informed decisions, delivering this in a timely manner and at the appropriate level to achieve the strategic objectives. Strategy thus needs a structure which requires a system. Strategy transfers through policy into structures consisting of people who take decisions based on communication which is generated through the set of systems and procedures.

Understanding expectations and translating them into tangible, deliverable outcomes or results requires that the 3Ss be invoked to ensure performance. The 3Ss aid effective strategy definition and set the stage for strategy oriented execution. However, even though a firm has executed the 3Ss well, there is no guarantee that on this basis alone the firm will deliver sustained performance. To translate the conceptual content of strategy into practice, the 3Ss are guided by 3Ps — policy, people and processes. The 3Ps can aid efficient delivery of the outcomes as defined by the 3Ss. The 3Ps form the main tasks of the board and define the board's supervisory role.

Together, the 3Ss and 3Ps establish the boundaries within which the firm should work, to perform, comply and conform. Boards and directors need to develop a way of working for a practical manifestation of the benefits of performance oriented governance to the firm. Because the 3S–3P dimensions are central to performance governance, they are the focus of the remainder of the chapter and are explained in further detail below.

14.2 The 3 Dimensions of Governance

As stated above, the performance dimension, the conformance dimension, and the compliance dimension, together with the two nested sets of dimensions (the 3Ss and 3Ps) constitute the three dimensions of the overall 3D model (see Figure 14.1) of performance governance.

14.2.1 *The Compliance Dimension*

Compliance in this context can be defined as the way the board works to translate strategy into policy using an accepted system for board functioning. This includes the processes, procedures and rules that boards work with. Much of this can be contained in a board manual, to capture the intent of the regulators. According to this definition, the compliance dimension is seen as being

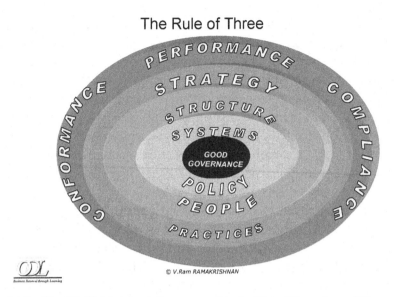

Figure 14.1 The 3S–3P Model as it Integrates with the Three Dimensions of Governance.

rules-based and focuses on adhering to processes that meet regulatory requirements and comply with legal and statutory frameworks. Compliance requires
the directors to accept and facilitate a disciplined working environment.

14.2.2 *The Conformance Dimension*

This dimension addresses the structural needs of the firm, including the relationship between the board and the CEO, between the board and the market
and the firm and its people as well as the policies developed by the board to
meet these needs. Every board is charged with ensuring that resources are uti-
lized wisely, if not profitably. To ensure threshold profitability, boards are
required to oversee the appointment of the CEO as well as the creation of a
management team and operational structure. The CEO, in turn, must conform to what the board has outlined in terms of strategy, structure and
systems. In other words, the CEO must execute policy faithfully and efficiently to ensure that the strategic objectives or key result areas (KRAs) set by,
or in conjunction with, the board are met or exceeded. The CEO can and
does have a say in developing the strategic objectives, but the board, and not
the CEO, owns the KRAs.

The conformance dimension indexes the efficiency with which the firm
uses resources, primary among them being capital, cash and assets (both tangible, such as land building, plant and machinery, and intangible, such as

people, skills, knowledge, brand, relationships, and so on). In this framework, the conformance dimension must coexist with the compliance dimension; it is complementary to and not a substitute for compliance.

The 3D performance governance framework implies that the need to separate compliance from conformance — often missed by many boards — is essential to drive growth in revenue, cost management and control procedures. The focus is on ensuring avoidance of waste and a system of sound internal controls to define, assess, analyze and mitigate risk.

14.2.3 *The Performance Dimension*

Enterprises are incorporated to perform (Garratt, 2003a) and the acid test of performance is the value created in relation to a promise made to the stakeholders. While value can be defined using any measure or combination of measures from a variety of different financial, non-financial or market ratios, whichever of these the board wishes to use will provide a starting point within the framework. Achieving the value promise requires a clear, well-enunciated and measurable strategy, which is at the core of this dimension.

Strategy is fundamentally about the planned actions the directors oversee to effectively improve the firm's ability to compete in the market place. Competitiveness demands the productive use of resources. Competitiveness and productivity are central to performance governance.

Figure 14.1 demonstrates that performance combines with conformance and compliance for effective delivery of strategy. This 3D approach also emphasizes the need for separation of the role of chairman of the board, who oversees the effectiveness of the strategy and that of the CEO, who delivers the results desired efficiently. The 3D framework thus provides a practical approach to the oversight-supervisory role of the board.

14.2.4 *Overseeing the 3Ss and 3Ps Constitutes the Three Main 'Duties' and 'Tasks' of the Board*

The strategy-structure-systems and people-policy-processes, or 3S–3P component of the framework starts by focusing on the effectiveness with which strategy can be developed, deployed and implemented effectively through appropriate policies by capable and motivated people using efficient systems. As indicated earlier in this chapter, the 3S–3P combination drives the three main duties (which are the creation of a viable strategy, appropriate and dynamic structures and ethical systems) that deliver effective direction, define the three main tasks (policy, people and processes) which ensure efficient direction, and facilitate board performance in the three dimensions of good governance, that is, compliance, conformance and performance (refer to Figure 14.1).

14.3 Duties and Tasks of the Board: Measuring Performance by Proxy

Effective boards combine performance with compliance at the board level. Often poor compliance is a consequence of poor performance, which can be defined as falling short of expectations. 'Effectiveness' at this level means that shareholder and stakeholder expectations are met or exceeded, for which the primary objectives must be achieved. Effective boards deliver on the strategy.

To be effective, the three dimensions of compliance, performance and conformance require a sound management AND executive structure that is designed to work with and through appropriate systems for efficient use of limited resources, the productive deployment of which is the basis for strategic success. Mr. Narayana Murthy, the founder and retired Chairman of Infosys, a company that has grown from start-up in the mid-1980s, to 2bn USD in 2006 and 4.5 bn in 2008, states emphatically that the rigorous implementation of internal controls required to meet Sarbanes-Oxley (SOX) guidelines has helped the firm improve its control system. Infosys has become the poster firm globally for quality performance and top class governance. Their compliance and conformance standards are high, based on the quality of reporting in the annual reports.

To help develop, deploy and implement strategy to deliver sustained value, boards need to have a profound understanding of the external factors that drive the current business and the changes that are likely to challenge the business in the near and long term, as stated above. Boards need to 'pace' the organization and fine tune the internal structures to ensure the quality and timeliness of the decisions and systems for communication, to be ready to identify, address and exploit emerging opportunities. This process is captured by the three main duties of the board (or 3Ss) stated above (see also Figure 14.1). The deployment of these three duties necessarily requires an interactive process that defines the three main tasks (or 3Ps) for directors, and a mechanism that helps operationalize these tasks.

Direction of this 'external-internal' or the 'oversight-supervisory' role of the board requires management of a critical interface by the directors without interfering with the executive. As shown in Figure 14.1, the instruments that boards need to focus on to direct-manage the interface are defined within the 3D model as the 3Ps: policies to implement strategy, develop and productively use people and assets, and disciplined use of systematic, formal processes.

Policy defines how the board expects the company to deploy capital to generate revenue, manage costs and use the tangible and intangible assets to create a cash surplus. It establishes the framework within which the CEO has to work and sets out the boundary conditions for day-to-day operations as expected by the directors. Policy defines the productivity benchmarks to guide the CEO in seeking profitable growth.

Typically, policy reflects, if not enshrines, the value systems under which the founders or owners expect the CEO and executive team to work. Policy sets the cultural tone and codifies the belief systems that ought to dominate the workings of the firm. Policy is also the basis of a framework for defining the expectations of value to be delivered to stakeholders, the raising, deployment and use of capital, specific thresholds for cash generation and retention, expected returns on fixed assets, deployment of intangible assets like people, knowledge and brands.

Policy derives from strategy; for example, if a firm wishes to be product-centric, the strategy has to be worked around acquiring and improving product-related competencies, whereas a firm that is service-centric presupposes a good product and invests resources in understanding and improving its service quality. A product-centric firm focuses mainly on developing quality products and technology; Intel is a firm that comes readily to mind. A process-centric firm is one in which processes and the understanding of processes is seen as vital. Many Japanese firms fit this bill, as would General Electric. The process thinking has to be deeply rooted and an intrinsic part of the value system of decision making, communication and execution. A customer-centric firm hugs the customer with whom planning begins and ends. These firms know and spend enormous amounts of time and effort in understanding customers. Service quality, both external and internal, is the watch-word. Toyota is a prime example. While much is made of the Toyota production system, the effort Toyota makes to stay close to its customers often sits below the horizon. Many a long-time Toyota car owner would attest to the efforts made by the company to stay close; the products are reliable, a complaint is taken seriously and the company reaches out continually to the owner to offer better service. To set and achieve high service standards, a firm must have excellent processes and quality products.

As stated earlier, to implement strategy and support it with suitable policy a sound structure is needed that will provide the communication hierarchy to ensure that decisions, information and ideas flow to and fro through the system. This involves a collection of processes which has to be managed by people. Toyota exemplifies well the 3Ps which enable the board to carry out its three main tasks in support of its strategy.

Combining the three Ss and three Ps provides a basis for developing performance governance. The 3S–3P component of the framework starts by focusing on the effectiveness with which strategy can be developed, deployed and implemented effectively through appropriate policies by capable and motivated people using efficient systems. Idealistic as this may sound, most high performance firms (Gerstner, 2002; Bossidy & Charan, 2002; Welch & Welch, 2005; Garratt, 2001a) seem to use the combination in some mix, one way or the other. Overall, this combination (3S–3P) is integral to a 3D system for developing the high level internal controls essential for ethical performance which, at the board level, enables delivery of agreed strategic objectives.

The 3S–3P component of the performance governance framework balances oversight by the directors with feedback from the internal audit to ensure effective use of resources and efficient transactional integrity. It is also a useful structure for developing an open approach to assessing board processes. Its purpose and objective is to ensure that the board discharges its primary duty, which is to deliver on expectations, through results that are generated at least risk. Given that all almost all transactions today are recorded in the IT backbone of an organization, ensuring a balance between effective resource deployment and efficient transactions is relatively easy and very assuring. As there is no direct index of strategic success, transactions when rolled up represent, by proxy, the success of the strategy. Audits can highlight system failures and structural shortcomings. Between them, transactions and audits ensure that directors keep to their tasks and fulfil their duties.

Figure 14.2 illustrates the three components of strategy, structure and systems in practice within the 3S dimension of the performance governance framework. Together, these three components are required for effective board performance and provide a platform for creating a learning organization that can be directed toward developing new competitiveness.

Prerequisites for sustaining competitiveness are:

1. Effective direction which requires development of strategy and setting out an execution framework through policies. This requires the board to identify the key result areas (KRAs) that are necessary to achieve the stated objectives.

2. Ensure management excellence through structures that will help ensure quality execution. Structure is about how people communicate to make decisions that will help the enterprise perform. People work optimally when measured. Using a set of key performance indicators (KPIs) that are

The 3 Dimensions In Practice

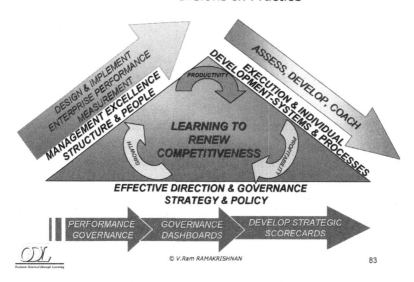

Figure 14.2   Concept of Direction in 3D — Creating a Learning Organisation

aligned with and linked through the KRAs into a governance or directoral dashboard (Garratt, 2006), helps navigate and steer simultaneously.

3. Assess and develop suitable systems. Communication-reliant systems such as Six-Sigma, Total Quality Management (TQM), European Foundation for Quality Management (EFQM) excellence model, Balanced Score Card (BSC), International Standards Organization (ISO) framework, or similar holistic continuous improvement and quality conformance approaches (the utilities of which are explained later) should be board level decisions because they commit the firm's resources including people, time and money for a considerable duration and hence cannot be left to executive teams.

The 3S–3P approach helps build a learning enterprise which fosters the firm's competitiveness derived from the ability to outperform competition continuously, over time.

Effective governance centres on performance and sound performance ensures that the firm is competitive. Remaining competitive requires productivity management which, in turn, demands efficient management of and by people. People work best when their competencies are channeled through appropriate structures, ones that facilitate decision making focused on delivery of value. Structures will, therefore, necessarily have to change when there is a shift in strategic focus. Productive execution happens when people believe that systematic processes work best in delivering strategy within a structural design that favours communication and encourages decision making. At the core of this approach is the ability to learn to improve competitiveness on an organic basis (Garratt, 2001b).

14.4 The Integrated 3D Model in Practice

While the 3D concept is simple enough, it is the practice that poses immense challenges, much of it limited by bounded rationality. The practice may also suffer because of fad-based narrow applications of powerful techniques and frameworks which, when applied diligently and with clarity, in their pristine forms yield tremendous synergies. The solution lies in boards recognizing what they do not know but acknowledge as essential for progress and then seeking the relevant competencies to assist them in using such frameworks, for optimal results. Figure 14.3 represents an attempt at integration, using tools such as EVA, Balanced Scorecard and Six-Sigma, that has benefited proponents of the 3S–3P dimensions of the framework. These tools are explained in further detail below. The framework takes time and persistence to implement but plucks the low hanging fruits easily and encourages the user to reach higher and beyond ordinary performance.

The 3S and 3P in Figure 14.3 have been explained in detail earlier. Other elements in the Figure 14.3 (Enterprise Resource Planning (ERP), Customer

Figure 14.3   The 3S–3P Model for High Quality Execution.

Relationship Management (CRM), and Supply Chain Management (SCM)) refer to commonly used operational support systems, while P&L refers to profit and loss as a result of operational outputs or activity.

The small gap between output-driven working and strategy-driven execution appears small, initially. The gap remains wide when policy and execution have no common ground. Strategy oriented execution provides the base for policy-driven or outcome-based execution.

14.4.1 *Economic Value Added as an "Effectivity" Index*

The application of the 3D concept requires the definition of expectations. One such overarching measure is economic value added or EVA (Ramakrishnan, 2003). When stripped of its accounting complications, EVA has the potential to encapsulate the needs and expectations of all stakeholders.

Whichever way it is calculated, EVA is an excellent index of factor productivity as a measure of the effective use of capital and people. When used as an "effectivity" index, economic value drives strategy well, in that all consequences ultimately are captured and reflected in this index. The trick is to employ an index appropriate to the business and cascade the implications within all measurements of strategy expressing these in a high level profit value chain, or cause-and-effect, diagram or map. The cause-and-effect diagram, or 'strategy map' (Kaplan & Norton, 1996; 2000), is a single sheet definition showing the relationships between the various strategic objectives or KRAs that have been set. It is an elegant method of identifying both the outcomes vital for delivery of the strategy and the interplay between the various outcomes.

While useful as an indicator of a firm's ability to deliver sustained value, EVA is simplistically defined as the returns a business delivers in excess of the cost of capital, and requires a complex set of accounting adjustments making it difficult to measure on a regular basis. However, while it may be difficult to interpret initially, EVA can provide insights into where there is a loss of productivity within the firm. In practice, it can be reduced to a metric that is easily understood such as return on capital, return on net assets, contribution margin, gross margin and similar familiar metrics that have a strong correlation to EVA. Such metrics can be derived from the EVA and hurdle rates set for the CEO to achieve. The implication is that if these hurdle rates are achieved, economic value at the desired level is added.

A measure such as EVA helps validate the formulated strategy because it offers a well accepted test of the performance quality relative to competition and industry norms. EVA also aids the coherent deployment of strategy in terms of capital expenditure and cash management. When used as a high level measure of strategic success and combined with specific, replicable methodologies such as SEXTANT® (Garratt, 2003b) and a proprietary framework to develop strategic thinking, EVA helps develop a quantified strategy that is measurable and replicable. This happens because the strategy is focused on the main value delivery mechanisms inside the enterprise and is developed through a systematic understanding of the environment and market forces that define the value expectations.

14.4.2 *The Balanced Score Card as an Alignment Framework*

The balanced scorecard aligns, a process of establishing the relationship between the performance, conformance, compliance dimensions and the 3S–3P framework. It helps create a strategy focused enterprise.

Strategy can be measured by proxy only and hence requires translation for effective deployment. The Balanced Score Card (BSC) (Kaplan & Norton, 1996; 2000) (see Figure 14.3) is a comprehensive tool that helps 'translate' the strategy and express it as outcomes meaningful to the executive team, then make it visible throughout the organisation. This 'line of sight' capability of the scorecard, arising from its focus on cause and effect between outcomes or KRA's, when combined with a strategy map, is its most outstanding quality and can be used make strategy happen. The BSC helps define the KRAs the CEO and executive team have to deliver to achieve the desired results.

A limitation often is that the scorecard assumes the existence of a defined and definite strategy, which is arguable in many organisations! The BSC also does not define an implementation framework. A superb translator, the BSC needs to align with a strategy development framework upstream and an execution system downstream, to unlock its true potential.

When the balance is well designed and measurements included that effectively index progress against strategy (and not simply a set of 'available' measures with which people are familiar and comfortable) the scorecard is a comprehensive indicator of progress. When linked to a quality, action-oriented execution system and married to a sound data base, the BSC can identify and address imperfections and potential shortcomings (www.odpl.net) in the initiatives taken for delivering value.

The last feature for which the scorecard is a powerful indicator is as an indicator of the bottlenecks based on the lag measures, identifying where the lead measures lie and the road blocks are likely to occur. This forms the basis for improving operational efficiency using Six-Sigma. Strategic success lies in effective execution, which is about the efficient use of resources at the operational level. This implies that the resources like capital, cash, people, plant, machinery, technology, when invested in and deployed yield the best results with minimal loss or waste. Six-Sigma is a technique that aids effective deployment of resources to optimize performance.

14.4.3 *Six-Sigma as a Framework for Creating a Learning Organization*

Also shown in Figure 14.3, Six-Sigma (Bhote, 2003) and all its variants including Lean Six-Sigma, as well as its complementary interventions like Total Productive Management (TPM), Total Quality Management (TQM) and so on, are about accountability for continuous improvement. Essentially, Six-Sigma demands a transparent system that identifies problems, states them and solves them on a lasting basis to optimize yields. It sounds much like the three main constituents of good governance which are accountability, transparency and probity! For this reason the fit of Six-Sigma with the 3S–3P component of the 3D framework is especially useful.

When linked to a strategy-derived balanced scorecard, Six-Sigma is, in the experience of the author, a powerful tool to implement strategy, although by no means is it the only quality framework. Nevertheless, Six-Sigma requires a conscious elevation as a strategy implementation tool because in practice it is seen as a tool for the shop floor and hence designed for improving operational rather than strategic effectiveness! Six-Sigma bases great stress on root cause driven solution around a customer expectation. Hence, in practice, the principles of Six-Sigma, as explained above, are especially well-suited for use in the boardroom.

Combining EVA, BSC and Six-Sigma provides a very effective methodology to bridge the gap between efficiency and effectiveness. Used in this way, the methodology can differentiate between good execution and top class execution, where the shortfalls may be small but the impact can be large. For example, a small fall in EVA could translate into a large loss in profit after tax. The idea behind the integration of the three methods is that these gaps can be recognized and corrected before they lead to less than ideal performance.

The integration of strategy with policy for deployment through adaptive structures and adaptable people, systematically through quality processes creates a coherence that is vital for maximizing limited available resources. In a sense this is the ideal or gold standard for productivity where capital, cash, assets, people and knowledge work in unison. Such cogent thinking helps create a replicable strategic thinking process in the firm (Bhote, 2003), helps translate strategy using frameworks like the balanced scorecard (Kaplan & Norton, 2000) and, with holistic approaches like Six-Sigma, to effectively deploy strategy.

The 3D formula, while not simplistic, is simple enough to address vital issues of performance and promote quality governance, making a complex effort a systematic process. When fully integrated and practiced it aids the setting up of an elegant dashboard — the Directorial Dashboard (Garratt, 2006; Ramakrishnan, 2003) or Governance Dashboard (www.odpl.net) — comprising a series of core metrics that boards and directors can use to navigate and to assess their own contribution. The directorial dashboard then becomes the practical manifestation of the 3S–3P framework in operation.

14.5 Practice in the Asian Context

In Asia, given its mix of 'nouveau' entrepreneurs (as in SE Asia) and old world entrepreneurs (as in India), strategy is seen as a wasteful and pointless exercise. Much development has been 'me too' and, given the nascent markets, any seed sown has grown entrepreneurial businesses beyond the wildest dreams of many. Directors on the boards of these firms find the governance task onerous and, sitting as they do on anything up to 20-plus boards, have neither the time nor inclination to delve deeply into the workings of the enterprises. With the exception of a few companies such as INFOSYS, where the board deliberates regularly on strategic issues, this situation is not changing fast enough. Hence, policy in many Asian firms tends to concentrate on micro concerns such as Human Resource matters related to travel, leave, promotion and so on, and seldom, if ever, addresses critical strategic issues like revenue growth, productivity or capital deployment, or the way capital and cash are invested.

Given a predilection among Asians for hierarchy and a deep respect for authority, structures hardly relate to the needs of the business. In many firms, senior management is characterized by fealty and loyalty — factors of great importance in a restricted environment, but which are losing importance in a competitive world.

An additional factor in determining structures is that much of Asian business is product-centric, with most firms taking the copycat approach. Hence, the primary differentiation is cost, not technology, not process, not service. The result is either very lean structures to achieve cost efficiency, as with many Singapore manufacturing firms, or at the other end, companies with bloated middles, many of whom are time servers who have outlived their utility. The latter is typical of many Chinese and Indian firms.

Cruel as these observations may seem, they reflect reality and have restricted the development of truly world-class players in Asia, including Japan (with a few exceptions like Toyota, and Korea, with the exception of Samsung) where Boards have muffled the ability of Asian entrepreneurial development. Progress has been further stymied by lack of due process arising from inadequate systems. Most Asian firms have all the certificates attesting to their quality standards, their quality in controlling emissions and so on. Very rarely do the firms follow the procedures as a matter of course. Systems are seen by many Asian firms as bureaucratic but, paradoxically, in practice are stifled to sustain the bureaucracy that ensures longevity of the old guard. Yet the same firms, when forced to adhere to systems, perform well. India, for example, has the maximum number of US Food and Drug Administration (FDA) approved pharmaceutical companies, globally, and process rigour is tightly managed by regulators like the FDA. In such instances, the system works because due process is a strategic necessity. The voluntary approach to systemic excellence is not seen often but is successful, as shown in the case study on TATA Motors, a leading Indian automaker with global reach and ambitions.

The solution lies in instilling in Asian managers the positive stimulation that a well-thought-through strategy has on performance, which is the core of performance governance and the challenge for performing boards.

14.5.1 *How TATA Motors has 'Paced' its Growth*

TATA Motors (the renamed truck maker, Telco) took a strategic decision many years ago to diversify into cars. Government regulation stymied the move in the 1980s. Today, TATA is among the top three car makers in India despite its major competitor, a Suzuki-owned company, Maruti, having had a 20-year head start in the small car segment. When freed of a stifling regulatory regime, the firm has designed and made the cheapest car in the world — the Nano.

While the strategy was given a fillip by deregulation in the Indian economy, TATA took a policy decision to design and make cars from scratch, in-house. Today, they are a feared competitor in the small car segment and are tipped to become a globally competitive firm by 2010.

The strategy was backed with purposeful management of its decision to select and work with suppliers who shared their vision of a low-cost car for India and the world. TATA's structures and systems for selection and manufacturing have been designed around the strategic imperative to make an affordable, low-cost car. A study of their resource use is revealing.

TATA's capital productivity, the sales to total capital employed ratio, improved from an anemic 1.06 in 2001 to a headline grabbing 2.77 in 2005 (as a comparison Toyota turns its capital around at a steady 1.39 times). This level of productivity will, in all likelihood, decline as TATA matures but it remains a stellar use of capital. In 2001, TATA consumed cash and hence retained very little; in 2005, it was generating 10 percent of revenues as cash and retaining around 17 percent. The numbers for Toyota are 14 percent generated and 22 percent retained. TATA has a way to go to become a global player as it has to generate significantly more cash than hitherto, but is well on its way to achieving this status. The TATA story is a significant lesson in performance governance where cash generation is vital and where cash retention is critical to fund growth.

In 2005, the sales per employee at TATA went from US$77000 per person to an astounding US$193000 per employee. In that year, the people at TATA improved the value they added per person from US$20000 in 2001 to US$62000. The comparative figures for Toyota are lower (sales per person US$63000 and value added per employee at US$14000). These numbers will also fall as the company funds and fuels global expansion.

At the process level, TATA improved its inventory turns from around six in a year to 10 — a solid improvement but significantly short of Toyota at 16 per year. Increasing this figure is an enormous task and should concern the senior team and directors. It requires a systemic upgrade. However, the board at TATA Motors has improved its use of capital, generated more cash, improved asset productivity and the return on capital employed. ROCE grew from a low 6 percent in 2002 to a remarkable 26 percent in 2005.

The TATA Motors story reflects the importance of performance governance. Dell in the US is also a good example, while Ford (which, notwithstanding a new CEO and being the only US auto firm not needing an injection of US Federal capital, is far from stability) and GM, sadly, are examples of companies with non-performing boards that have destroyed value.

14.6 Conclusion

It seems inevitable that, sooner rather than later, boards have to deliver, that is, to perform to expectations laid down in law and frequently overlooked. The current crisis will accelerate the demand for boards to oversee performance and one possible outcome of the G20 meeting in March 2009 is a regulatory demand for firms to better manage capital and cash.

An effective board would, therefore, ensure that sound processes are in place to develop, execute and oversee implementation of strategy. The board should create appropriate structures in the enterprise that ensure continuity and adaptability to capture and exploit opportunities productively at acceptable levels of risk.

Boards and directors should ensure that:

- strategy is dynamic and relevant to the circumstances;
- structures are flexible to respond to and exploit change;

- systems are adaptable but robust; and
- their performance is measured and strategic course correction made in real time.

This 3D approach is strategic in orientation and focus, helps attain effective oversight and avoids meddling by the board. Practice and experience indicate that the 3S–3P framework is a good predicator of what to expect (Ramakrishnan, 2004) from the firm in terms of performance.

Chapter 15

THE UNFINISHED AGENDA: TWO LEVELS OF CORPORATE GOVERNANCE REFORM

BOB GARRATT

Media Projects International and Imperial College

15.1 The Big Picture

15.1.1 *Towards Risk and Sustainability*

The banking crisis and its subsequent credit crunch was followed by international public anger about the current nature of governance, capitalism, risk management, ethics, and the fallible nature of humans and their organisations. These have all led to strident demands for a massive reconsideration of the nature and purpose of those socio-economic systems by which we currently create and distribute wealth.

Currently, there are many ill-considered demands for instant solutions to such problems which have grown and festered over many years and for which no rapid solutions exist. However, there are the outlines of possible national and international systems of the governance of wealth creation and distribution which have two consistent themes. These themes involve the careful integration of systems of thought and behaviour which have been previously assumed to have no direct connection. Specifically, these centre on risk and sustainability, two areas many would regard as diametrically opposed. In the first part of this chapter, a more conceptual case is put forward for future developments in corporate governance.

Life is both risky and fragile. Risk is an essential part of the human condition. Without risk being taken, life would be static; especially when launching a business venture there will always be risks. Many of these are calculable but some are fraught with uncertainty. The differentiation made by Knight (1921) in the 1920s is helpful in understanding the corporate governance aspects of this under-explored issue. Knight defined *risk* as those conditions 'where the probabilities of different outcomes is known, but not the outcome itself'; and *uncertainty* as 'where the probabilities themselves are unknown.' He further stated that 'It is difficult to rationalise uncertainty even using "bounded rationality" (rational decision making with limited information).' The management of risk is the domain of the executives of an organisation. The drive to understand and use for its benefit the uncertainties within which an organisation exists, however, is arguably a primary role of the board of directors.

Often a board will be initially uncomfortable with the intellectual process of becoming sensitised to the changing trends in a messy external environment where political, physical, environmental, economic, social/demographic, technological and globalisation trends conflict with each other. But it is the directors' duty to do the best job they can of unscrambling this "fog" before taking policy and strategic decisions. Many boards regard this task as being too hard, and so drop back into the relative executive certainty of managing narrowly defined "risks."

Any healthy organisation needs to balance continuously both risks and uncertainties at the head of the organisation. That "head" is where the board and the executives meet to determine the broad strategies of the enterprise, public or private. Indeed, an enterprise cannot develop without assessing risk and, hopefully, reward and is the essence of our economic system. The very word "risk" derives from the Italian *riscare* — to dare. This is what executives do. Their risk-taking is kept in balance by the board of directors who are there to assess, usually on a monthly basis, whether they are balancing the age-old *Director's Dilemma* of how they drive the enterprise forward whilst keeping it under prudent control. The executives manage the day-to-day business of risk management. The directors ensure the steering of the total business direction in relation to the changing and uncertain external environment. They ensure the connectedness of the internal control systems so that they can see quickly the results of their direction-giving.

In the end, it is the directors who "bet the business" and are held liable for this. In the current crisis, however, it was the executives who had mis-priced risk through their lack of understanding of the complexity of the financial instruments they were developing, who bet the business instead. This is the major accusation against many directors internationally: that they were so lacking in the key duties of effective corporate governance — care, skill and diligence — that they were unable to fulfil their fiduciary duty to ensure a healthy future for their organisation. The examples are legion as greed and short-termism, boosted by unrealistic reward systems which, for example, "guaranteed" annual performance bonuses irrespective of company perform-ance, took command. Even the notionally unbiased credit rating agencies joined in by giving Triple A ratings to questionable derivative packages in which they had a commercial interest.

This leads to the seemingly opposite concept of *Sustainability*, the simple basis of which is that people and their organisations should do no harm to a frag-ile and living world. Whether one follows the Gaia thesis of life on the planet as a single, self-regulating, living system (see http://www.gaiatheory.org) or any other similar concept, there is now little doubt that the Earth is being impacted and changed for the worse by human activity on it and that, therefore, this use and abuse of the world's natural resources needs urgent rebalancing. Although the management of specific risks lies with the executives, the enterprise's politi-cal will in facing up to the wider uncertainties involved is firmly rooted in the Board, as mining and energy companies are finding. This seems to be a problem because not enough is known about the wider trends and the subsequent changes needed. There is a risk that we are betting the world on a lack of knowl-edge and consensus about how to address the issues.

The notion of *Sustainability* is of increasing importance and is just beginning to be reflected in the corporate governance world. The current corporate governance debate is most strongly advanced in South Africa with its latest consultation document "King 3" where sustainability is first mentioned officially at a national level (see http://www.iodsa.co.za/downloads/reports/King%20Report%2025%20Feb%202009.pdf); and in the United Kingdom where the 2006 Companies Act is paving the way towards all registered companies needing to prepare for "Triple Bottom Line Reporting" (see http://www.opsi.gov.uk/acts/acts2006/pdf/ukpga_20060046_en.pdf) although many directors are unaware of this. Both initia-tives have similar objectives. The underlying thought is that no organisation is a truly independent entity with the unlimited right to do what it likes with its people, resources, the environment or the communities in which its "stakeholders" live. In the future, a company's "licence to operate" will be granted nationally, subject to satisfactory behaviour on three annually assess-able dimensions:

- its financial performance;
- its impact on the physical environment; and
- its impact on its stakeholder communities.

This Triple Bottom Line approach is not just good news for auditors but has a much more profound meaning for the directors and managers of any organisation, public or private. It requires a corporate mindset by the Board which seeks to balance three variables which have been considered previously quite distinct from each other. From a strategic thinking perspective, it is difficult to see why they have not been considered connected. The use of any resource can only be maximised until it is exhausted. The more subtle concept of *optimising* resources brings at least the notion of balancing variables. Now the notion of sustainability takes optimisation further, to the point where any resources used need to be replaced or substituted in a renewable way. This idea is the opposite of rapaciousness amongst unlimited resources, including people, which Mel Brookes satirised in his fictional title, *Engulf and Devour Corporation*.[1] The concept of sustainability acknowledges the fragility of the Earth whilst simultaneously encouraging enterprise and innovation. Indeed, the business opportunities generated by a sustainability approach seem manifest.

15.1.2 *A Risk Tax?*

This raises the question of whether there is a way to square this apparent circle. One way that looks promising is to accept the existing business model and the need to refine it, and then for nations and international organisations to develop a "risk tax" for organisations. This would be targeted initially at financial institutions so that banks, insurance companies, fund managers and their like would pay a levy aligned to the extent by which they increase risk in the economic system. It would be similar in flavour to the carbon taxes which are gaining ground internationally and would be underpinned by the development of Triple Bottom Line reporting. The Risk tax concept is being developed by Professor Andrew Lo at the Sloane School of Management at MIT. He accepts the frailties and excesses of the human condition but seeks to moderate them through systematically reducing ill-considered risk "by governments treating systemic risk as a negative externality and setting a limit for it via the price mechanism."[2] It is an idea that could be worth developing and one which would mean that both executives and directors could be much more questioning of the risks they undertake.

---

[1] Engulf and Devour Corporation was a fictional company featuring in the 1976 comedy film directed by and starring Mel Brookes and released by 20th Century Fox on June 17. The film entitled "Silent Movie" is a parody of the silent film genre and a play on the 1970s trend of large corporations buying up smaller companies. See en.wikipedia.org/wiki/Silent_Movie.
[2] See www.ft.com, "Call for levy on risk pollution", 24/05/09, Financial Times.

15.2 The Corporate Governance Picture

15.2.1 *Back To Basics — But this Time With All the Players*

Changing the perspective of this chapter to that of the existing world of corporate governance and Board development, it may be that many of the participants are so shocked by the anger and revolutionary demands generated by an angry public that they have the dazed expression described by PG Wodehouse as 'one who, picking daisies on the railway, has just caught the down express in the small of the back.'[3]

First, a general point. Effective corporate governance applies to all organisations. It is a historical quirk that, in all the major countries trying to develop effective corporate governace, the approach has been to see it only as necessary for companies listed on their stock exchanges. This is curious as listed companies form only a tiny percentage of the registered organisations in their nation. If corporate governance really matters then non-listed companies, their charities and not-for-profits, their government agencies and departments also need to be included, all of whom are asking for better corporate governance. Indeed, taking the UK as an example of what was held out as an international standard of corporate governance, then it is odd that the new Companies Act 2006 covers many of those types of organisations listed above (even some government agencies) but does not incorporate the Combined Code of Corporate Governance (2006) which applies only to listed companies and in a few ways is contradictory to the new Act. The two pieces of legislation could be complementary with a few adjustments, but are not.

15.2.2 *Care, Skill and Diligence — The Professionalisation of Directors*

It is noticeable that in the King Reviews in South Africa and now in the UK's 2006 Companies Act the basic concepts of good corporate governance have been consolidated around the notion of directors' basic duties of care, skill and diligence so that they may fulfil their fundamental fiduciary duty — to ensure that their organisation has a healthy future. Surprisingly, little time is spent on most boards ensuring processes exist so that directors are careful, skillful, and diligent in their work. But without these attributes, how can a director fulfill their duty? Many still regard care, skill and diligence as optional extras for busy people, but with an increasingly angry public and the likelihood of years of bad

---

[3] The Inimitable Jeeves — a semi-novel collecting Jeeves stories by P.G. Wodehouse first published in the UK by Herbert Jenkins, London, May 17, 1923.

publicity from trials and jailings of recalcitrant directors, especially in the US and UK, the notion of directors needing to be trained in the future as disinterested professionals is being debated.

Within that debate, certain issues stand out as a need of returning to their roots at law. Interestingly, given the current furore over director and executive pay, little is said in either primary or secondary legislation about this — and rightly so. This is a matter of judgement by the board and active participation by the owners who need to exert more frequently their right to dismiss the underperformers and overpaid. Arguably much greater leverage can be made in all types of organisation by stressing the chairman's role as "the architect of the Board," ensuring that a professional company secretary is employed, and that a chairman's office (real or virtual) is created which then supervises and assesses, at least annually, the performance of the board, its committees, and each individual director, including executives who are also statutory directors.

The chairman would be held accountable by the owners for such issues as:

- the selection and deselection of the directors subject to owner approval; the mandatory and detailed induction of each director; and their re-induction after any three-year term.
- a transparent (to the owners and regulators) annual evaluation of the performance of the board, its committees and each individual director to cover categories specified by the regulator.
- a transparent annual development plan for the three parties above, as seen in the 2007 BAE annual report following the Woolf Committee investigation.[4]

15.3 Tightening the Director's Role and Contract

It is a curiosity that in the UK, and copied by many other countries, there is a disconnect between the Company Law and the Listed Company Code. This is found in the hard statements made in Company Law of the roles and duties of a statutory director — essentially that "a director is a director, full-stop" — and the misconstruction of this term to allow two categories of director — "Executive Director" and Non-Executive Director" in the Code. It is arguable that to obey the law, any statutory director must put aside the

---

[4] In June 2007, the Board appointed Lord Woolf to lead an independent expert committee to study and publish a report on the BAE Systems Group's ethical policies and processes. BAE Systems is a global company engaged in the development, delivery and support of advanced defence, security and aerospace systems. BAE Systems Annual Report 2007, http://production. investis.com.

executive role on entering the boardroom. They can then fulfill their legal duties to put the future of the organisation first, to demonstrate a primary loyalty to it, and act collegially around the boardroom table before using their single vote to decide the board proposition before them.

To do this well, all directors should have the same contract for services for one year, which specifies their roles, time commitments and primary loyalty. If a statutory director is also an executive of the company, then they should have a separate contract of employment for the majority of their time. In the few cases where executives have these two contracts, the board's performance has improved noticeably — following some intense induction of the executives under the chairman's supervision.

15.3.1 *Can Directors' Values and Ethics Ever be Reformed?*

The answer to this question is yes, if directors understand and are trained for a very different role than being an executive. Many directors have created a career by having a fixed focus on getting the day-to-day projects and systems sorted. That is fine. It is their duty to design, install, maintain and refine the prudent control systems of their business. But directing an organisation requires much higher levels of strategic thinking and, more uncomfortably, of grappling with uncertainty whilst still giving direction; which is why there is a need for a Board. Many "executive directors" find making the shift from executing to directing difficult after a career that has developed very different tendencies in them as executives.

So the notion that their role around the boardroom table is not mainly to say "yes" or "no" to executive proposals but to budget time to track and consider external trends in the uncertain worlds of politics, the physical environment, economics as well as the social/demographic, technological and globalisation contexts, is almost impossible to bear for many executives. Yet effective directors have to constantly make judgements with fuzzy data and this requires a psychological temperament which is not "executive." It requires comfort in creating time to reflect; and it also requires having a value set and consequent behaviours which reflect prudence, justice, mercy and courage. These are developable ethical behaviours which can lead to the creation of both a personal and corporate conscience.

Now there's a challenge for future directors! Such initiatives to improve corporate governance practise could even lead to a sustainable future, and to dramatically reducing the current and justified public anger. But it would also require specification of the need to set out the duties and liabilities of the owners to complete the task, as well as a strong system of regulation which ensures prudent behaviour.

GLOSSARY

Active Investment — A form of traditional portfolio management whereby frequent decisions are made regarding stock selection based on specific characteristics or beliefs indicating whether the stock is under or over-valued.

Anti-Dilution Provisions — Provisions designed to protect investors in the event that a company issues further capital at a lower valuation than earlier financing rounds in the future.

Anti-Director Rights — Refers to an index developed by La Porta, Lopez-de-Silanes, Shleifer, and Vishny (1998) to measure legal protections available to shareholders in different countries.

Anti-Takeover Procedures — The specific techniques and strategies available to target companies to defeat or frustrate a takeover offer.

Availability Hueristic — A phenomenon in which people's expectations about the probability of an event occurring is based on the ease with which they can come up with an example.

Behavioural Finance — A field of finance that proposes psychological based theories to explain stock market anomalies. A central tenant of behavioural finance is the fact that markets are not rational.

Chaebols — South Korean family-run conglomerates.

Control Premiums — The extra value that investors are willing to pay above the current market price to acquire a controlling interest in a firm.

Corporate Social Responsibility — A concept whereby companies integrate social and environmental concerns in their business operations and in their interaction with their stakeholders on a voluntary basis.

Creditors Rights Index — An index identifying the legal protections available to creditors developed in La Porta, Lopez-de-Silanes, Shleifer, and Vishny (1998).

Cumulative Voting — When shareholders are able to pool their votes to concentrate them on the election of a small number of directors rather than apply their votes to all directors.

Dual-Board Structure — A board structure where shareholders appoint a Supervisory Board who is then responsible for the appointment of a management board.

Dual-Class Shares — A situation where a company has more than one class of equity with differing voting rights or ownership restrictions. This structure often has the goal of consolidating control in the hands of management.

Enhanced Analytics Initiative — An international collaboration between asset owners and managers aimed at encouraging better investment research, including the inclusion of extra-financial issues on long-term investment.

Extra-Financial Information — Information beyond purely financial information that analysts may use to evaluate companies. This can include information on environmental, social and governance factors.

Going Private Transactions — A transaction whereby a publicly listed company is purchased and then delisted from the public exchanges. This is typically achieved by means of a leveraged buyout, often initiated by management.

Gray directors — Refer to non-employee directors who have some other connection to the company, often financial, which impairs their ability to be independent.

Insider Trading — Trading by a director, executive or large block holder in the shares of their own company. Where this trading is based on, as yet undisclosed material or price sensitive information by these individuals or anyone to whom they have passed on information, is considered illegal in most countries.

Integrative Social Contract Theory — A theory proposed by Donaldson and Dunfee in the 1980s that applied Social Contract Theory to businesses.

Inter-locking Directorships — Situations where executives sit on one another's boards as directors.

Investor Protection Laws — Covers the range of legislation that a country has implemented to prevent shareholders from being exploited and ensuring that a suitable return is returned to shareholders.

Legal Bonding — Refers to companies choosing to list in other countries with stronger investor protection laws so that they become bound by the more rigorous legal environment of that country.

Mandatory Bid Rule — A regulatory requirement that when a new shareholder takes control of a company that they have to make an offer to all remaining shareholders at a fair price.

Material Information — Information that, if it were to become known to the investing public, would be expected to have a significant price impact.

Microfinance — Refers to a movement to make high quality financial products, including credit, savings and insurance, available to groups traditionally viewed as too poor to have access to regular banks and financial prodicts.

Minority Freeze-outs — Takeovers designed by majority shareholders to seize the remaining portion of the company as yet unowned and in the process divorce minority shareholders from their ownership in the company and thus from any future gains of the company.

REITS — Real Estate Invesment Trust; a financial product which specialises in investing in property.

Reputational Bonding — Refers to companies choosing to list in other countries with stricter investor protection laws in an effort to foster a reputation for not exploiting shareholders.

Revolving-door Appointments — Situations where a former employee or partner of a company's external auditors is appointed to the board of the company shortly after their retirement or leaving the audit firm.

Soft Information — Information that is difficult to quantify and or collect except through an in-depth knowledge of an organisation and its key personal.

SRI — Socially Responsible Investing is a movement towards mutual funds considering more than financial performance before investing in a company. Other factors like environmental record, social factors and governance are all considered important and which impact investment decision making.

Sustainability Reporting — The practise of measuring, disclosing and being accountable to internal and external stakeholders for organisational performance towards the goal of sustainable development.

Targeted Share Repurchases — Also known as Greenmail; is a takeover defence where a company will repurchase shares exclusively from a potential hostile acquirer at a rate well above the current market price.

Tunneling — A type of fraud whereby assets or profits of a firm are taken out of a firm for the benefit of controlling shareholders exclusively. There are considered to be three types of tunnelling: asset, equity and cash flow tunnelling.

REFERENCES

Abbott, LJ, S Parker & GF Peters (2000). The effects of audit committee activity and independence on corporate fraud. *Managerial Finance*, 26, 55–67.

Abbott, LJ, S Parker & GF Peters (2004). Audit committee characteristics and restatements. *Auditing: A Journal of Practice & Theory*, 23, 69–87.

Adams, RB & D Ferreira (2007). A theory of friendly boards. *Journal of Finance*, 62, 217–250.

Agrawal, A & S Chadha (2005). Corporate governance and accounting scandals. *Journal of Law and Economics*, 48, 371–406.

Aguilera, RV (2005). Corporate governance and director accountability: An institutional comparative perspective. *British Journal of Management*, 16, 39–53.

Alexander, I & C Mayer (1997). Creating incentives for private infrastructure companies to become more efficient, *World Bank Policy Research Working Paper*, No. 1736.

Allcock, D & I Filatotchev (2009). Executive incentive schemes in initial public offerings: The effects of multiple-agency conflicts and corporate governance. *Journal of Management OnlineFirst*. doi: 10.1177/0149206308329962.

Andres, L, J Guasch, T Haven & V Foster (2008). *The Impact of Private Sector Participation in Infrastructure, Lights, Shadows, and the Road Ahead.* Washington, DC: World Bank.

Archambeault, DS, FT DeZoort & DR Hermanson (2008). Audit committee incentive compensation and accounting restatements. *Contemporary Accounting Research*, 25, 965–992.

Arthurs, JD, RE Hoskisson, LW Busenitz & RA Johnson (2008). Managerial agents watching other agents: Multiple agency conflicts regarding underpricing in IPO firms. *Academy of Management Journal*, 52, 277–294.

Atanasov, V (2005). How much value can blockholders tunnel? Evidence from the Bulgarian mass privatization auctions. *Journal of Financial Economics*, 76, 191–234.

Atanasov, V, B Black, C Ciccotello & S Gyoshev (2010a). How does law affect finance: An examination of equity tunneling in Bulgaria. *Journal of Financial Economics*, 96, 155–173.

Atanasov, V, A Boone & D Haushalter (2010b). Is there shareholder expropriation in the U.S.? An analysis of publicly-traded subsidiaries. *Journal of Financial and Quantitative Analysis*, 45, 1–26.

Atanasov, V, B Black & C Ciccotello (2008). Unbundling and measuring tunneling. *Working Paper*.

Atanasov, V, C Ciccotello & S Gyoshev (2006). Learning from the general principles of company law for transition economies: The case of Bulgaria. *Journal of Corporation Law*, 31, 1003–1033.

Atanasov, V, A Durnev, L Fauver & K Litvak (2008). The anatomy of preemptive rights and other anti-dilution provisions in emerging markets. *Working paper*.

Atanasov, V, V Ivanov & K Litvak (2007). The Impact of Litigation on Venture Capitalist Reputation. *NBER Working Paper* 13641. Available from: http://www.nber.org/papers/w13641.

Australian Prudential Regulation Authority (2009a). Remuneration — Proposed extensions to governance requirements for APRA-regulated institutions. Discussion Paper. Available at http://www.apra.gov.au/Policy/Remuneration-requirements-consultation-May-2009.cfm.

Australian Prudential Regulation Authority (2009b). Prudential Practice Guide PPG 511 — Remuneration. Available at http://www.apra.gov.au/Policy/Remuneration-requirments-consultation-May-2009.cfm.

Australian Government Productivity Commission (2009). Regulation of Director and Executive Remuneration in Australia. Issues Paper. Available at http://www.pl.gov.au/projects/inquiry/executive-remuneration.

Australian Shareholders Association (2009). Policy Statement Executive Remuneration. 23 March. Available at http://www.asa.asn.au/I_Policy Statements.asp.

Australian Stock Exchange (2007). *Principles of Good Corporate Governance and Best Practice Recommendations*. Australian Stock Exchange Corporate Governance Council, Sydney.

Ausubel, L (1990). Insider trading in a rational expectations economy. *The American Economic Review*, 80(5), 1022–1039.

Ayyagari, M, T Beck & A Demirguc-Kunt (2007). Small and medium enterprises across the globe. *Small Business Economics*, 29, 415–434.

Backman, M (2002). *The Asian Eclipse: Exposing the Dark Side of Business in Asia*. Singapore: John Wiley and Sons.

Bae, KH & V Goyal (2009). Creditor rights, contract enforcement and costs of loan financing. *Journal of Finance, 84*, 823–860.

Bae, KH, JK Kang & JM Kim (2002). Tunneling or value added? Evidence from mergers by Korean business groups. *Journal of Finance, 57*, 2695–2740.

Bae, K, R Stulz & H Tan (2008). Do local analysts know more? A cross-country study of the performance of local analysts and foreign analysts. *Journal of Financial Economics, 88*, 581–606.

Baek, J, J Kang & I Lee (2006). Business groups and tunneling: Evidence from private securities offerings by Korean chaebols. *Journal of Finance, 61*, 2415–2449.

Baesel, J & G Stein (1979). The value of information: Inferences from the profitability of insider trading. *Journal of Financial and Quantitative Analysis, 14*, 553–571.

Bailey, W, A Karolyi & C Salva (2006). The economic consequences of increased disclosure: Evidence from international cross-listings. *Journal of Financial Economics, 81*, 175–213.

Bainbridge, S (2000). Insider trading: An overview. In B. Bouckaert & G. De Geest (eds.). *The Regulation of Contracts Encyclopedia of Law and Economics* Vol. III, pp. 772–812. Edward Elgar: Cheltenham.

Barro, RJ & RM McCleary (2003). Religion and economic growth. *American Sociological Review, 68*, 760–781.

Baker, K, J Nofsinger & D Weaver (2002). International cross-listing and visibility. *Journal of Financial and Quantitative Analysis, 37*, 495–521.

Bates, TW, M Lemmon & J Linck (2006). Shareholder wealth effects and bid negotiation in freeze-out deals? Are minority shareholders left out in the cold? *Journal of Financial Economics, 81*, 681–706.

Bauer, R, J Derwall & W Jaworski (2007). Extra-financial Information in Financial Communication of European Companies, *ECCE Report,* Maastricht University.

Bauer, R, P Eichholtz & N Kok (2010). Corporate governance and performance: The REIT effect. *Real Estate Economics, 38*, 1–29.

Bauer, R, P Frentrop, N Günster & H de Ruiter (2004). Corporate governance: A review of the debate in the Netherlands and empirical evidence on the link with financial performance. *VBA Journal, 20*, 19–34.

Bauer, R, B Frijns, R Otten & A Tourani-Rad (2008). The impact of corporate governance on corporate performance: Evidence from Japan. *Pacific Basin Finance Journal, 16*, 236–251.

Bauer, R, N Günster & R Otten (2004). Empirical evidence on corporate governance in Europe: The effect on stock returns, firm value and performance. *Journal of Asset Management, 5*, 91–104.

Bauer, R, D Hann & J Derwall (2009). Employee Relations and Credit Risk. *ECCE Working Paper,* Maastricht University.

Bauer, R, CG Koedijk & R Otten (2005). International evidence on ethical mutual fund performance and investment style. *Journal of Banking and Finance*, 29, 1751–1767.

Beasley, MS, JV Carcello, DR Hermanson & PD Lapides (2000). Fraudulent financial reporting: Consideration of industry traits and corporate governance mechanisms. *Accounting Horizons*, 14, 441–454.

Bebchuk, L & C Fershtman (1994). Insider trading and the managerial choice among risky projects. *Journal of Financial and Quantitative Analysis*, 29(1), 1–14.

Bebchuk, L & C Jolls (1999). Managerial value diversion & shareholder wealth. *Journal of Law, Economics, and Organization*, 15, 487–502.

Becht, M, P Bolton & A Roell (2002). Corporate governance and control. *European Corporate Governance Institute*. Working Paper No. 02.

Beck, T, A Demirguc-Kunt & V Maksimovic (2004). Bank competition and access to finance: International evidence. *Journal of Money, Credit, and Banking*, 36, 627–648.

Becker, B (2007). Geographical segmentation of US capital markets. *Journal of Financial Economics*, 85, 151–178.

Becker, B, H Cronqvist & R Fahlenbrach (2008). Estimating the effects of large shareholders using a geographic instrument. *Working paper*.

Becker, B, Z Ivkovic & S Weisbenner (2009). Local dividend clienteles. *Journal of Finance*, forthcoming.

Becker, G (1968). Crime and punishment: An economic approach. *The Journal of Political Economy*, 76, 169–217.

Becker, GS (1975). *Human capital*. Chicago, IL: The University of Chicago Press.

Bedard, J, SM Chtourou & L Courteau (2004). The effect of audit committee expertise, independence, and activity on aggressive earnings management. *Auditing: A Journal of Practice & Theory*, 23, 13–35.

Bello, ZY (2005). Socially responsible investing and portfolio diversification. *Journal of Financial Research*, 28, 41–57.

Beny, L (1999). A Comparative Empirical Investigation of Agency and Market Theories of Insider Trading (Vol. Discussion Paper No. 264). www.ssrn.com: *John M. Olin Center for Law, Economics and Business*.

Beny, L (2005). Do insider trading laws matter? Some preliminary comparative evidence. *American Law and Economics Review*, 7, 144–183.

Berger, AN, NH Miller, MA Petersen, RG Rajan & JC Stein (2005). Does function follow organizational form? Evidence from the lending practices of large and small banks. *Journal of Financial Economics*, 76, 237–269.

Berkman, H, R Cole & J Fu (2008). Expropriation Through loan guarantees to related parties: Evidence from China. *Journal of Banking and Finance*, forthcoming.

Bernhadt, D, B Hollifield & E Hughson (1995). Investment and insider trading. *The Review of Financial Studies*, 8, 501–543.

Bertrand, M, P Mehta & S Mullainathan (2002). Ferreting out tunneling: An application to Indian business groups. *Quarterly Journal of Economics*, 117, 121–148.

Bertrand, M, S Johnson, K Samphantarak & A Schoar (2008). Mixing family with business: A study of Thai business groups and the families behind them. *Journal of Financial Economics*, 88, 466–498.

Bezemer, P-J, GF Maasen, FAJ Van den Bosch & HW Volberda (2007). Investigating the development of the internal and external service tasks of non-executive directors: The case of the Netheirlands (1997–2005). *Corporate Governance: An International Review*, 15, 1119–1129.

Bhargava, R, A Bose & D Dubofsky (1998). Exploiting international stock market correlations with open-end international mutual funds. *Journal of Business Finance and Accounting*, 25, 765–773.

Bhasa, MP (2004). Global corporate governance: Debates and challenges. *Corporate Governance: The International Journal of Effective Board Performance*, 4, 5–17.

Bhattacharya, U & H Daouk (2002). The world price of insider trading. *Journal of Finance*, 57, 75–108.

Bhattacharya, U, H Daouk & M Welker (2003). The world price of earnings opacity. *The Accounting Review*, 78, 641–678.

Bhattacharya, U & H Daouk (2009). When no law is better than a good law. *Review of Finance*, 13, 577–627.

Bhote, K (2003). The Power of Ultimate Six Sigma, American Management Association.

Bigelli, M, V Mehrotra & R Rau (2006). Expropriation through unification? Wealth effects of dual class share unifications in Italy. *Working Paper*.

Black, B (1998). Shareholder robbery, Russian style. *Institutional Shareholder Services: Issue Alert*, 3–14.

Black, B (2001). The legal and institutional preconditions for strong securities markets. *UCLA Law Review*, I, 781–855.

Black, B (2001a). The corporate governance behavior and market value of russian firms. *Emerging Markets Review*, 2, 89–108.

Black, B, W Kim, H Jang & K Park (2008). How corporate governance affects firm value: Evidence on channels from Korea. *Working paper*. Available from: http://ssrn.com/abstract=844744.

Black, B, R Kraakman & A Tarassova (2000). Russian privatization and corporate governance: What went wrong? *Stanford Law Review*, 52, 1731–1808.

Blair, MM (1995). *Ownership and Control: Rethinking Corporate Governance for the Twenty-First Century*. Washington, DC The Brookings Institution.

Blumentritt, T (2006). The relationship between boards and planning in family businesses. *Family Business Review*, 19, 65–72.

Blundell-Wignall, A & P Atkinson (2008). The Sub-price Crisis: Causal Distortions and Regulatory Reform, Paper Presented at the Reserve Bank of Australia Conference, Sydney, Australia.

Blundell-Wignall, A, P Atkinson & S Hoon Lee (2008). The Current Financial Crisis: Causes and Policy Issues. *Financial Market Trends*, OECD.

Boeker, W & J Goodstein (1993). Performance and successor choice: The moderating effects of governance and ownership. *Academy of Management Journal, 36*, 172–186.

Borch, OJ & M Huse (1993). Informal strategic networks and the board of directors. *Entrepreneurship: Theory and Practice, 18*, 23–36.

Bossidy, L & R Charan (2002). *Execution, The Discipline of Getting Things Done*, Crown Business.

Boyd, R & PH Richerson (1985). *Culture and the evolutionary process*. Chicago: University of Chicago Press.

Bradbury, M, Y Mak & S Tan (2004). Board characteristics, audit committee characteristics and abnormal accruals. *Working paper, Massey University*.

Bris, A (2005). Do insider trading laws work? *European Financial Management, 11*, 267–312.

Brockman P & E Unlu (2009). Dividend policy, creditor rights, and the agency costs of debt. *Journal of Financial Economics*, forthcoming.

Brown, JR, Z Ivković, P Smith & S Weisbenner (2008). Neighbors matter: Causal community effects and stock market participation. *Journal of Finance, 63*, 1509–1531.

Brown, T & M Potoski (2003). Managing contract performance: A transaction cost approach. *Journal of Policy Analysis and Management, 22*, 275–297.

Brudney, V (1979). Insiders, outsiders, and information advantages under the federal securities laws. *Harvard Law Review, 93*, 322–376.

Brunninge, O & M Nordqvist (2004). Ownership structure, board composition and entrepreneurship: Evidence from family firms and venture-capital-backed firms, *International Journal of Entrepreneurial Behavior & Research, 10*, 85–105.

Brunninge, O, M Nordqvist & J Winlund (2007). Corporate governance and strategic change in SMEs: The effects of ownership, board composition and top management teams. *Small Business Economics, 29*, 295–308.

Buchanan, B (1974). Building organizational commitment: The socialization of managers in work organizations. *Administrative Science Quarterly, 19*, 533–546.

Burger, P, J Tyson, I Karpowicz & M Coelho (2009). The effects of the financial crisis on public-private partnership, *Working Paper no 09/144*, Washington, DC: IMF.

Burkart, M, D Gromb & F Panunzi (1998). Why higher takeover premia protect minority shareholders. *Journal of Political Economy, 106*, 172–204.

Bushman, R, J Piotroski & A Smith (2005). Insider trading restrictions and analyst's incentives to follow firms. *Journal of Finance, 60*, 35–66.

Business in the Community in partnership with Accenture (2007). *An MP's Guide to Responsible Business*. Available at http://www.accenture.co.uk/corporatecitizenship.

Butler, A (2008). Distance still matters: Evidence from municipal bond underwriting. *Review of Financial Studies, 21*, 763–784.

Cadbury, A (1992). *Report of the Committee on the Financial Aspects of Corporate Governance*. Gee & Co. Ltd, London.

Carcello, JV & TL Neal (2003). Audit committee characteristics and auditor dismissals following "new" going-concern reports. *The Accounting Review, 78*, 95–117.

Carlsson, RH (2001). *Ownership and Value Creation: Strategic Corporate Governance in the New Economy*. Chichester, John Wiley.

Carlton, D & D Fischel (1983). The regulation of insider trading. *Stanford Law Review, 93*, 857–895.

Carter, CB & JW Lorsch (2004). *Back to the Drawing Board: Designing Corporate Boards for a Complex World*. Boston: Harvard Business School Press.

Carter, DA, BJ Simkins & GW Simpson (2003). Corporate governance, board diversity, and firm value. *The Financial Review, 38*, 33–53.

Carvalhal-da-Silva, AL & A Subramanyam (2007). Dual-class premium, corporate governance, and the mandatory bid rule: Evidence from the Brazilian stock market. *Journal of Corporate Finance, 13*, 1–24.

Carver, J (2000). Does your board need its own dedicated support staff? *Non-profit World, 18*, 6–7.

Carver, J (1997). *Boards That Make a Difference: A New Design for Leadership in Non-Profit and Public Organizations*, 2nd ed. New York: Jossey-Bass, John Wiley & Sons Inc.

Castaldi, R & MS Wortman (1984). Boards of directors in small corporations: An untapped resource. *American Journal Small Business, 9*, 1–10.

Celent (2007). Socially responsible investing in the US and Europe: Same goals but different paths. 13 March, Paris, France. http://reports.celent.com/PressReleases/2007.313/SRI.htm.

Celent Financial Consultancy cited in P Manoje "Establishing Buddhist Investment Criteria: The analysis through Product Differentiation Theory and the Case Study of Thailand SET 50 Index," Paper 490464081 Available at: http://www.scribd.com/doc/20898424/Buddhist-Investment-Criteria-by-Manoje.

Cetorelli, N & PE Strahan (2006). Finance as a barrier to entry: Bank competition and industry structure in local U.S. markets. *Journal of Finance, 61*, 437–461.

Chakravarty, S & J McConnell (1997). An analysis of prices, bid/ask spreads, and bid and ask depths surrounding Ivan Boesky's illegal trading in carnation's stock. *Financial Management Association*, 26, 18–34.

Chakravarty, S & J McConnell (1999). Does insider trading really move stock prices? *Journal of Financial and Quantitative Analysis*, 34(2), 191–209.

Chalmers, J, R Edelen & G Kadlec (2002). On the perils of financial intermediaries setting security prices: The mutual fund wild card option. *Journal of Finance*, 56, 2209–2236.

Chang, SW & D Suk (1998). Stock prices and secondary dissemination of information: The wall street journal's insider trading spotlight column. *The Financial Review*, 33, 115–128.

Cheatham, B & W Oblin (2007). Private investment opportunities in public transport. *The McKinsey Quarterly*. Web exclusive.

Chen, D, M Jian & M Xu (2008). Dividends for tunneling in a regulated economy: The case of China. *Pacific-Basin Finance Journal*, forthcoming.

Cheung, Y, PR Rao & A Stouraitis (2006). Tunneling, propping and expropriation: evidence from connected party transactions in Hong Kong. *Journal of Financial Economics*, 82, 343–386.

Cheung, Y, Y Qi, PR Rao & A Stouraitis (2008). Buy high, sell low: How listed firms price asset transfers in related party transactions. *Working paper*.

Chiarella v. United States, 455 222 (US 1980).

Child, J & SB Rodrigues (2003). Corporate governance and new organizational forms: Issues of double and multiple agency. *Journal of Management & Governance*, 7, 337–360.

Chung, K & C Charoenwong (1998). Insider trading and bid ask spread. *The Financial Review*, 33, 1–20.

Citigroup (2006) "Demystifying responsible investment performance: a review of key academic and broker research on ESG factors," A joint report by The Asset Management Working Group of the United Nations Environment Programme Finance Initiative and Mercer https://www.ethicalfunds.com/SiteCollection Documents/docs/demystifying_responsible_investment_performance.pdf.

Clarke, AD (2006). SMEs and Corporate Governance: Politics, Resources and Trickle-Down Effects, Paper presented at the Corporate Law Teachers' Association Conference, University of Queensland, February 5–7.

Clarke, T (2007). The materiality of sustainability: corporate social and environmental responsibility as instruments of strategic change? In S Benn & D Dunphy (eds.). *Corporate Sustainability: Challenges for Theory and Practice*, pp. 219–251, London: Routledge.

Clarke, T (2005). Accounting for Enron: shareholder value and stakeholder interests. *Corporate Governance: An International Review*, 13, 598–612.

Claessens, S, S Djankov, J Fan & L Lang (2002). Disentangling the incentive and entrenchment effects of large shareholdings. *Journal of Finance, 57,* 2379–2408.

Claessens, S & L Klapper (2005). Bankruptcy around the world: Explanations of its relative use. *American Law and Economics Review, 7,* 253–283.

Coffee, J (1999). The future as history: The prospects for global convergence in corporate governance and its implications. *Northwestern University Law Review, 93,* 641–708.

Coffee, J (2006). *Gatekeepers: The Professions and Corporate Governance.* Oxford University Press.

Combined Code (1998). *Combined Code, Principles of Corporate Governance.* Gee & Co. Ltd., London.

Combined Code (2003). *The Combined Code on Corporate Governance.* Financial Reporting Council, London.

Combined Code (2006). *The Combined Code on Corporate Governance.* Financial Reporting Council, London.

Combined Code (2008). *The Combined Code on Corporate Governance.* Financial Reporting Council, London.

Comelli, F & O Yosha (2003). Stage financing and the role of convertible securities. *Review of Economic Studies, 70,* 1–32.

Companies Act 2006. HM Treasury, London.

Consolandi, C, A Jaiswal-Dale, E Poggiani & A Vercelli (2009). Global standards and ethical stock indexes: the case of the Dow Jones Sustainability STOXX Index. *Journal of Business Ethics, 87,* 185–197.

Conway, E (2009). Brutal Truths in the Banqueting Hall. The Telegraph, 18 June. Available at http://www.telegraph.co.uk/finance/comment/edmundconway/5571646/Brutal-truths-in-the-banqueting-hall.html.

Copeland, T & D Galai (1988). Information effects and the bid-ask spread. *Journal of Finance, 38,* 1457–1469.

Corbetta, G & C Salvato (2004a). Self-serving or self-actualizing? Models of man and agency costs in different types of family firms: A commentary on "Comparing angency costs of family and non-family firms: Comparing issues and exploratory evidence." *Entrepreneurship: Theory & Practice, 28,* 355–362.

Corbetta G & CA Salvato (2004b). The board of directors in family firms: One size fits all? *Family Business Review, 17,* 119–134.

Corbetta G & D Montemerlo (1999). Ownership, governance and management issues in small and medium size family business: A comparaison of Italy and the United States, *Family Business Review, 12,* 361–374.

Core, J, W Guay & T Rusticus (2006). Does weak governance cause weak stock returns? An examination of firm operating performance and investors' expectations. *Journal of Finance, 61,* 655–687.

Core, JE, RW Holthausen & DF Larcker (1999). Corporate governance, chief executive officer compensation, and firm performance. *Journal of Financial Economics, 51*, 371 – 406.

Cornell, B & E Sirri (1992). The reaction of investors and stock prices to insider trading. *Journal of Finance, 47*(3), 1031–1059.

Coulson-Thomas, C (2007). SME directors and boards: The contribution of directors and boards to the growth and development of Small and Medium-sized Enterprises (SMEs). *International Journal of Business Governance and Ethics, 3*, 250–261.

Council on Corporate Disclosure and Governance (2005). *The Code of Corporate Governance.* Singapore.

Council on Ethics for the Government Pension Fund — Global, *Annual Report 2006*, Oslo.

Counterparty Risk Management Policy Group (2008). Containing Systemic Risk: The Road to Reform, The Report of the CRMPG III. Available at http://www.crmpolicygroup.org/.

Coval, JD & TJ Moskowitz (1999). Home bias at home: Local equity preference in domestic portfolios. *Journal of Finance, 54*, 2045–2073.

Coval, JD & TJ Moskowitz (2001). The geography of investment: Informed trading and asset prices. *Journal of Political Economy, 109*, 811–841.

Cramer, A & M Hirschland (2006). The socially responsible board. *The Corporate Board, 161*, 20–24.

Cremers, M & V Nair (2005). Governance mechanisms and equity prices. *Journal of Finance, 60*, 2859–2894.

Cremers, M, V Nair & J Wei (2007). Governance mechanisms and bond prices, *Review of Financial Studies, 20*, 1359–1388.

Crystal, G (1991). *In Search of Excess: The Overcompensation of American Executives.* New York: W.W. Norton.

Cumming, DJ (2004). The determinants of venture capital portfolio size: Empirical evidence. *Journal of Business*, 1083–1126.

Daft, R & K Weick (1984). Toward a model of organizations as interpretation systems. *Academy of Management Journal, 9*, 284–295.

Dahiya, S, A Saunders & A Srinivasan (2003). Financial distress and bank lending relationships. *Journal of Finance, 58*, 375–399.

Dahya, J, O Dimitrov & J McConnell (2008). Dominant shareholders, corporate boards, and corporate value: A cross-country analysis. *Journal of Financial Economics, 87*, 73–100.

Daily CM & DR Dalton (1992). The relationship between governance structure and corporate performance in entrepreneurial firms. *Journal of Business Venturing, 7*, 375–386.

Daily, CM, PP McDougall, JG Covin & D Dalton (2002). Governance and strategic leadership in entrepreneurial firms. *Journal of Management, 28*, 387–412.

D'Aloisio, T (2009). Regulatory Issues Arising from the Financial Crisis for ASIC and for Market Participants, ASIC.

Davidson, R, J Goodwin-Stewart & P Kent (2005). Internal governance structures and earnings management. *Accounting & Finance, 45*, 241–267.

Davies, M & B Schlitzer (2008). The impracticality of an international "one size fits all" corporate governance code of best practice. *Managerial Auditing Journal, 23*, 532–644.

Davila, A, G Foster & M Gupta (2003). Staging venture capital: Empirical evidence on the differential role of early versus late rounds. *Working Paper*, Stanford University.

Davis, GF (1996). The significance of board interlocks for corporate governance. *Corporate Governance, 4*, 154–159.

Davis, GF & HR Greve (1997). Corporate elite networks and governance changes in the 1980s. *American Journal of Sociology, 103*, 1–37.

Davis, GF & TA Thompson (1994). A social movement perspective on corporate control. *Administrative Science Quarterly, 38*, 141–173.

Davis, J & JV Henderson (2004). The agglomeration of corporate headquarters. *Working paper*, Brown University.

Davis, JH, FD Schoorman & L Donaldson (1997). Toward a stewardship theory of management. *Academy of Management Review, 22*, 20–47.

Davis, P & K Eustice (2005). Delivering the PPP Promise: A Review of PPP Issues and Activity. *A PriceWaterhouse Coopers Report*.

Davis, P (2009). A Review of Lending Appetite for Public–Private Partnership Financings. *Talking Points*. London: Public Sector Research Centre — PricewaterhouseCoopers.

de Larosiere, J (2009). *High-Level Group on Financial Supervision in the EU*. Brussels, EU.

de Palma, A, L Leruth & G Prunier (2009). Towards a principal-agent based typology of risks in public–private partnerships. *International Monetary Fund Working Paper*, WP/09/177.

Degryse, H & S Ongena (2005). Distance, lending relationships, and competition. *Journal of Finance, 60*, 231–266.

Del Brio, E, A Miguel & J Perote (2002). An investigation of insider trading profits in the Spanish stock market. *Quarterly Review of Economics and Finance, 42*, 73–94.

Demb, A & FF Neubauer (1992). *The Corporate Board: Confronting the Paradoxes*. New York: Oxford University Press.

Demb, A, D Chouet, T Lossius & FF Neubauer (1989). Defining the role of the board. *Long Range Planning, 22*, 61–68.

Demirgüç-Kunt, A & R Levine (2001). *Financial Structure and Economic Growth: Cross-country Comparisons of Banks, Markets, and Development*. Cambridge, MA: MIT Press.

Deng, J, J Gan & J He (2008). Privatization, large shareholders' incentive to expropriate, and firm performance. *Working paper*. Available from: http://ssrn.com/abstract=970056.

Derwall, J, N Günster, R Bauer & CG Koedijk (2005). The Eco-Efficiency Premium Puzzle. *Financial Analysts Journal*, *61*, 51–63.

Desai, M, A Dyck & L Zingales (2007). Theft and taxes. *Journal of Financial Economics*, *84*, 591–623.

Devapriya, K (2006). Governance issues in financing of public-private partnership organisations in network infrastructure industries, *International Journal of Project Management*, *24*, 557–566.

Diamond, DW (2004). Presidential address, committing to commit: Short-term debt when enforcement is costly. *Journal of Finance*, *59*, 1447–1479.

Dittmar, A, J Mahrt-Smith & H Servaes (2003). International corporate governance and corporate cash holdings. *Journal of Financial and Quantitative Analysis*, *38*, 111–133.

Djankov, S, R La Porta, F Lopez-de-Silanes & A Shleifer (2008). The law and economics of self-dealing. *Journal of Financial Economics*, *88*, 430–465.

Djankov, S, C McLiesh & A Shleifer (2007). Private credit in 129 countries. *Journal of Financial Economics*, *84*, 299–329.

Doidge, C, A Karolyi & R Stulz (2004). Why are foreign firms listed in the U.S. worth more? *Journal of Financial Economics*, *71*, 205–238.

Doidge, C, A Karolyi, KV Lins, DP Miller & R Stulz (2009a). Private benefits of control, ownership, and the cross-listing decision. *Journal of Finance*, *64*, 425–466.

Doidge, C, A Karolyi & R Stulz (2009b). Has New York become less competitive than London in global markets? Evaluating foreign listing choices over time. *Journal of Financial Economics*, forthcoming.

Donaldson, L (1990). The ethereal hand: organisational economics and management theory', *Academy of Management Review*, *15*, 369–382.

Donaldson, L & JH Davis (1991). Stewardship theory or agency theory: CEO governance and shareholder returns. *Australian Journal of Management*, *16*, 49–65.

Donaldson, L & JH Davis (1994). Boards and company performance: Research challenges the conventional wisdom. *Corporate Governance: An International Review*, *2*, 151–160.

Donaldson, T & T Dunfee (1999). *Ties that Bind: A Social Contracts Approach to Business Ethics*. Boston: Harvard Business School Press.

Donaldson, T & LE Preston (1995). The stakeholder theory of the corporation: concepts, evidence, and implications. *Academy of Management Review*, *20*, 65–91.

Dowdell, TD & J Krishnan (2004). Former audit firm personnel as CFOs: Effects on earnings management. *Canadian Accounting Perspectives, 3*, 117–142.

du Plessis, J, J McConroll & M Bagaric (2005). *Principles of Contemporary Corporate Governance*. New York: Cambridge University Press.

Durnev, A & H Kim (2005). To steal or not to steal: Firm attributes, legal environment, and valuation. *Journal of Finance, 60*, 1461–1493.

Durnev, A & A Nain (2004). The effectiveness of insider trading regulation around the globe. Willam Davidson Institute Working Paper #695.

Dyck, A & L Zingales (2004). Private benefits of control: an international comparison. *Journal of Finance, 59*, 537–600.

Dyck, A, N Volchkova & L Zingales (2008). The corporate governance role of the media: Evidence from Russia. *Journal of Finance, 63*, 1093–1113.

Eichholtz, P, N Kok & J Quigley (2008). Doing well while doing good: Green office buildings. *ECCE Working Paper*, Maastricht University.

Employee Retirement Income Security Act 1974 Department of Labor, Washington, DC.

Environmental Agency UK (2004). *Corporate Environmental Governance: A Study into the Influence of Environmental Governance and Financial Performance*. Online. Available at http://www.environment-agency.gov.uk/business/444255/887223/1251983/?lang=_e.

Errunza, V & D Miller (2000). Market segmentation and the cost of capital in international equity markets. *Journal of Financial and Quantitative Analysis, 35*, 577–600.

Esterbrook, F (1981). Insider trading, secret agents, evidentiary privileges, and the production of information. *Supreme Court Review, 1981*, 309–365.

Esty, B & WL Megginson (2003). Creditor rights, enforcement, and debt ownership structure: evidence from the global syndicated loan market. *Journal of Financial and Quantitative Analysis, 38*, 37–59.

Etebari, A, A Tourani-Rad & A Gilbert (2004). Disclosure regulation and the profitability of insider trading: Evidence from New Zealand. *Pacific-Basin Finance Journal, 12*, 479–509.

European Union (2007). *Directive 2007/36/EC Shareholders' Rights*, EU, Brussels.

Faccio, M, L Lang & L Young (2001). Dividends and expropriation. *American Economic Review, 91*, 54–78.

Fama, EF (1980). Agency problems and the theory of the firm. *The Journal of Political Economy, 88*, 288–307.

Fama, EF & MC Jensen, (1983). Agency problems and residual claims. *Journal of Law & Economics, 26*, 327–350.

Farrar, JH (2008). The corporate governance of SMEs and Unlisted companies. *New Zealand Business Law Quarterly, 14*, 213–230.

Farrar, JH and J du Plessis (2009). Business structures: Are SMEs and family business currently served by the legislation? Keynote presentation at SME and Family Business Conference, University of Auckland, August 14.

Fernandes, N & M Ferreira (2008). Does international cross-listing really improve the information environment? *Journal of Financial Economics, 88*, 216–244.

Ferreira MA & P Matos (2008). The colors of investors' money: The role of institutional investors around the world. *Journal of Financial Economics, 88*, 499–533.

Financial Stability Forum (2008). *Report of the Financial Stability Forum on Enhancing Market and Institutional Resilience: Follow-up on Implementation.* Available at http://www.fsforum.org/press/pr_081009f.pdf.

Financial Stability Forum (2009a). Financial Stability Forum decides to broaden its membership. Press Release Ref: no: 10/2009. Available at http://www.financialstabilityboard.org/list/fsb_press_releases/index.htm.

Financial Stability Forum (2009b). Mandate. Available at http://www.financialstabilityboard.org/about/mandate.htm.

Financial Services Authority (2009). The Turner Review, A Regulatory Response to the Global Banking Crisis. Available at http://www.fsa.gov.uk/pages/library/corporate/turner/index.shtml.

Financial Reporting Council (2009). Review of the Effectiveness of the Combined Code: Call for Evidence.

Finkelstein, S & DC Hambrick (1996). *Strategic Leadership: Top Executives and their Effects* on Organizations. West, Minneapolis, MN.

Finkelstein S, DC Hambrick & AA Cannella Jr. (2009). *Strategic Leadership: Theory and Research on Executives, Top Management Teams, and Boards.* UK: Oxford University Press.

Finkelstein, S & AC Mooney (2003). Not the usual suspects: How to use board process to make boards better. *The Academy of Management Executive, 17*, 101–113.

Finnerty, J (1976). Insiders and market efficiency. *Journal of Finance, 31*, 1141–1148.

Fishman, M & K Hagerty (1992). Insider trading and the efficency of stock prices. *Rand Journal of Economics, 23*, 106–122.

Fishman, M & K Hagerty (1995). The mandatory disclosure of trades and market liquidity. *The Review of Financial Studies, 8*, 637–676.

Forbes, DP & FJ Milliken (1999). Cognition and corporate governance: Understanding boards of directors as strategic decision-making groups. *Academy of Management Review, 24*, 489–505.

Ford, RH (1992). *Boards of Directors and the Privately Owned Firm.* New York: Quorum Books.

Foucault, T & T Gehrig (2008). Stock price informativeness, cross-listings, and investment decisions. *Journal of Financial Economics, 88*, 146–168.

Francis, B, I Hasan & M Waisman (2008). Does geography matter to bondholders? *Working paper*, Rennsealer Polytechnic Institute.

Freeman, RE (1984). *Strategic management: a stakeholder approach.* Boston: Pitman.

Freeman, RE & WM Evans (1990). Corporate governance: a stakeholder theory interpretation. *The Journal of Behavioral Economics, 19*, 337–359.

Fried, VH, GD Bruton & RD Hisrich (1998). Strategy and the board of directors in venture capital-backed firms. *Journal of Business Venturing, 13*, 493–503.

Freiderich, S, A Gregory, J Matatko & I Tonks (2002). Short run returns around the trades of corporate insiders on the London Stock Exchange. *European Financial Management, 8*, 7–30.

Friedman, M (1970, September 13). The Social Responsibility of Business is to Increase its Profits. *The New York Times Magazine*, New York.

Frijns, B, A Gilbert & A Tourani-Rad (2008). Insider trading, regulation and the components of the bid-ask spread. *Journal of Financial Research, 31*, 225–246.

Frijns, B, A Gilbert & A Tourani-Rad (2009). Elements of effective insider trading regulation. *AUT University Working Paper.*

Gabrielsson, J & M Huse (2005). "Outside" directors in SME boards: A call for theoretical reflections. *Corporate Board: Role, Duties & Composition, 1*, 28–37.

Gabrielson, J & M Huse (2002). The venture capitalist and the board of directors in SMEs: role and process. *Venture Capital, 4*, 125–146.

Gabrielsson, J & H Winlund (2000). Boards of directors in small and medium-sized industrial firms: Examining the effects of the board's working style on board task performance. *Entrepreneurship & Regional Development, 12*, 311–330.

Galaskiewicz, J & S Wasserman (1989). Mimetic process within an interorganizational field: An empirical test. *Administrative Science Quarterly, 34*, 454–479.

Gallo, MA (2005). Independent board directors: How to improve their contribution to the family business. *IESE Working Paper* No. 589.

Gao, L & G Kling (2008). Corporate governance and tunneling: Empirical evidence from China. *Pacific-Basin Finance Journal*, forthcoming.

Gao, W, L Ng & Q Wang (2008). Does geographic dispersion affect firm valuation? *Journal of Corporate Finance, 14*, 674–687.

Garmaise, M & T Moskowitz (2006). Bank mergers and crime: The real and social effects of credit market competition. *Journal of Finance, 61*, 495–538.

Garratt, B (2001a). *The Twelve Organizational Capabilities.* New York: Harper Collins Business.

Garratt, B (2001b). *The Learning Organization, Developing Democracy at Work.* New York: Harper Collins Business.

Garratt, B (2003a). *The Fish Rots from the Head.* London: Profile Books Ltd.

Garratt, B (2003b). *Developing Strategic Thought: A Collection of Best Thinking on Business strategy.* UK: Profilebooks.

Garratt, B (2006). *Thin On Top, Why Corporate Governance Matters and How to Measure and Improve board performance.* London: Nicholas Brealey.

Garratt, B (2007). Dilemmas, uncertainty, risks and board performance. *BT Technology Journal*, 25, 11–18.

Gaspar, J & M Massa (2007). Local ownership and private information: Evidence on the monitoring-liquidity trade-off. *Journal of Financial Economics*, 83, 751–792.

Geczy, C, RF Stambaugh & D Levin (2005). Investing in socially responsible mutual funds, *Working Paper*. University of Pennsylvania.

Geiger, MA, DS North & BT O'Connell (2005). The auditor-to-client revolving door and earnings management. *Journal of Accounting, Auditing and Finance*, 20, 1–26.

Geiger, MA & DS North (2006). Does hiring a new CFO change things? An investigation of changes in discretionary accruals. *The Accounting Review*, 81, 781–809.

George, G, DR Wood & R Khan (2001). Networking strategy of boards: Implications for small and medium-sized enterprises. *Entrepreneurship & Regional Development*, 13, 269–285.

Gerstner, L (2002). *Who Said Elephants Can't Dance*. Harper Collins.

Gilbert, A, A Tourani-Rad & TP Wisniewski (2006). Do insiders crowd out analysts? *Finance Research Letters*, 3, 40–48.

Gilson, R & J Gordon (2003). Controlling controlling shareholders. *University of Pennsylvania Law Review*, 152, 785–850.

Glaeser, E, S Johnson & A Shleifer (2001). Coase v. the Coasians. *Quarterly Journal of Economics*, 116, 853–899.

Glaeser, E & J Scheinkman (2003). Non-market interactions. In M Dewatripont, M Hansen & S Turnovsky (eds.). *Advances in Economics and Econometrics: Theory and Applications*. Eight World Congress, Cambridge University Press.

Global Reporting Initiative (GRI) (2002). *Sustainability Reporting Guidelines*, Amsterdam: GRI. Online. Available at http://www.globalreporting.org.

Glosten, L & P Milgrom (1985). Bid, ask and transaction prices in a specialist market with heterogeneoulsy informed traders. *Journal of Financial Economics*, 14, 71–100.

Golden, BR and EJ Zajac (2001). When will boards influence strategy? Inclination x power = strategic change. *Strategic Management Journal*, 22, 1087–1111.

Goldman, M (2003). *The Piratization of Russia: Russian Reform Goes Awry*. New York: Routledge.

Gompers, P (1995). Optimal investments, monitoring, and the staging of venture capital. *Journal of Finance*, 50, 1461–1489.

Gompers, P, JL Ishii & A Metrick (2003). Corporate governance and equity prices. *Quarterly Journal of Economics*, 188, 107–155.

Gompers, P, J Lerner & D Scharfstein (2005). Entrepreneurial spawning: Public corporations and the formation of new ventures. *Journal of Finance*, 60, 577–614.

Gordon, E, E Henry & D Palia (2004). Related party transactions: Associations with corporate governance and firm value. *Advances in Financial Economics*, 9, 1–27.

Gozzi, J, RL Levine & S Schmukler (2008). Internationalization and the evolution of corporate valuation. *Journal of Financial Economics, 88,* 607–632.

Grayson, D & A Hodges (2004). *Corporate Social Opportunity: 7 Steps to Make Corporate Social Responsibility Work for Your Business.* Sheffield: Greenleaf Publishing.

Greenbury, R (1995). *Directors' Remuneration.* Gee & Co. Ltd., London.

Greene, J & C Ciccotello (2006). Mutual fund dilution from market timing trades. *Journal of Investment Management, 4,* 31–54.

Greiner, LE (1972). Evolution and revolution as organizations grow. *Harvard Business Review.* Jul–Aug., 397–409.

Greiner, LE (1998). Evolution and revolution as organisations grow. *Harvard Business Review,* May–June, 55–67.

Grinblatt, M & M Keloharju (2001). How distance, language, and culture influence stockholdings and trades? *Journal of Finance, 56,* 1053–1073.

Grossman, BR & W Sharpe (1986). Financial implications of South African divestment. *Financial Analysts Journal, 42,* 15–29.

Gruber, MJ (1996). Another puzzle: The growth in actively managed mutual funds. *Journal of Finance, 51,* 783–810.

Guillen, MF (2000). Convergence in global governance? *Corporate Board, 21,* 17–21.

Günster, N, J Derwall, R Bauer & CG Koedijk (2006). The economic value of corporate eco-efficiency. *ECCE Working Paper,* Maastricht University.

Guiso, L, P Sapienza & L Zingales (2006). Does culture affect economic outcomes? *Journal of Economic Perspectives, 20,* 23–49.

Guiso, L, P Sapienza & L Zingales (2008). Trusting the stock market. *Journal of Finance, 63,* 2557–2600.

Gulati, R & JD Westphal (1999). Cooperative or controlling? The effects of CEO-board relations and the content of interlocks on the formation of joint ventures. *Administrative Science Quarterly, 44,* 473–506.

Gupta, AK & HJ Sapienza (1992). Determinants of capital firms' preferences regarding the industry diversity and geographic scope of their investments. *Journal of Business Venturing, 7,* 347–362.

Gupta, M & LP Fields (2009). Board independence and corporate governance: Evidence from director resignations. *Journal of Business, Finance and Accounting, 36,* 161–184.

Gupta, M, IK Khurana & R Pereira (2008). Legal enforcement, short maturity debt, and incentive to manage earnings. *Journal of Law and Economics, 51,* 619–639.

Hackethal, A, RH Schmidt & M Tyrell (2005). Banks and German corporate governance: On the way to a capital market-based system? *Corporate Governance: An International Review, 13,* 397–407.

Hall, C (2007). Are emerging market TNCs sensitive to corporate responsibility issues? *Journal of Corporate Citizenship, 26,* 30–37.

Hammami, M, J-F Ruhashyankiko & EB Yehoue (2006). Determinants of public-private partnerships in infrastructure. *Working paper No. 06/99*, Washington, DC: IMF.

Hampel, R (1998). *Committee on Corporate Governance: Final Report.* Gee & Co. Ltd., London.

Harris, C (2003). Private participation in infrastructure in developing countries: Trends, impacts, and policy lessons. *Working paper*.

Hart, O (1995). *Firms, Contracts, and Financial Structure.* London: Oxford University Press.

Hart, O & J Moore (1994). A theory of debt based on the inalienability of human capital. *Quarterly Journal of Economics, 109*, 841–879.

Harvey, CR, KV Lins & AH Roper (2003). The effect of capital structure when expected agency costs are extreme. *Journal of Financial Economics, 74*, 3–30.

Haunschild, PR (1993). Interorganizational imitation: The impact of interlocks on corporate acquisition activity. *Administrative Science Quarterly, 38*, 564–592.

Hermalin, BE & MS Weisbach (2003). Boards of directors as an endogenously determined institution: A survey of the economic literature. *Economic Policy Review, 9*, 7–26.

Higgs, D (2003). *Review of the Role and Effectiveness of Non-Executive Directors.* Department of Trade and Industry, London.

Hilary, G & KW Hui (2009). Does religion matter in corporate decision making in America? *Journal of Financial Economics, 93*, 455–473.

Hilb, M (2008). *New Corporate Governance: Successful Board Management Tools.* Berlin: Springer.

Hill, S (1995). The social organization of boards of directors. *British Journal of Sociology, 46*, 245–278.

Hillman, AJH & M Hitt (1999). Corporate political strategy formulation: A model of approach participation, and strategy decisions. *The Academy of Management Review, 24*, 825–842.

Hilmer, FG & RI Tricker (1994). An Effective Board. In RI Tricker, *International corporate governance: Text readings and cases,* pp. 285–296. Singapore: Prentice Hall.

Hochberg, Y, A Ljungqvist & Y Lu (2007). Whom you know matters: Venture capital networks and investment performance. *Journal of Finance 62*, 251–301.

Hodge, G (2000). *Privatization: An International Review of Performance.* In Theoretical Lenses on Public Policy, Westview Press.

Hodge, G (2004). The risky business of public-private partnerships. *Australian Journal of Public Administration, 63*, 37–49.

Hong, H & M Kacperczyk (2009). The price of sin: The effect of social norms on markets. *Journal of Financial Economics, 93*, 15–36.

Hong, H, JD Kubik & JC Stein (2004). Social interaction and stock market participation. *Journal of Finance, 59*, 137–163.

Hong, H, JD Kubik & JC Stein (2008). The only game in town: Stock price consequences of local bias. *Journal of Financial Economics, 90,* 20–37.

Hoskisson, R, M Hitt, R Johnson & W Grossman (2002). Conflicting votes:
The effects of institutional ownership heterogeneity and internal governance
on corporate innovation strategies. *Academy of Management Journal, 45,*
697–716.

Huberman, G (2001). Familiarity breeds investment. *Review of Financial Studies, 14,*
659–680.

Hummels, H (2007). De Kracht van Pensioenfondsen. *ECCE Report,* Maastricht
University.

Hummels, H & R Bauer (2006). Van Stille Kracht naar Stille Macht: Pensioenfondsen
in Gesprek met Ondernemingen over Corporate Governance en Maatschappelijk
Handelen. *van Gorcum,* Assen.

Huse, M (1994). Board-management relations in small firms: The paradox of simul-
taneous independence and interdependence. *Small Business Economics, 6,* 55–72.

Huse, M (2000). Boards of directors in SMEs: A review and research agenda.
Entrepreneurship and Regional Development, 12, 271–290.

Huse, M (2005). Accountability and creating accountability: A framework for exploring behavioural perspectives of corporate governance. *British Journal of
Management, 16,* S65–S79.

Huse, M (2005). Corporate governance: Understanding important contingencies.
Corporate Ownership & Control, 2, 41–50.

Huse, M (2007). *Boards, governance and value creation: The human side of corporate
governance.* UK: Cambridge University Press.

Hung, (1998). A typology of theories of the roles of governing boards. *Corporate
Governance: An International Review, 6,* 101–110.

Ingley, C (2004). From conformance to performance: The strategic role of the board
and its involvement in corporate leadership. Unpublished Doctoral Thesis,
RMIT University, June. Melbourne, Australia.

Ingley, C & K McCaffrey (2007). Effective governance for start-up companies:
Regarding the board as a strategic resource. *International Journal of Business
Governance and Ethics, 3,* 308–329.

Ingley CB & NT van der Walt (2004a). Corporate governance, institutional investors
and conflicts of interest. *Corporate Governance: An International Review, 12,*
534–551.

Institutional Shareholders' Committee (2002). *The Responsibilities of Institutional
Shareholders and Agents — Statement of Principles.* ISC, London.

Institutional Shareholders' Committee (2005). *Review of the Institutional Shareholders'
Committee Statement of Principles on the Responsibilities of Institutional
Shareholders and Agents.* London: ISC.

Institutional Shareholders' Committee (2007). *The Responsibilities of Institutional Shareholders and Agents — Statement of Principles.* London: ISC.

Ivković, Z & S Weisbenner (2005). Local does as local is: Information content of the geography of individual investors' common stock investments. *Journal of Finance, 60,* 267–306.

Jaffe, J (1974). Special information and insider trading. *Journal of Business, 47,* 410–428.

Jaworski, W (2007). The use of extra-financial information by research analysts and investment managers. *ECCE Report,* Maastricht University.

James, C (1987). Some evidence on the uniqueness of bank loans. *Journal of Financial Economics, 19,* 217–235.

Jeffers, E (2005). Corporate governance: Toward converging models? *Global Finance Journal, 16,* 221–232.

Jensen, M & W Meckling (1976). Theory of the firm: Managerial behavior, agency costs, and ownership structure. *Journal of Financial Economics, 3,* 305–360.

Jensen, M & EJ Zajac (2004). Corporate elites and corporate strategy: How demographic preferences and structural position shape the scope of the firm. *Strategic Management Journal, 25,* 507–524.

Jiang, G, C Lee & H Yue (2005). Tunneling in China: The surprisingly pervasive use of corporate loans to extract funds from Chinese listed companies. *Working Paper,* Johnson School Research Paper Series No. 31–06.

Johanisson, B & M Huse (2000). Recruiting outside board members in the small family business: An ideological challenge. *Entrepreneurship & Regional Development, 12,* 353–378.

John, K & A Knyazeva (2008). Corporate governance and commitment. *Working paper,* University of Rochester.

John, K, A Knyazeva & D Knyazeva (2008). Do shareholders care about geography? *Working paper,* New York University.

Johnson, S, P Boone, A Breach & E Friedman (2000a). Corporate governance in the Asian financial crisis. *Journal of Financial Economics, 58,* 141–186.

Johnson, JL, CM Daily & AE Ellstrand (1996). Boards of directors: A review and research agenda. *Journal of Management, 22,* 409–438.

Johnson, S, R La Porta, A Shleifer & F Lopez-de-Silanes (2000b). Tunneling. *American Economic Review Papers and Proceedings, 90,* 22–27.

Jones, JJ (1991). Earnings management during import relief investigations. *Journal of Accounting Research, 29,* 193–228.

Jonker, J (2003). In search of society: Redefining corporate social responsibility, organisational theory and business strategies. *Research in International Business and Finance, 17,* 423–439.

Kahneman, D & A Tversky (1973). On the psychology of prediction. *Psychological Review, 80,* 237–251.

Kang, J & J Kim (2008). The geography of block acquisitions. *Journal of Finance*, 63, 2817–2858.

Kaplan, R & D Norton (1996). *The Balanced Scorecard, Translating Strategy into Action*. HBS Press.

Kaplan, R & D Norton (2000). *The Strategy Focused Organisation, How Balanced Scorecard Companies Thrive in the New Environment*. HBS Press.

Kaplan, S & P Stromberg (2004). Characteristics, contracts, and actions: Evidence from venture capitalist analyses. *Journal of Finance*, 59, 2177–2210.

Kedia, S, V Panchapagesan & V Uysal (2008). Geography and acquirer returns. *Journal of Financial Intermediation*, 17, 256–275.

Kedia, S & S Rajgopal (2009). Neighborhood matters: The impact of location on broad based stock option plans. *Journal of Financial Economics*, 92, 109–127.

Kesner, IF (1988). Directors' characteristics and committee membership: An investigation of type, occupation, tenure and gender. *Academy of Management Journal*, 31, 66–84.

Khanna, N & S Slezak (1994). Insider trading, outside search and resource allocation: Why firms and society may disagree on insider trading restrictions. *The Review of Financial Studies*, 7, 575–608.

Kidd, C (1992). The evolution of sustainability. *Journal of Agricultural and Environmental Ethics*, 5, 1–26.

Kiel, G & G Nicholson (2003). *Boards That Work: A New Guide for Directors*. Australia: McGraw-Hill.

King, R & R Levine (1993). Finance and growth: Schumpeter might be right. *Quarterly Journal of Economics*, CVIII, 717–738.

Kirchmaier, T & J Grant (2004). Who governs? Corporate ownership and control structures in Europe. Available at SSRN: http://ssrn.com/abstract=555877.

Kirchmaier, T & J Grant (2005). Financial tunneling and the revenge of the insider system: How to circumvent the new European corporate governance legislation. *London School of Economics Discussion Paper 536*.

Kirtpatrick, G (2009). *The Corporate Governance Lessons from the Financial Crisis*, OECD.

Klapper, L & I Love (2004). Corporate governance, investor protection, and performance in emerging markets. *Journal of Corporate Finance*, 10, 703–728.

Klein, A (2002). Audit committee, board of director characteristics, and earnings management. *Journal of Accounting and Economics*, 33, 375–400.

Knight, F (1921). *Risk, Uncertainity and Profit*. Boston: Hart, Schaffner & Marx.

Knoepfel, I (2001). Dow Jones sustainability group index: A global benchmark for corporate sustainability. *Corporate Environmental Strategy*, 8, 6–14.

Kraakman, R (1991). The Legal Theory of Insider Trading Regulation in the United States. In K Hopt & E Wymeerisch (eds.). *European Insider Dealing* (pp. 39–54).

Kyle, A (1985). Continuous auctions and insider trading. *Econometrica*, 53, 1315–1335.

La Porta, R, F Lopez-de-Silanes & A Shleifer (1998). Law and finance. *Journal of Political Economy*, 106, 1133–1155.

La Porta, R, F Lopez-de-Silanes, A Shleifer & R Vishny (1997). Legal determinants of external finance. *Journal of Finance*, 52, 1131–1150.

La Porta, R, F Lopez-de-Silanes, A Shleifer & R Vishney (1999). The quality of government. *Journal of Law, Economics and Organisation*, 15, 222–279.

La Porta, R, F Lopez-de-Silanes, A Shleifer & R Vishny (2000). Agency problems and dividend policies around the world. *Journal of Finance*, 55, 1–33.

La Porta, R, F Lopez-de-Silanes, A Shleifer & R Vishny (2002). Investor protection and corporate valuation. *Journal of Finance*, 57, 1147–1170.

La Porta, R, F Lopez-de-Silanes & A Shleifer (2006). What works in securities laws? *Journal of Finance*, 61, 1–32.

Lakonishok, J & I Lee (2001). Are insiders trades informative? *The Review of Financial Studies*, 14, 79–111.

Landier, A, V Nair & J Wulf (2008). Trade-offs in staying close: Corporate decision making and geographic dispersion. *Review of Financial Studies*, forthcoming.

Lang, M, K Lins & D Miller (2004). Concentrated control, analyst following, and valuation: Do analysts matter most when investors are protected least? *Journal of Accounting Research*, 42, 589–623.

Leavitt, J (2005). Burned angels: The coming wave of minority shareholder oppression claims in venture capital start-up companies. *North Carolina Journal of Law and Technology*, 6, 223–288.

Lel, U & D Miller (2008). International cross-listing, firm performance, and top management turnover: A test of the bonding hypothesis. *Journal of Finance*, 63, 1897–1937.

Lennox, C (2005). Audit quality and executive officers' affiliations with CPA firms. *Journal of Accounting and Economics*, 39, 201–231.

Lerner, J & A Schoar (2005). Does legal enforcement affect financial transactions? The contractual channel in private equity. *Quarterly Journal of Economics*, 120, 223–246.

Leuz, C, D Nanda & PD Wysocki (2003). Earnings management and investor protection: An international comparison. *Journal of Financial Economics*, 69, 505–527.

Leuz, C, A Triantis & T Wang (2008). Why do firms go dark? Causes and economic consequences of voluntary SEC deregistration? *Journal of Accounting and Economics*, 45, 181–208.

Lie, E (2005). On the timing of CEO stock option awards. *Management Science*, 51, 802–812.

Lins, KV (2003). Equity ownership and firm value in emerging markets. *Journal of Financial and Quantitative Analysis, 38*, 159–184.

Lins, KV, D Strickland & M Zenner (2005). Do non-U.S. firms issue equity on U.S. exchanges to relax capital constraints? *The Journal of Financial and Quantitative Analysis, 40*, 109–133.

Litvin, D (2004). *Empires of Profit: Commerce, Conquest and Corporate Responsibility.* Thomson. Mason.

Liu, Q & Z Lu (2004). Earnings management to tunnel: Evidence from Chinese listed companies. *Working paper.*

Lorsch, JW (1995a). Empowering the board. *Harvard Business Review, 73,* 107–117.

Lorsch, JW (1995b). The board's balancing act. *Harvard Business Review, 73,* 190–192.

Louden, JK (1982). *The Director: A Professionals Guide to Effective Board Work.* New York: Amacom.

Loughran, T (2008). The impact of firm location on equity issuance. *Financial Management, 37,* 1–21.

Loughran, T & P Schulz (2005). Liquidity: Urban versus rural firms. *Journal of Financial Economics, 78,* 341–374.

Loughran, T & P Schulz (2006). Asymmetric information, firm location, and equity issuance. *Working paper,* University of Notre Dame.

Lummer, S & J McConnell (1989). Further evidence on the bank lending process and the reaction of the capital market to bank loan agreements. *Journal of Financial Economics, 25,* 99–122.

Mace, ML (1948). *The board of directors in small corporations.* Graduate School of Business Administration, Harvard University, Boston, MA.

Macey, J (1991). *Insider Trading: Economics, Politics. Policy.* American Enterprise Institute Press.

Madhavan, A, M Richardson & M Roomans (1997). Why do security prices change? A transaction-level analysis of NYSE stocks. *The Review of Financial Studies, 10,* 1035–1064.

Maharaj, R (2008). Crtiquing and contrasting "moral" stakeholder theory and "strategic" stakeholder: Implications for the board of directors. *Corporate Governance, 8,* 115–127.

Makower, J (2006). Milton Friedman and the social responsibility of business. *World Changing.* Online. Available at http://www.worldchanging.com/archives/005373.html.

Malan, D (2005). Corporate citizens, colonialists, tourists or activists? Ethical challenges facing South African corporations in Africa. *Journal of Corporate Citizenship, 18,* 49–60.

Malizia, DJ (2008). Big fish, little pond: How large-company execs best fit into smaller businesses... and their board rooms. *Directors and Boards, 2,* 24–27.

Malkiel, BG (1995). Returns from investing in equity mutual funds from 1971 to 1991. *Journal of Finance, 50,* 549–572.

Malloy, CJ (2005). The geography of equity analysis. *Journal of Finance, 60,* 719–755.

Manoje, P (n.d.). Establishing buddhist investment criteria: The analysis through product differentiation theory and the case study of Thailand SET 50 Index. Paper 490464081. Available at: http://www.scribd.com/doc/20898424/Buddhist-Investment-Criteria-by-Manoje.

Manove, M (1989). The harm from insider trading and informed speculation. *The Quarterly Journal of Economics,* 823–845.

Manne, H (1966). *Insider Trading and the Stock Market.* New York: The Free Press.

Marquis, C, MA Glynn & GF Davis (2009). Community isomorphism and corporate social action. *Academy of Management Review,* forthcoming.

Marosi, A & NZ Massoud (2007). Why do firms go dark? *Journal of Financial and Quantitative Analysis, 42,* 421–442.

Marosi, A & N Massoud (2008). You can enter but you cannot leave: US securities markets and foreign firms. *Journal of Finance, 63,* 2477–2506.

Massa, M & A Simonov (2006). Hedging, familiarity and portfolio choice. *Review of Financial Studies, 19,* 633–685.

Massie, RK (2002). Engage, disclose and act! The future of sustainable governance. Keynote address at SRI, Colorado Springs: *Investors and Environmentalists,* Ceres, October 16. Available at http://www.ceres.org/Page.aspx?pid=777.

Massie, RK (2003). The irresistible rise of sustainable governance. World Economic Forum, Davos, Switzerland.

Maurer, N & S Haber (2003). Bank concentration, related lending, and economic performance: Evidence from Mexico. *Mimeo,* Stanford University.

Mayne, S (2009). Season of revolt. Business Day, 30 March. Available at http://www.businessday.com.au/business/season-of-revolt-20090330-9fwo.html?page=-1.

McCahery, JA & EPM Vermeulen (2008). Corporate governance of non-listed companies: The way forward. Available at http://www.icc-corporategovernance.org/uploadedFiles/Corporate%20Governance%20-%20The%20Way%20Forward.pdf.

McDermott, D (2009). Corporate agenda 21: A unified global approach to CSR and sustainability. *Corporate Communications: An International Journal, 14,* 286–302.

McKinsey & Company (2002). *Global Investor Opinion Survey* (www.McKinsey.com).

McPeak, C & N Tooley (2008). Do corporate social responsibility leaders perform better financially? *Journal of Global Business Issues, 2,* 1–6.

Menon, K & DD Williams (2004). Former audit partners and abnormal accruals. *The Accounting Review, 79,* 1095–1118.

Mercer Investment Consultants (2007). *Defined contribution plans and socially responsible investing in the United States: a survey of plan sponsors, administrators and consultants.* www.mercer.com.

Merton, R (1974). On the pricing of corporate debt: The risk structure of interest rates. *Journal of Finance, 29,* 449–471.

Meulbroek, L (1992). An empirical analysis of illegal insider trading. *Journal of Finance, 47,* 1661–1699.

Michelson, G, N Wailes, S van der Laan & G Frost (2004). Ethical investment processes and outcomes. *Journal of Business Ethics, 52,* 1–10.

Milgrom, P & J Roberts (1992). *Economics, Organization and Management.* Englewood Cliffs: Prentice Hall.

Miller, D (1999). The market reaction to international cross-listings: Evidence from depositary receipts. *Journal of Financial Economics, 51,* 103–123.

Millstein, I & S Katsh (2003). *The Limits of Corporate Power: Existing Constraints on the Exercise of Corporate* Discretion. Washington: BeardBooks.

Ming, J & T Wong (2003). Earnings management and tunneling through related party transactions: Evidence from Chinese corporate groups. *Working Paper.*

Mizruchi, MS (1989). Similarity of political behavior among large American corporations. *American Journal of Sociology, 95,* 401–424.

Mizruchi, M & L Stearns (1994). A longitudinal study of borrowing by large American corporations. *Administrative Science Quarterly, 39,* 118–140.

Mo Ibrahim Foundation (2008). *2008 Ibrahim Index of Governance.* President and Fellows of Harvard College. Boston.

Monks, RAG & N Minow (2008). *Corporate Governance.* West Sussex, England: John Wiley.

Morck, R, B Yeung & W Yu (2000). The information content of stock markets: Why do emerging markets have synchronous stock price movements? *Journal of Financial Economics, 58,* 215–260.

Mueller, J, C Ingley & G Cocks (2009). Where small business hits the big times: Good governance is more affordable than ever. Paper presented at the 2009 SEAANZ Conference, Wellington, September 2.

Mueller, J, C Ingley & G Cocks (2008). The blender approach to governance leadership: Do diverse director attributes contribute to board capital? Paper presented at the 22nd Annual Australian and New Zealand Academy of Management (ANZAM) Conference "Managing in the Pacific Century," Auckland, December 2–5.

Munnell, AH (2007). Should public pension funds engage in social investing? *Publication Center for Retirement Research,* Boston.

Muth, MM & L Donaldson (1998). Stewardship theory and board structure: A contingency approach. *Corporate Governance: An International Review, 6,* 5–29.

Myers, SC & NS Majluf (1984). Corporate financing and investment decisions when firms have information that investors do not have. *Journal of Financial Economics, 13,* 187–221.

Myners, P (2007). *Shareholder Voting Working Group.* London.

Nadler, DA (2004). What's the board's role in strategy development? Engaging the board in corporate strategy. *Strategy & Leadership, 32,* 25–33.

Naiker, V & DS Sharma (2009). Former audit partners on the audit committee and internal control deficiencies. *The Accounting Review, 84,* 559–587.

Nanto, DK (2009). The Global Financial Crisis: Analysis and Policy Implications Congressional Research Service.

National Association of Corporate Directors (NACD) (1996). *Report of the NACD Blue Ribbon Committee on Director Professionalism.* Washington, DC: NACD.

National Association of Securities Dealers (NASDAQ) (2009). *Listing rules.* New York: NASDAQ OMX Group.

Nenova, T (2003). The value of corporate votes and control benefits: A cross-country analysis. *Journal of Financial Economics, 68,* 325–351.

Nenova, T (2005). Control values and changes in corporate law in Brazil. *Latin American Business Review, 6,* 1–37.

Norton, E & B Tenenbaum (1993). Specialization versus diversification as a venture capital investment strategy. *Journal of Business Venturing, 8,* 431–442.

Nenova, T (2003). The value of corporate voting rights and control: A cross-country analysis. *Journal of Financial Economics, 68,* 325–352.

New York Stock Exchange (2008). *NYSE Listed Company Manual.* New York: New York Stock Exchange.

New Zealand Securities Commission (2004). *Corporate governance in New Zealand principles and guidance.* Wellington: New Zealand Securities Commission.

Obasanjo, O (1991). Opening Remarks. Democracy and Governance in Africa, (pp. 21–44). Ota.

OECD (2010). Corporate Governance and the Financial Crisis, Conclusions and emerging good practices to enhance implementation of the Principles.

OECD (2008). SME Policy Brief, 29 July 2008. Retrieved from www.scribd.com/doc/4237302/OECD-SME-policy-brief-ENG.

OECD (2004). *Principles of Corporate Governance,* Paris. http://www.oecd.org/dataoecd/32/18/31557724.pdf.

OECD (1999). Principles of Corporate Governance, OECD, Parris.

OECD Website (2009). Available at http://www.oecd.org/pages/0,3417,en_36734052_36734103_1_1_1_1_1,00.html.

Office of National Statistics (2007). *Share Ownership: A Report on Ownership of Shares as at 31st December 2006.* HMSO, London.

O'Neal, FH & R Thompson (2004). *Oppression of Minority Shareholders and LLC Members.* 2d Edition. Thomson-West.

Orlitzky, M, F Schmidt & S Rynes (2003). Corporate social and financial perform-ance: A meta-analysis. *Organization Studies*, 24, 403–441.

Orpurt, S (2004). Local analyst earnings forecast advantages in Europe. *Working paper*, University of Chicago.

Parsons, T (1960). *Structure and process in modern societies*. Free Press, Glencoe: IL.

Pendleton, A (2004). The real face of corporate social responsibility. *Consumer Policy Review*, http://www.allbusiness.com/legal/laws-government-regulations-environmental/946545.html.

Perrini, F (2006). The practitioner's perspective on non-financial reporting. *California Management Review*, 48, 73–103.

Peterson, MA & RG Rajan (1994). The benefits of lending relationships: Evidence fromsmall business data. *Journal of Finance*, 49, 3–37.

Peterson, MA & RG Rajan (2002). Does distance still matter? The information revolution in small business lending. *Journal of Finance*, 57, 2533–2570.

Peyer, U & T Vermaelen (2005). The many facets of privately negotiated stock repurchases. *Journal of Financial Economics*, 75, 361–395.

Pfeffer, J (1973). Size, composition and function of hospital boards of directors: A study of organization-environmental linkage. *Administrative Science Quarterly*, 18, 349–364.

Pfeffer, J (1972). Size and composition of corporate boards of directors: The organ-ization and its environment. *Administrative Science Quarterly*, 17, 218–228.

Pfeffer, J & G Salancik (1978). *The external control of organizations*. New York: Harper and Row.

Phillips, K (2009). Obama signs financial bill, creating investigative panel. New York Times. Available at http://thecaucus.blogs.nytimes.com/2009/05/20/obama-signs-financial-bill-creating-investigative-panel/.

Pirinsky, C & Q Wang (2006). Does corporate headquarters location matter for stock returns? *Journal of Finance*, 61, 1991–2015.

Pirinsky, C & Q Wang (2009). Market segmentation and the cost of capital: Evidence from the municipal bond market. *Working paper*, George Washington University and Georgia Institute of Technology.

Pistor, K & C Xu (2005). Governing stock markets in transition economies: Lessons from China. *American Law and Economics Review*, 7, 184–210.

Pollitt, C (2003). *The Essential Public Manager*. Maidenhead: Open University Press.

Ponssard, J-P, D Plihon & P Zarlowski (2005). Towards a convergence of the shareholder and stakeholder models. *Corporate Ownership & Control*, 2, 11–18.

Pope, P, R Morris & D Peel (1990). Insider trading: Some evidence on market effi-ciency and directors share dealings in Great Britian. *Journal of Business, Finance and Accounting*, 17, 359–380.

Porter, M & S van der Linde (1995). Green and competitive, ending the stalemate. *Harvard Business Review*, September–October, 120–135.

Porter, M & M Kramer (2003). The competitive advantage of corporate philanthropy. *Harvard Business Review on Corporate Responsibility*, 27–64.

Powley, T (2009). SRI funds "holding up" social businesses. Available at http://www.iii.co.uk/articles/articledisplay.jsp?article_id=10040110&section=SRI.

Prendergast, C (1999). The provision of incentives in firms. *Journal of Economic Literature*, 37, 7–63.

Qian, J & P Strahan (2007). How laws & institutions shape financial contracts: The case of bank loans. *Journal of Finance*, 62, 2803–2834.

Raghunandan, K, WJ Read & DV Rama (2001). Audit committee characteristics, "gray" directors, and interaction with internal auditing. *Accounting Horizons*, 15, 105–118.

Rahman, R & F Ali (2006). Board, audit committee, culture and earnings management: Malaysian evidence. *Managerial Auditing Journal*, 21, 783–804.

Ramakrishnan, V (2003). *Directorial Dashboards and Directors Accounts: Why We Need Them and What They Are,* Presented at the 6th International Conference on Corporate Governance and Board Leadership, Henley 6–8 October.

Ramakrishnan, V (2004). *Predictive Preformance Management — Binocular Vision, Ambidextrous Implementation,* Paper presented at the 4th International conference of the Performance Management Association, Edinburgh, July.

Rajan, RG & L Zingales (1998). Financial dependence and growth. *American Economic Review*, 88, 559–586.

Reese, W & M Weisbach (2002). Protection of minority shareholder interests, cross-listings in the United States, and subsequent equity offerings. *Journal of Financial Economics*, 66, 65–104.

Rindova, V (1999). What corporate boards have to do with strategy. *Journal of Management Studies*, 36, 953–975.

Riskmetrics (2009). *Credit Crisis and Corporate Governance Implications*, Riskmetrics.

Roberts, J, T McNulty & P Stiles (2005). Accountability and creating accountability: A framework for exploring behavioural perspectives of corporate governance. *British Journal of Management*, 16, S65–S79.

Rosenbaum, P (2005). Bargaining on board structure at the Initial Public Offering. *Journal of Management Governance*, 9, 171–198.

Rozeff, M & M Zaman (1988). Market efficiency and insider trading: New evidence. *Journal of Business*, 61, 25–43.

Rucker, P & R Younglai (2009). Obama financial reform, yet unwritten, faces battles. Reuters. Available at http://www.reuters.com/article/companyNews/idUKTRE5455KS20090529.

Rudd, K (2008). Address to the United Nations General Assembly, New York, 25 September. Available at http://www.pm.gov.au/media/Speech/2008/speech_0502.cfm.

Russell, S, N Haigh & A Griffiths (2007). Understanding corporate sustainability: recognizing the impact of corporate governance systems." In S Benn & D Dunphy, *Corporate Sustainability: Challenges for Theory and Practice*. London: Routledge. pp. 36–56.

Salancik, G (1977). Commitment and control of organizational behavior and belief. In *New Directions in Organizational Behavior*, edited by BM Staw & GR Salancik. pp. 1–54. Chicago: St. Claire Press.

Sapienza, HJ, MA Korsgaar, P Goulet & JP Hoogendam (2000). Effects of agency risks and procedural justice on board process in venture capital-backed firms. *Entrepreneurship and Regional Development, 12*, 331–352.

Sapienza, HJ, S Manigart & W Vermier (1996). Venture capitalist governance and value added in four countries. *Journal of Business Venturing, 11*, 439–469.

Sarbanes, P & M Oxley (2002). Sarbanes-Oxley Act of 2002. Washington, DC: US Congress.

Schacter, M (2005). Boards face new social responsibility. *CA Magazine*, May 12.

Scheinkestel, L (1997). The debt-equity conflict: Where does the project finance fit? *Journal of Banking and Finance Law Practice*, 102–124.

Scheinkman, J (2008). Social Interactions. In S Durlauf & L Blume(eds.). *The New Palgrave Dictionary of Economics*. 2nd ed. Palgrave Macmillan.

Schnatterly, K & SG Johnson (2008). Competing to be CEO in high-tech firms: Insider, board member, or outsider candidates. *The Journal of High Technology Management Research, 18*, 132–142.

Schroeder, M (2007). Is there a difference? The performance characteristics of SRI equity indices. *Journal of Business Finance and Accounting, 34*, 331–348.

Schultz, P (2003). Who makes markets. *Journal of Financial Markets, 6*, 49–72.

Schumpeter, JA (1911). *The Theory of Economic Development*. New York: Oxford University Press.

Schwartz, R (2009). Cited in "SRI funds "holding up" social businesses," interviewed by Tanya Powley. Available at http://www.iii.co.uk/articles/articledisplay.jsp?article_id=10040110&section=SRI.

Sethi, P (2003). *Setting Global Standards: Guidelines for Creating Codes of Conduct in Multinational Corporations*. Hoboken: John Wiley & Sons, Inc.

Seyhun, N (1986). Insider profits, costs of trading and market efficiency. *Journal of Financial Economics, 16*, 189–212.

Seyhun, N (1998). *Investment Intelligence from Insider Trading*. Cambridge: MIT Press.

Siegel, J (2005). Can foreign firms bond themselves effectively by renting U.S. securities laws? *Journal of Financial Economics, 75*, 319–359.

Sharma, VD & ER Iselin (2006). Reputation, tenure and compensation of independent audit committee members and financial restatements. *Paper presented at the American Accounting Association Annual Conference*, Washington DC, US.

Sharma, VD & C Kuang (2008). Voluntary audit committee characteristics and aggressive earnings management: Evidence from New Zealand. *Paper presented at the American Accounting Association Mid-Year International Accounting Conference*, San Diego, US.

Shleifer, A & R Vishny (1997). A survey of corporate governance. *Journal of Finance*, 52, 737–783.

Shleifer, A & D Wolfenzon (2002). Investor protection and equity markets. *Journal of Financial Economics*, 66, 3–27.

Short, H, K Keasey, M Wright & A Hull (1999). Corporate governance: From accountability to enterprise. *Accounting and Business Research*, 29, 337–352.

Smith, R (2003). *Audit Committees Combined Code Guidance*. Financial Reporting Council, London.

Smith, R (2008). *Guidance on Audit Committees*. Financial Reporting Council, London.

Sorenson, O & TE Stuart (2001). Syndication networks and the spatial distribution of venture capital financing. *American Journal of Sociology*, 106, 1546–1588.

Spanish Securities Markets Commission (2006). *Unified Code on Good Corporate Governance*. Spanish Securities Markets Commission, Spain.

Stein, J (2002). Information production and capital allocation: Decentralized versus hierarchical firms. *Journal of Finance*, 57, 1891–1921.

Stenzel, J & C Stenzel (2005). The payoffs for corporate social responsibility: A conversation with Marc J. Epstein. *Journal of Cost Management*, July/August, 5–9.

Stiles, P (2001). The impact of the board on strategy: An empirical examination. *Journal of Management Studies*, 38, 627–650.

Stiles, P & B Taylor (2001). *Boards At Work: How Directors View Their Roles and Responsibilities*. UK: Oxford University Press.

Stulz, R (1999). Globalization, corporate finance, and the cost of capital. *Journal of Applied Corporate Finance*, 26, 3–28.

Stulz, RM (2005). The limits of financial globalization. *Journal of Finance*, 60, 1595–1638.

Stulz, R & R Williamson (2003). Culture, openness, and finance. *Journal of Financial Economics*, 70, 313–349.

SustainAbility Group. *Tomorrow's Value: The Global Reporters 2006 Survey of Corporate Sustainability Reporting*. Available at: http://www.sustainability.com/aboutsustainability/article_previous.asp?id=865.

Teen, MY, J Sequeira, J Yipin & L Luh (2008). Does the Adoption of an Information-connected Approach reduce Insider Trading. http://ssrn.com/abstract=1156143.

Teksten, EL, SB Moser & DB Elbert (2005). Boards of directors for small businesses and small private corporations: The changing role, duties and expectations. *Management Research* News, 28, 50–68.

The Economist (2002). Lots of it about. *Economist: Special Report*, 14 December, 365, 62–63.

The Global Compact (2004). *Who cares wins: Connecting financial markets to a changing world.* Report for Swiss Federal Department of Foreign Affairs and United Nations.

Thomas, J & M Coleman (2005). Development and maintenance of board structures and practices in small to medium sized family businesses: An exploratory study. Paper presented at ICSB World Conference, 15–18 June, Washington DC.

Tian, X (2008). Geography and the structure of venture capital financing. *Working paper,* Kelley School of Business, Indiana University.

Torres, O & PA Julien (2005). Specificity and denaturing of small business. *International Small Business Journal, 23,* 355–377.

Transparency International (2009). *2009 Global Corruption Barometer.* Transparency International. Berlin.

Trowbridge, J (2009). Executive Renumeration: The Regulatory Debate. CGI Glass Lewis and Guerdon Associates, Sydney. Available at http://www.apra.gov.au/Speeches/upload/Executive-renumeration-in-the-financial-sector-Apr-09.pdf.

Turnbull, N (1999). *Internal Control: Guidance for Directors on the Combined Code.* Institute of Chartered Accountants in England and Wales, London.

Turnbull, N (2005). *Internal Control: Revised Guidance for Directors on the Combined Code.* Financial Reporting Council, London.

Tyson, L (2003). *The Tyson Report on the Recruitment and Development of Non-Executive Directors.* London Business School.

UK Social Investment Forum (2008). *European SRI Study 2008: United Kingdom,* Available from Eurosif at http://www.eurosif.org/sri/sri_country_resources/united_kingdom and UKSIF: www.uksif.org.

United States v. O'Hagan, 521 642 (U.S. 1997).

US Department of the Treasury (2009). Treasury Outlines Framework for Regulatory Reform. Available at http://www.ustreas.gov/press/releases/tg72.htm.

US Senate (2002). *The role of the board of directors' in Enron's collapse.* Report prepared by the Permanent Subcommittee on Investigations of the Senate of the United States.

Uysal, VB, S Kedia & V Panchapagesan (2008). Geography and acquirer returns. *Journal of Financial Intermediation, 17,* 256–275.

Vafeas, N (2003). Length of board tenure and outside director independence. *Journal of Business Finance & Accounting, 30,* 1043–1064.

Valor, C (2005). Corporate social responsibility and corporate citizenship: Towards corporate accountability. *Business and Society Review, 110,* 191–212.

Van den Heuvel, J, A van Gils & W Voordeckers (2006). Board roles in family businesses: Performance and importance. *Corporate Governance: An International Review, 14,* 467–485.

Van der Walt, NT, CB Ingley & G Diack (2002). Corporate governance: Implications of ownership, performance requirements and strategy. *Journal of Change Management*, 2, 319–333.

Voordeckers, W, A van Gils & J van den Heuvel (2007). Board composition in small and medium-sized family firms. *Journal of Small Business Management*, 45, 137–156.

Wade, J, CA O'Reily & I Chandratat (1990). Golden parachutes: CEOs and the exercise of social influence. *Administrative Science Quarterly*, 35, 587–603.

Walsh, JP & JK Seward (1990). On the efficiency of internal and external corporate control mechanisms. *Academy of Management Review*, 42, 7–25.

Weber, M (1930). *The Protestant Ethnic and the Spirit of Capitalism*. New York: Harper Collins.

Wehinger, G (2008). Lessons from the Financial Market Turmoil: Challenges ahead for the Financial Industry and Policy Makers. OECD.

Welch, J & S Welch (2005). *Winning*. Harper Collins.

Welsh, JA & JF White (1981). A small business is not a little big business. *Harvard Business Review*, July/August, 18–32.

West, A (2009). Corporate governance convergence and moral relativism. *Corporate Governance: An International Review*, 17, 107–119.

Westphal, JD (1999). Collaboration in the boardroom: Behavioural and performance consequences of CEO-board social ties. *Academy of Management Journal*, 42, 7–24.

Williams, O (2007). *Responsible Corporate Citizenship and the Ideals of the UN Global Compact* (unpublished chapter).

World Bank/PPIAF (2002). *Emerging Lessons in Private Provision of Infrastructure Services in Rural Areas: Water and Electricity Services in Gabon*. Washington, DC: World Bank.

World Economic Forum (2009). *The Future of the Global Financial System*, Geneva.

Wurgler, J (2000). Financial markets and the allocation of capital. *Journal of Financial Economics*, 58, 187–214.

Xie, B, WN Davidson & PJ Dadalt (2003). Earnings management and corporate governance: The roles of the board and the audit committee. *Journal of Corporate Finance*, 9, 295–316.

Zahra, SA, DO Neubaum & L Naldi (2007). The effects of ownership and governance on SME's international knowledge-based resources. *Small Business Economics*, 29, 309–327.

Zahra, SA & JA Pearce (1989). Boards of directors and corporate financial performance: A review and integrative model. *Journal of Management*, 15, 291–334.

Zhu, N (2002). The local bias of individual investors. *Working paper.* Yale School of Management.

Zingales, L (2007). Is the U.S. capital market losing its competitive edge? *Working paper*, University of Chicago Graduate School of Business.

Zitzewitz, E (2003). Who cares about shareholders? Arbitrage-proofing mutual funds. *Journal of Law, Economics, and Organization, 19*, 245–280.

INDEX